T0386241

THE ZAMBEZI

MALYN NEWITT

The Zambezi

A History

HURST & COMPANY, LONDON

First published in the United Kingdom in 2022 by
C. Hurst & Co. (Publishers) Ltd.,
New Wing, Somerset House, Strand, London, WC2R 1LA
© Malyn Newitt, 2022
All rights reserved.

Distributed in the United States, Canada and Latin America by
Oxford University Press, 198 Madison Avenue, New York, NY 10016,
United States of America.

The right of Malyn Newitt to be identified as the author of
this publication is asserted by him in accordance with the
Copyright, Designs and Patents Act, 1988.

A Cataloguing-in-Publication data record for this book
is available from the British Library.

This book is printed using paper from registered sustainable
and managed sources.

ISBN: 9781787387003

www.hurstpublishers.com

Printed in Great Britain by Bell and Bain Ltd, Glasgow

CONTENTS

ACKNOWLEDGMENTS

This book was written during the Covid epidemic when visits to archives and libraries were very difficult and travel to and around Africa impossible. As my first book on Africa appeared exactly fifty years ago, this book is the result of a lifetime of living in, writing about and visiting central Africa.

I would like to acknowledge what I owe to the remarkable scholars I have known and from whom I have learnt all that has enabled me to write this book. My first experience of Africa was as a lecturer in the History Department of what was then the University College of Rhodesia and Nyasaland. There were five other members of the department—Eric Stokes, Terence Ranger, Richard Brown, Ian Henderson and Hilary Jenkins. Two other notable scholars, John McCracken and Ronald Robinson, came to lecture there for a year. From this remarkable assembly of scholars I learnt in depth about the issues and arguments of African history. I also met George Fortune and Peter Garlake with whom I travelled to the Zambezi valley and the Comoros Islands. Magnus McLeod, still irrepressibly in the land of the living, accompanied me on my first major expedition to Mozambique and was with me when we crossed the Zambezi behind a hired steam locomotive.

When carrying out research in Lisbon I got to know Stan Mudenge and Gerhard Liesegang both of whom were scholars

ACKNOWLEDGMENTS

whose influence I gratefully acknowledge. I had the extraordinary privilege of being almost the only PhD student to be surpervised by Charles Boxer while he was Camoens Professor at King's College London. At King's I worked in the same department as Patrick Chabal, one of the most influential political scientists to have addressed the problems of modern Africa.

I would also like to acknowledge the inspiration I received from the generations of students I either taught or examined, especially Corrado Tornimbeni, Afzal Ahmed, Hilary Palmer, Ana Afanasyeva, Isabel Ferreira, Joel Neves Tembe, Nuno Vidal and Kaykay Marivate.

Others whose help and friendship I gratefully acknowledge and whose ideas I have shamelessly plundered include Elizabeth Mancke, Jill Dias, Landeg White, Liazzat Bonate, Maria Allen, Alexander Keese, Alex Vines and Allen Isaacman—and a special thanks to Philip Havik for his scholarship and for his friendship over many years.

Finally I need to express my gratitude to Hurst and Co – to Christopher Hurst and his successor Michael Dwyer who have continued to publish what I write and even to commission books from me.

LIST OF ILLUSTRATIONS

1. Victoria Falls by Thomas Baines, 1865. Source: Thomas Baines, Public domain, via Wikimedia Commons.
2. Cahora Bassa dam and gorge. Source: (WT-en) Nic Roets at English Wikivoyage, Public domain, via Wikimedia Commons.
3. Postcard of Chinde during floods. Every effort was made to trace the source and the publisher would be grateful if anyone with information would contact them.
4. The Courthouse Lealui during the annual floods. Source: Catharine Winkworth Mackintosh, *Coillard of the Zambesi* (London: T. Fisher Unwin, 1907), p. 324.
5. The Dona Ana Bridge, spanning the Lower Zambezi. Source: Erik Cleves Kristensen, CC BY 2.0, via Wikimedia Commons.
6. Ma Robert, D. Livingstone's steamboat on which he explored the Zambezi River, 1858. Source: Lithograph by T. Picken after S. Walters, 1858. Wellcome Collection, Public Domain Mark.
7. Nalikuanda. Ceremonial barge of the Litunga of Barotseland. Source: Catharine Winkworth Mackintosh, *Coillard of the Zambesi* (London: T. Fisher Unwin, 1907), p. 344.
8. Portuguese gunboat on the Zambezi, 1913. Source: Courtesy of the Smithsonian Libraries and Archives (https://library.si.edu/digital-library/book/bondsofafricaim00letc). Owen Letcher, *The Bonds of Africa* (London: J. Long, 1913).

LIST OF ILLUSTRATIONS

9. Map of the Lower Zambezi by João Teixeira Albernaz II. Source: *Atlas de 1665*, Archives Nationales, Paris.

10. Canoe on the Lower Zambezi at Bandar, 1964. Source: photo by author.

11. Site of the *aringa* of Massangano. Site of repeated battles between Portuguese and the da Cruz, 1964. Source: photo by author.

12. Author crossing the Zambezi by bridge, behind a steam locomotive, 1964. Source: photo by author.

13. A traditional Lower Zambezi house at Tete, 1964. Source: photo by author.

14. District Commissioner Balovale departing by boat, 1935. Source: photo by AJ Board, reprinted with his daughter's permission.

15. Barotseland boatmen, 1935. Source: photo by AJ Board, reprinted with his daughter's permission.

16. A river boat on the Upper Zambezi, 1935. Source: photo by AJ Board, reprinted with his daughter's permission.

GLOSSARY

Aldeamentos	protected village settlements established by the Portuguese during the Mozambique war of independence.
Almadias	canoes.
Aringa	large, fortified stockade in Zambezia.
Bares	mining camp. Also, a measurement of weight used for ivory or cloth. A *bare* of cloth amounted to 400 *panos*, each *pano* consisting of approximately 6 feet of cloth.
Caciz	a Muslim *qadi*. Used by Africans for Christian priests.
Cafre	Portuguese version of 'kaffir'. Widely used in Portuguese texts to describe all Africans.
Capitães	captains. Often also used for the headman of a group of workers.
Capitão-mor	captain major.
Cartaz	pass recording the tax and labour record of Africans in Mozambique in the twentieth century.
Chicote	whip.
Chicunda	slaves or clients of the *prazo senhores*. Now the name of an ethnic group in Zimbabwe, Zambia and Mozambique.

GLOSSARY

Choriro	disorderly funeral celebrations.
Chuambo	stockaded settlement. Especially applied to Quelimane.
Colonos	free African inhabitants of the *prazos*.
Cuama	name of one of the rivers of the Zambezi delta. The whole of Zambezia was sometimes called the Rios de Cuama.
Cypaes	similar to 'sepoy'. Term used for African police in Mozambique.
Dona	lady. Title given to female holders of *prazos*.
Engagés	contract labourers recruited for the French Indian Ocean islands.
Feira	fair.
Fumo	headman or minor ruler.
Gero	building where adolescents lived.
Grumetes	Africans who became servants or clients of the Portuguese in Upper Guinea.
Impis	regiments.
Kotla	royal council of the Barotse kingdom.
Lançados	Portuguese living among the African population in Upper Guinea.
Luanes	rural houses and properties of the *prazo senhores*.
Luzios	decked boats in use on the Lower Zambezi in the sixteenth and seventeenth centuries.
Machilla	palanquin or hammock for carrying people.
Machiras	cotton cloth woven on the Lower Zambezi.
Mambo	African king or paramount ruler.
Manilhas	copper bracelets.
Mapira	grain.
Mhondoro	spirit of a dead ruler inhabiting a lion.
Missonco	tribute paid by the *colonos* to a *prazo senhor*.
Moradores	settlers or residents.

GLOSSARY

Mucazambos	leaders of groups of slaves or *chicunda*.
Murimo	God or supreme being.
Mussambazes	traders in the service of Portuguese creoles.
Mussoco	head tax.
Muzimos (midzimus)	spirits of the ancestors.
Muzinda	town or large village.
Muzungus	used for white people and their descendants.
Nomi	organisations of adolescents among the A-Sena.
Pangayo	dhow.
Pataca	Spanish silver coin minted in Mexico.
Pataxo	pinnace or small sailing craft.
Pombe	African beer made from millet.
Prazos	land held from the Portuguese Crown on long (usually three life) leases.
Quite	ceremonial chair or throne.
Rabo da Guerra	literally 'war tail'. Animal tail carried by traditional medicine men in battle.
Régulo	minor ruler.
Senado da Câmara	town council.
Senhor	seigneur. Used for lessees of the *prazos*.
Sesmarias	vacant lands.
Vanhai (singular Munhai)	servant, messenger or soldier of the Monomotapa.

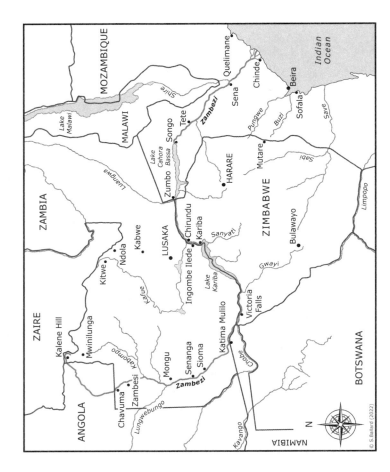

Zambezi Valley

Upper Zambezi

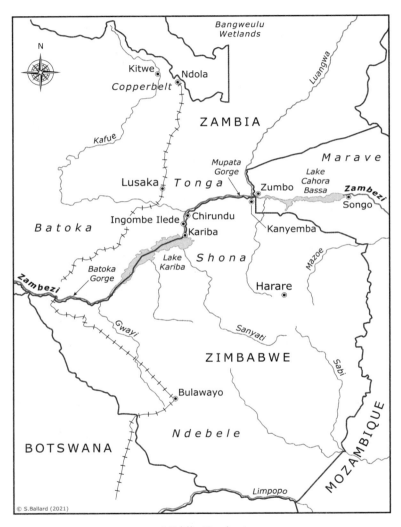

Middle Zambezi

Lower Zambezi

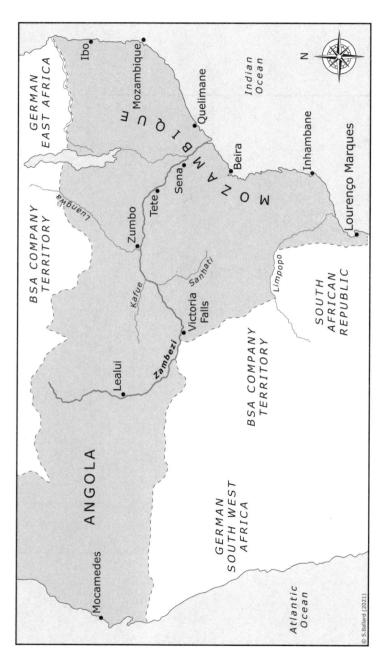

Mapa Cor de Rosa

INTRODUCTION

Rivers carry with them a weight of symbolism. To some, they have been a metaphor for human life itself: its youth represented in some small spring or meandering stream which increases to the full volume of adulthood as it follows a course full of twists, waterfalls and cataracts until finally it reaches its end in the ocean. As Swinburne wrote, "even the weariest river winds somewhere safe to sea." Navigable rivers have often been appropriately compared to the arteries of the body, with trade and human interaction being the blood that flows through them.

For the ancient world, the river Styx was the portal to the underworld, with the dead rowed across by Charon the ferryman, their fare paid for by a silver coin placed in the mouth of the dead. In Norse mythology, it was the river Gjöll. Once across the river, there was no return. For Heraclitus, a river represented the truth about nature, that the world was in a constant state of flux. It is not possible to step into the same river twice. In Buddhist and Hindu belief, a river is not a linear course from a beginning to an end but a cyclical process. As the waters of the river reach the sea, so they are taken up again to form clouds and fall as rain to renew the flow of the river: just as human life reaches its end only for there to be rebirth.

Crossing the river Rubicon became a standard metaphor to describe the taking of an irrevocable decision, while many writers have seen the state as a boat being carried along on the stream of history, with the role of political leaders being confined to giving an occasional touch to the rudder. Rivers are often boundaries separating 'them' from 'us'—perhaps national frontiers like the Cunene river separating Angola from Namibia or the river Tamar confining the Cornish in their rocky peninsula between its waters and the ocean. To live south of the Thames has a special meaning for Londoners, just as the 'left bank' has for Parisians. But rivers also unite, with those upstream travelling down through their neighbour's territory to reach the outside world, and in some cases—as with Egypt—those downstream depending on the goodwill of those who control the waters upstream for the continuing flow of life-giving water. Access to rivers and the use of their waters is central to much of the network of treaties that guide and even determine international relations.

One consequence of the ebb and flow of traders, boatmen, hunters, porters, refugees and migrants has been an extremely fluid and constantly changing ethnic identity among the inhabitants of river valleys. Different languages and dialects are spoken and evolve; ethnicities come and go with a shake of history's kaleidoscope. The river valley becomes the artery for cultural exchange, trade bringing with it new consumer goods, new technologies, new ideas and new human relations.

The Lower Zambezi has certainly acted as a highway into the interior, and for those living inland it has provided an opening to the influences of the outside world. For 300 miles from the sea it is navigable, even during the dry season. It is then blocked by the Cahora Bassa rapids, but those travelling to and from the interior followed a well-worn road round the rapids, after which there was a further 200 miles of navigation, past the Luangwa confluence to the Kariba gorge. In fact, it was only once they reached the gorges carved by the Victoria Falls that the trade routes and the Zambezi river parted company. The region above the Falls, a thousand miles of the Zambezi's course, remained relatively cut off until the nineteenth century, more accessible from the west and the south than from the river valley downstream.

If the Zambezi acted as an artery for trade and migration, it was also, confusingly, a frontier between two cultural systems. North of the river, the various ethnic and linguistic groups share a common matrilineal system of family relations. Children belong to the mother's lineage, not the father's; married couples usually reside in the mother's village, and male responsibility for the children ultimately rests with the mother's brother. Such systems are common throughout the central and western parts of Africa and historically have had an uneasy relationship with the legal and cultural ideas that have accompanied the spread of Islam.

South of the Zambezi, patrilineal systems prevail where children belong to the father's lineage, a practice which had also been predominant in Europe since Roman times. These contrasting systems helped to shape the history of the region. In matrilineal communities, the incorporation of slaves or outsiders is difficult to achieve and the consolidation of political authority in a male dynasty almost impossible. In patrilineal societies, by contrast, female slaves can be incorporated as secondary wives, and dynasties of male rulers have aided the emergence of state systems that have, in some cases, proved very resilient.

The history of rivers can be told in geological time, lasting millions of years; or in human time, over a few thousand; or in the time during which humans have recorded their activities, which can sometimes be only a few hundred years. In the case of the Zambezi, the archaeological and written record extends back 600 years, but only in the last hundred have humans imposed themselves on the river in such a way as totally to transform its nature. The first bridge across the Zambezi was built in 1905. In 1959, a dam was completed across the Kariba gorge. As the lake behind the dam filled, earth tremors were felt as far away as Salisbury, the capital of what was then Southern Rhodesia. The Kariba lake backed up 225 kilometres along the Gwembe valley and eventually covered 5,580 square kilometres of valley floor, adding another lake to Africa's inland waterways. Of the Tonga population who had inhabited the valley for many hundreds of years, 57,000 had to be forcibly removed, their villages replaced by safari lodges and holiday resorts. Where once wild floodwaters had poured through the gorge, there was now a placid inland sea.

No sooner was Lake Kariba filled than planning began for a second dam. This was to be in Mozambique further down the river, and it was to prove highly controversial. The Cahora Bassa gorge, which a hundred years earlier had thwarted Livingstone's plan for a commercial highway, was now the site of a second Zambezi dam. Completed in 1974, the dam was larger than Kariba, and the lake behind the dam extended for 240 kilometres and flooded 2,700 square kilometres. Forty years were to pass before tentative plans were announced for a third dam below Cahora Bassa at Mphanda Nkua. A fourth dam was proposed 47 kilometres below the Victoria Falls, known as the Batoka Gorge dam, which would flood the valley gorges to within half a mile of the Falls.

From one perspective, this book is an elegy for the grandeur and rich diversity of one of the natural world's richest environments. Like the Douro river in Portugal, where six dams have turned a wild and tempestuous river into a string of long, thin lakes hardly ruffled by a sluggish current, the Zambezi will soon cease to be a natural river whose floodwaters carved gorges through mountain ranges and will instead become a string of placid lakes, destined to gradually become ever shallower as they silt up. Viewing these lakes in the future will require an exercise of the historical imagination to recapture the deep history of the river and the valley through which it flowed, and to reimagine how this river directly and indirectly shaped the destiny of central Africa.

1

RHYTHMS OF HISTORY

The Zambezi river

The Zambezi drains 540,000 square miles of central Africa, hundreds of tributary streams and rivers feeding into the 1,600-mile length of the river. It ranks fourth among Africa's rivers after the Nile, the Niger and the Zaire, and, like them, it changes character as it passes through different geographical zones. The Zambezi flows through floodplains, rocky narrows, vast sandy beds in which the river is almost lost during the dry season and finally a delta with a hundred-mile face on the seaward side. In order to describe the river and its history, it is a convention to consider it in three distinct sections: the Upper Zambezi, which extends from its source as far as the Victoria Falls; the Middle Zambezi, extending from the Victoria Falls to the Cahora Bassa rapids; and the Lower Zambezi from Cahora Bassa to the sea. Throughout its course, the river passes through a number of gorges that have been carved through the mountains that barred its way. The most important of these were the Batoka gorge below the Victoria Falls and the Kafue, Kariba, Cahora Bassa and Lupata gorges. With the exception of the Lupata gorge on the lower river, it was not possible to navigate through these narrows, and in between them there were many smaller rapids and falls, many of them exposed only during the dry season, but all presenting hazards for navigation.

However, the nature of the river is not only determined by geology. More important is the seasonal nature of the rains of central Africa, which swell the Zambezi and transform it from a modestly flowing stream into a huge torrent which overflows its banks and in parts creates extensive floodplains. Rainclouds travel in from the Indian Ocean during the months of October to April, during which time up to 50 inches of rain can fall on the upper reaches of the river and 30–40 inches on the central African plateau further east. Half an inch of rain can fall in a single thunderstorm and two inches in the course of a day. The floods last from January to mid-May, during which time the Zambezi can rise 20–30 feet above the dry-season level. The flooding of the Barotse plain is well known, but extensive flooding can also occur higher up the river as well, where the numerous streams entering the Zambezi form a network of waterways.

In December 1885, Frederick Arnot, a Plymouth Brothers missionary who in 1884 had been the first European known to have identified the source of the Zambezi, travelled through country on the right bank of the upper river and described the floods in his diary.

13th Started *wading* today, and all got into camp very tired I found some huts ... built on dry mounds, the work of former travellers.

14th Water about knee-deep all day; got to another group of half-dry mounds; I pitched my tent with great care, and by setting each foot of my chair on an ant hill, managed to keep above water.

21st Crossed the Lutembwa Valley today. It is flooded, and covered with a forest of immense trees, which have large spreading roots like the mangrove. We waded for some hours through this dense forest. The emerald green mosses, shining through the water, contrasted beautifully with the pale ferns clustering round and among the tree-roots, and with icicle-like mosses, which hung in long delicate festoons from the branches at every opening in the forest.[1]

The source of the Zambezi is located in the Mwinilunga district in the north-west corner of Zambia, now officially termed the Zambezi Source National Monument, part of the Zambezi Source National Forest, a protected botanical reserve. This point is near the summit of the great watershed which separates the river systems of the Zaire from those of the Zambezi. These two giant waterways are not just rivers but whole drainage systems, fed by countless streams and major rivers that discharge into them from the surrounding plateaux. On its upper reaches, the Zambezi is joined by the Kabompo and the Lungwebungu as well as numerous smaller streams that flow into it every 10 to 15 miles. It is these tributaries that turn what begins as a small stream into a major river which, even a thousand miles from the sea, can be up to a mile wide.

The rains produce a notable rise in the level of the river, but the descent of the water from the upper reaches can take weeks to reach the sea, leading to a number of rises and falls in the level of the main stream in a single year. Moreover, rains are not always regular, so that there may be considerable variations between one year and the next, with prolonged dry periods that may last many years. The rain mostly falls on the high ground of the plateau so that the valley itself can sometimes suffer from drought conditions, and the average annual rainfall at Tete on the Lower Zambezi is only 25 inches. Matthew Hannaford has researched in great detail the cycle of dry and wet periods in south-east Africa over the period 1500 to 1830 and has shown how important they were in their influence on political developments, especially at the end of the sixteenth century and in the early nineteenth century—themes that are discussed in subsequent chapters.[2]

During the period from April to September little rain falls. Many of the streams on the plateau run dry or are reduced to stagnant pools with sometimes only a trickle of water. At the height of the dry season, the Zambezi itself shrinks in depth and in many places in width. On the lower reaches, it can become a stream less than a hundred yards wide, meandering through a waste of sand, and so shallow that people can cross it on foot.

The vast drainage basin of the Zambezi is a major determinant of the region's history. The river valleys that feed floodwaters into the Zambezi are sites of settlement, allowing people easy access to water and, although often marshy and liable themselves to flooding, also lines of communication. These valleys are often backed by rocky escarpments or by forested land which can be dense, hostile and sometimes almost impenetrable. The people who live in these river valleys have their lives structured by the seasons, which are not so much the spring, summer, autumn and winter of the northern hemisphere but seasons marked by the dry months and the coming of the rains.

The impassable barriers of the gorges, together with the nature of the delta, which did not provide any reliable navigation channels, and the extreme changes in the flow of the river all served to make navigation difficult and at times impossible, preventing the Zambezi from acting satisfactorily as a major highway from the sea into the interior. As hazardous as navigation of the Zambezi could be, the course of the river did include long navigable stretches. On the lower river, it was possible to sail from the Cahora Bassa gorge downstream to the point where the river splits into the streams of the delta; on the Middle Zambezi between Cahora Bassa and the beginnings of the Batoka gorge, there were long, relatively clear stretches which could be navigated by locally built canoes, while on the upper river the Barotse floodplain provided unbroken navigation from the Ngonye Falls almost as far as the river's source.

However, nowhere on the Zambezi was navigation easy. During the dry season when the level of the river fell, numerous sandbanks and rocky outcrops diverted the stream into tortuous channels. Then, when the river rose as a result of the rains, the Zambezi would overflow its banks and create extensive shallows and marshes which could disguise the path of the main stream, while the passage over cataracts and through the gorges produced currents and whirlpools that could play havoc with small boats.

When the floods subsided, the peoples who lived on or near the river used canoes, which enabled them to negotiate the shallows and the smaller cataracts, as boats drawing more than a foot could not find enough water in which to float. On most of the river, the dugout canoe was the craft of choice. These varied from small canoes holding two or possibly three people to larger canoes able to carry nine or ten people or the equivalent in tonnage. Canoes operated without difficulty when the river was low, but when the water rose and the flow increased they became less easy to use. On the Middle Zambezi, they were more often employed to cross the river from one side to the other than to travel up- or downstream. On the Lower Zambezi, when the level of the river permitted, traders travelled in boats which writers in the seventeenth century called *luzios*. These were described in some detail by the Jesuit António Gomes in the middle of the seventeenth century.

> They sail on the rivers in boats made of the trunks of trees, both small and big, the big ones being made of nice planks of which there are plenty. They are trimmed and are not made with nails. They are put together with coir and are so tight and expertly made that they do not seem to have been made by cafres and they can be heavily loaded. They are divided into three sections: one is the shelter, in the middle; the stern section is where the rowing is done by the sailors, who are twenty-four [in number] apart from the helmsman; the prow section carries a big stove where the passengers and the

crew cook their food. The middle shelter has a raised floor. Underneath they carry the goods in the bow and in the stern section they load barrels and boxes with the goods that must not get wet. The shelter is divided into two parts: one is for accommodation and can hold two bunks, writing bureaux, baskets and other such things, the other is a verandah with room for four chairs and a table and it is also used to steer the ship. When the sails are in use, the ropes are controlled from here and it is very comfortable for the people travelling in it.[3]

The *luzio* seems to have been an adaptation of the seagoing dhow. When Francisco de Lacerda, who undertook the first Portuguese mission to Kazembe's Lunda kingdom in 1798, travelled up the Zambezi from Quelimane he went in a boat he called a *ballão*.

Ballões are also made from a single trunk and differ from the *coches* [small canoes] in having a deck and in having the cafres row seated in the waist ... but they have short oars made so that the hand in the centre serves as a pivot and the other as the power for this lever. That in which I travelled was 48 *palmos* long and 8½ *palmos* in the beam. They are only used for passengers and for such things as must not be damaged ... My *ballão* had nine seats and eighteen rowers apart from the pilot (*mallemo*) and the man in the prow (*mucadão*).[4]

Anything bigger than the *luzio* or the *ballão* experienced huge problems. In 1858, Livingstone brought the first steamer to the Zambezi, and the diaries he and his companions kept are filled with the seemingly endless problems caused by running aground on sandbanks and hidden shallows. In 1898, Major A. St H. Gibbons tried to take a steamer up the middle reaches of the Zambezi as far as the Batoka gorge. He succeeded, just, but the experience underlined the impracticality of this kind of boat. Eventually, special shallow-draft stern-wheel steamers were introduced on the lower river, but their use ran up against another problem. During much of its course between the Cahora

Bassa rapids and the sea, the Zambezi has no well-defined or stable banks where jetties, warehouses and mooring facilities could be built to service the steamers. The course of the river changed from year to year, meaning one year's shoreline might be eaten away by next year's floods and disappear altogether.

As with transport on land, the internal combustion engine brought about a revolution. In the twentieth century, the outboard motor enabled a large variety of boats of shallow draft to be used, making travel on the river more of a possibility. However, as late as the mid-1930s, travel on the Upper Zambezi was still largely by means of canoes or barges manned by paddlers.

The difficulty of navigation on the Zambezi was a dominant theme in the history of the river. A deep, evenly flowing river would have become a main artery for trade and allowed towns to be built along its course. These could have then become the centres of large state systems, with the river providing vital transport and communication links. It is possible to see how such ports might have developed by looking at the Lower Zambezi, where two towns, Sena and Tete, grew up as river ports and trading hubs from the sixteenth century onwards. These became the urban centres around which the Portuguese creole state was formed, but the lack of secure connections with a sea port, due to the maze of the delta streams, limited the possibilities for commercial development.

Zumbo, at the confluence with the Luangwa, was the only trading town that grew up on the Middle Zambezi. However, this town was short-lived. Flourishing briefly in the eighteenth century, it never formed part of any state system and was abandoned early in the nineteenth century. On the upper river, navigation was relatively easy for a hundred-mile stretch beyond the Ngonye Falls. Here, quite large towns developed near the river—for example, Sesheke and Lealui—but for much of the year the Zambezi overflowed its banks and flooded the land, which made permanent settlements near the river difficult and led to seasonal migrations of the population.

If the course of the river and its difficult navigation made it unsatisfactory as a commercial highway and transport corridor, there were other features which made it an unfavourable environment for large state systems to flourish. Much of the middle and lower reaches of the Zambezi were flanked by rugged escarpments, which insulated it from the central African plateau. The escarpment was made up of barren, mountainous territory which in places was 20 or 30 miles deep. Much of the escarpment presented a very real barrier to easy movement and effectively cut off the people living in the valley from those on the plateau.

Much of the escarpment and the valley below remained without roads and was virtually unexplored through most of the colonial period. Between 1989 and 1991, a decade after the independence of Zimbabwe, Richard Hasler carried out research into resource utilisation in the Zambezi valley near the border between Zimbabwe and Mozambique. He described the difficulties of trying to access the communities in the valley:

> Vehicle access ... is via the gravel road down the Zambezi escarpment. The trip is six to seven hours by four-wheel drive vehicle from Harare to Kanyemba, four of which are on the dirt road. When descending from Guruve, the tar ends shortly before making the descent into the valley and the gravel road that traverses the valley floor is very badly corrugated in the dry season and can be impassable in the wet season.[5]

On the upper river there was no escarpment, but the Zambezi floodplain was bordered by dense forest and in the south by the marshes of the Chobe and the Okavango delta. The Zambezi valley also had an unfavourable disease environment which discouraged settlement. Mosquitoes bred in the marshes and pools left behind by the falling waters after April, and much of the valley was infested with tsetse flies, which made living there impossible for people whose economy was based on cattle rearing.

An overview of Zambezi history

Although the Zambezi is clearly divided into three segments, there is nevertheless a certain unity to its history. Just as the river valleys have attracted settlement, so they have also facilitated migration, and much of the discernible history of the people of the great central African plateaux is one of migration and conquest, as well as permanent settlement. The migrations were often the result of such natural causes as drought, famine and locusts. However, these causes were not easily distinguished from the wars of conquest of warrior elites, who subjected the populations of the river valleys to their overrule and exacted tribute from them. The history of the Zambezi valley reflects this interaction of the relative stability and permanence of the settled valley communities, whose agricultural society is characterised by small, lineage-based villages dependent on extended family networks, and the dominance imposed from above by warlike invaders who established the overrule of a tribute-taking state system.

These invaders, often warrior elites rather than large migrating populations, were able to create state systems governed through the central authority of a king, backed by his office holders and military commanders, and with an elaborate ritual developed to confer mystique and ancestral authority on the ruler. As well as tribute-taking, these were also slave-owning states. The conquerors invariably sought to increase the manpower at their disposal by capturing slaves, attracting clients and dependents and taking wives from the subject populations. However, the degree to which these states depended on slaves differed. The Barotse and Ndebele kingdoms raided extensively for slaves, while slaves were perhaps less important for the Karanga and Marave kingdoms of an earlier period.

The language of the conquerors was also not infrequently imposed as a way of improving communication in a culture that had few means of conveying information apart from word of mouth, and as a way of unifying and consolidating the state. These conquerors always, in the end, reached some accommodation with the settled communities, recognising and incorporating the local spirit cults and rain shrines of the long-settled village communities into their system of control. Ultimately, however, these Zambezian state systems depended on the ability of the elites to mobilise and monopolise the use of force.

The Zambezian states, unlike those that emerged in Europe, never had clearly defined frontiers (although the Zambezi provided a natural barrier to the expansion of raiding and tribute taking, and came to constitute a kind of informal frontier on the lower and middle reaches of the river). The African states that grew up north and south of the river were defined by the allegiance of populations rather than by territorial boundaries. The extent of a kingdom was only as large as the population from which its rulers were able to exact tribute. This inevitably meant that the size of kingdoms could fluctuate considerably over time and that it makes no sense to try to draw their exact boundaries as Europeans tried to do at the time of the partition of Africa. Nowhere were the attempts to define precise boundaries more controversial than in the case of the Lozi kingdom of Barotseland on the Upper Zambezi. When European rulers began to delineate the frontiers of their colonies on the Upper Zambezi, they were faced with all the fluctuating uncertainties that surrounded the claims of the Lozi kings to 'rule' vast stretches of the Zambezi valley and its surrounding lands. As Lawrence Flint explained, these claims could be extreme.

> At its maximum extent in the late nineteenth century, Lozi rule probably included all the people inhabiting the lands of the Upper Zambezi River basin from approximately 12° S as far downstream as

the Victoria Falls. This includes all of present-day Western and much of North-Western Province of Zambia, parts of Eastern Angola, northern Botswana and north-western Zimbabwe[6]

Although the ruling elites exacted tribute in kind or in slaves, this served to regularise to some extent what would otherwise have been random destructive depredations on communities too small and scattered to defend themselves. Submission to a higher authority bought some peace and stability. The tribute paid by subject populations was usually redistributed by the rulers among their principal followers, a process which provided some guarantee of loyalty and stability at the centre where authority resided with a ritual kingship, but which, in reality, depended on the consent and co-operation of local elites which were able to dominate the village communities, where the 'small society' tilled the land.

As well as tribute-taking, the rulers of the Zambezian states tried to control long-distance trade. This could take many forms: the organisation of 'fairs', controlled by the ruling elites, to which traders had to come; the organisation of trading caravans by members of the elites; regulations governing the hunting of elephants or the possession of the tusks of elephants found dead; and control over the gold mines, which could only be worked with the ruler's consent.

The history of the societies that live north and south of the Zambezi is, therefore, the story of small villages and clusters of villages and the overrule of military invaders who sought to control the key economic resources of the country. The central African region has seen the rise and decline of these major state systems, but—with the exception of the Barotse kingdom on the upper river and the state formed by the Portuguese creoles on the lower river—all these state systems have had their centres on the plateau, with the escarpment and Zambezi valley being a frontier region only partially incorporated.

The plateau south of the river saw the rise of the state system based on Great Zimbabwe, which appears to have gone into decline in the fifteenth century and was succeeded by a number of states ruled by Karanga dynasties, the most important of which was the kingdom of Monomotapa. The Karanga conquered the Tonga peoples who lived in the Zambezi valley but, in the late sixteenth century, allowed the Portuguese to secure control over the neighbourhood of the trading towns of Sena and Tete. The Monomotapa kingdom was superseded at the end of the seventeenth century by the Rosvi dynasty of Changamire, which, like its predecessor, was based on the ownership of cattle and on the gold trade. This in turn was conquered by Nguni raiders from the south in the early nineteenth century, and an Nguni kingdom, that of the Ndebele, was established there in the 1840s. North of the river, the Marave kingdoms of Lundu, Undi and Karonga came into being in the late sixteenth century and survived until they also were conquered by Nguni warbands and Portuguese creole warlords in the early nineteenth century. On the upper river, the Lunda kings gradually expanded their control over the upper reaches of the Zambezi, the Barotse kingdom—established in the seventeenth century—being an offshoot of this Lunda empire.

The states formed in the Zambezi valley by coastal Muslims, Europeans, Indians and their descendants in many respects followed the pattern of the central African states described above. In the sixteenth century, Islamic traders from the coast had penetrated the lower Zambezi and the gold-bearing plateau to the south and had founded trading towns on the river. However, it does not seem that they had consolidated their position so far as to create any state system, though they would do so in the Mozambique lowlands in the nineteenth century. The invasion of the Lower Zambezi by the Portuguese in the 1570s was different. Formal administration and government structures were established, and over the next century Portuguese creoles with their private armies gradually strengthened their position in the lowlands around Quelimane and Sofala, and along the south bank of the Zambezi as far as the Cahora Bassa rapids. From the mid-eighteenth century onwards, the Portuguese creoles also expanded their influence north of the river, at the expense of the Marave.

Although this creole state was an offshoot of the Portuguese maritime empire with its base in Goa in western India, it soon acquired many of the characteristics of a typical central African state. The Portuguese ruled through a narrow elite of creole landowners who acquired numerous slaves and clients. Their rule was made effective by agents of this ruling elite, and by members of the elite themselves, who resided in outlying areas, with relatively little power being exerted from the centre. This is a characteristic which can also be discerned in the Lunda states of the upper river and in the Marave kingdoms on the north bank of the Lower Zambezi. Tribute was taken from the population, and collection was enforced by private armies of slaves and clients. Through the Catholic Church, the religious cult of the creole society expanded its influence over the people of the valley and assimilated aspects of the pre-existing religious systems, creating a web of mystical beliefs and religious rituals—a mixture of European and African religious practice—which bound the population to the colonial state.

The similarity of the Portuguese creole state to the African kingdoms of the plateau was enhanced by the fact that the Portuguese did not introduce any European technology (except literacy), but traded, built houses, produced food, wove cloth, manufactured iron weapons and hoes, all using traditional African technology. At first, the possession by the Portuguese of firearms singled them out from their African counterparts, but firearms soon began to spread among the African population as well. Eventually, they would be acquired, though not always effectively used, by all the central African states during the nineteenth century.

These conquest states all have their separate histories. Some lasted for centuries, others barely survived the deaths of their founders, but the general pattern of their overrule is remarkably similar. The kings of these central African states surrounded themselves with the aura of divine kingship in which the king was deemed to have supernatural powers and direct access to powerful ancestral spirits. Graves of former rulers were preserved as sanctuaries, and traditions were remembered by spirit mediums designated to represent and consult with past rulers. The kings married wives from important subject lineages as a form of social and political insurance.

Many of these conquest-state systems extended over huge areas of land and took tribute from extensive populations. At the height of its power at the end of the nineteenth century, the extent of the Barotse kingdom was three times that of the British Isles. However, the effectiveness of these systems was somewhat limited. In fact, central control often amounted to little more than the regular collection of tribute and the less regular arrival of armed parties raiding the outlying frontier areas for cattle or slaves. All these states ruled through placing members of the elites on the ground in outlying areas, but government was very decentralised. With the exception of the creole Portuguese, the ruling elites had no literacy, a fact which limited their sources of knowledge, information and collective memory, and their technology was simple. In particular, they had no means of transport apart from canoes on the rivers and the occasional use of riding oxen. The construction of buildings and the production of minerals, food, textiles, metalware, pottery, baskets and woodwork was all dependent on human labour, without the assistance of machines of any kind. The lack of machinery meant that there were no windmills or watermills to assist grinding corn, irrigating fields or pumping out flooded mines. When traders from outside Africa eventually penetrated the interior with their offerings of luxury goods and manufactures, the elites of these states had little to exchange for them except slaves and the rapidly vanishing resource of ivory.

Even when the partition of Africa brought Central Africa under direct European control, many aspects of traditional politics remained. The population was still controlled by members of a culturally distinct ruling elite, with key individuals (District Commissioners) located in all outlying areas to supervise the payment of tribute (in the form of head or hut tax). Slavery and slave raiding was abolished, but forced labour and the systems of migrant labour meant that there was, in effect, a levy of labour on the population. Moreover, the new rulers introduced a lingua franca (English or Portuguese) and a new religious cult (Christianity). For many Africans in the rural areas, the British and Portuguese officials, settlers and missionaries had merely replaced the indunas of the previous regimes.

Whereas authority at the centre was focussed on the figure of a king and highly ritualised, at the local level village communities were often acephalous (literally 'headless'). Local authority resided collectively in councils of elders, or temporarily with elected headmen, aided by collaboration between village settlements on the basis of informal agreements and temporary confederations. There were no clear-cut cultural or ethnic differences among the inhabitants of the river valleys. The people called themselves by a variety of different names and spoke many different but related dialects. Cultural practices in such matters as initiation rituals, marriage, body markings, hair styles and artistic traditions differed from place to place but seldom to the extent that they prevented easy contact between peoples. When Europeans tried to divide the populations they met into distinct 'tribal' groupings, they were confronted with an endlessly shifting kaleidoscope of names, dialects and cultural practices. However, the gradual precipitation of this rich solution of names, languages and cultures into more defined ethnic identities can be observed, particularly in the nineteenth century when, faced by the tribute-taking demands of the larger political systems and the insecurity produced by the slave trade, people sought greater security by combining with others who had a shared cultural affinity.

This pattern of state formation provides, over time, a kind of rhythm to history. Just as the seasonal rains determined the life of the village, the recurring droughts and famines created waves of migration that imposed new elites of invaders to dominate and extract tribute from the small society. Most of the history of these states is lost. Traditional stories told at village level or by spirit mediums sometimes sketch a shadowy succession of events, but these traditions are the stories that people tell about themselves to explain natural phenomena, the peculiar characteristics of their societies and their relations with the land and their neighbours. They are not primarily concerned with that accurate recording of events which seems to be the, often pointless, obsession of Western culture. Indeed, these shadowy traditional narratives may say little about the past, but they are usually eloquent in telling how people feel and understand the present.

2

THE LOWER ZAMBEZI BEFORE THE 19th CENTURY

The Zambezi and the trade routes of the interior

Trade between the gold-bearing plateau of Zimbabwe and the peoples of the Indian Ocean goes back 1,500 years, and possibly more, but most of this trade passed through the seaports along the coast south of the Zambezi and used the Sabi river to access the interior. However, some long-distance trade did make use of the Zambezi before 1500. Excavations at Ingombe Ilede, a hilltop site on the Middle Zambezi near where the Kariba dam would later be built, revealed quantities of trade goods that were clearly being transported to and from regional markets. These included salt, ivory, gold, copper and, probably, slaves. There were also imported goods suggesting contacts with the Indian Ocean. The site may have been occupied as early as the twelfth century, but the finds indicate that its importance really dates from the fifteenth century and that it may have been a site linked to some state of considerable wealth and influence.

Apart from this important site, archaeology has focussed primarily on the civilisations of the Zimbabwe plateau to the south, where a chronological framework for the material cultures of the region has been established. Here it seems that the state system that had been responsible for the building of the major urban centre of Great Zimbabwe had gone into terminal decline, and that Great Zimbabwe itself was abandoned sometime in the middle of the fifteenth century. With its decline, the old trade routes from the Indian Ocean via the Sabi also fell into disuse, while dynasties that were offshoots of Great Zimbabwe's ruling elite had already begun to found states in the northern parts of the plateau. These new dynasties were certainly linked in some way to Great Zimbabwe. They may have been the supporters of those who had failed in succession disputes or younger branches of the ruling dynasty who sought to establish new 'houses', but always within the tradition of their common origin in Great Zimbabwe.[1]

With the establishment of these new kingdoms in regions which were rich in gold, the trade route up the Zambezi began to assume major importance and new coastal towns were formed by those participating in the Zambezi trade. It was probably in the second half of the fifteenth century that Angoche, halfway between the Zambezi delta and Mozambique Island, grew in importance while Muslim traders formed settlements at Quelimane and on the Zambezi river itself.

The Lower Zambezi described by the Portuguese

Although some writings by Islamic geographers refer to south-eastern Africa, it was only with the arrival of the Portuguese on the coast in 1498 that the written record really begins. Portuguese writers of the sixteenth and seventeenth centuries provide some of the best descriptions of the lower river that have ever been written. Like many Europeans of the time, the Portuguese were determined to record their experiences, and they wrote lengthy accounts of their exploits and the peoples they encountered. These writings were primarily existential exercises through which the Portuguese sought to affirm their own identities and to see their actions in the context of God's plan for the world which would validate the values of their society. In this they were no different from other Europeans of the time, though few non-Europeans shared this obsession with description, narrative record and self-examination. As a result, the written record that describes the world of the sixteenth and seventeenth centuries is overwhelmingly that of Europeans and the world seen through European eyes.

In 1498, the first Portuguese fleet to sail into the Indian Ocean from Europe put into the Qua Qua river for repairs. The Qua Qua was the northernmost stream of the Zambezi delta, only connected to the main river at the height of the annual floods. There the Portuguese sailors met Islamic traders who were clearly involved with the traffic on the river. As the Portuguese learned more about eastern Africa, the main features of trade with the interior became clearer. Merchants from the Gulf and India (not all of them Muslims) brought textiles, beads, pottery and metalware to the main coastal trading towns, Mombasa, Kilwa and Mozambique Island. There they were shipped onward for sale in the southern regions where the monsoon winds still blew, but which were too remote for a round trip to and from India to be made in a single year. Sofala was still a major port giving access to the plateau regions of modern Zimbabwe, but goods sent from Mozambique Island to Angoche were now being taken up the Qua Qua river and from there to the fairs and trading settlements on the main stream of the Zambezi.

In their desire to have bases on the African coast and control the gold trade, in the same way that they controlled the trade of the Mina coast in West Africa, the Portuguese built fortified bases at Sofala and Mozambique Island in 1506. A summary of a report by the captain of Sofala, written in 1511, told the Portuguese king all that was known at that time about the Zambezi trade route.

> All the trade lies in Angoxe and ... the merchandise is taken from there to [Cuama, which] is a very great river and ... they land goods six leagues upstream at the house of an honoured cafre, king of that land, and there pay his duties and ... he gives them canoes (*almadias*) to take the cloth upriver ... Further up there is a narrow pass through which the canoes go after they have been unloaded by him and then they load again and go another 20 leagues or so, where there is a mountain they call Otonga and there lies a fair where ... all the cafre and moorish merchants of the land gather together and where they sell and set up their markets.[2]

By the second half of the sixteenth century, there were permanent settlements of Muslim traders along the Zambezi, and the towns of Sena and Tete were already in existence. At Sena, the Jesuit Francisco Monclaro wrote in the 1570s that there were around twenty "turbaned Moors", and across the river lived a "very rich Moor, who had forty Moorish servants and more than five hundred cafres".[3] There were also Muslims living in the delta region. The Swahili mercantile culture of eastern Africa had clearly taken root along the river which had, in effect, become an inland extension of the coast.

In Lisbon, the earliest reports concerning the Zambezi region were assembled by João de Barros, the principal archivist of the Torre de Tombo, and in the 1550s he made the first attempt at a coherent description. Barros was principally interested in the 'empire' of Monomotapa which the Portuguese seemed determined to believe was similar to the great empires that the Spaniards had conquered in Central and South America. He has little to say about the great river, which formed the northern border of the Monomotapa kingdom, but what he does say is interesting. When they first heard of the Zambezi, the

Portuguese knew it as the Rio Cuama, the local name for one of the delta streams, but Barros adds that "in the interior other people call it Zambesi". The name of the river is, therefore, ancient, and so are the names of the main tributaries that feed into it. Again according to Barros, these are Panhames, Luamguoa, Arruya, Manjovo, Inadire and Ruenia, "all of which drain the land of Benomotapa". These names are easily recognisable as the Panhame, Luangwa, Ruia, Mazoe, Inyadire and Ruenya. All of these enter the Zambezi from the south, with the exception of the Luangwa, which enters from the north.[4]

The Dominican friar João dos Santos, in his famous *Etiópia Oriental*, published in 1609, thought that the name 'Zambezi' originated from the name of an African town. After repeating the old geographical legend, which goes back to Ptolemy and had been repeated by Barros, that the river originated in a great lake in the African interior, he goes on, "this river is called Zambesi because upon issuing from the lake it runs through a large cafre town so called, and from this the river takes the same name as the town".[5]

In 1966, the new government of independent Zambia renamed the colonial town that had been called Balovale and called it 'Zambesi'. This is, indeed, the largest town near to the source of the river, and it seems that someone in the Zambian government was familiar with the old Portuguese chronicles.

In the seventeenth century, the Zambezi and its tributaries were still often referred to as the Rivers of Cuama, or simply the Rivers. Manuel Barretto, writing in the 1660s, explains the usage of this term. Whereas the main stream was called the Zambezi,

we call Cuama the maritime belt which extends from the point of Quidango to the large bay where the lands of Luabo end; and as the great river discharges in this district by five mouths or outlets, at a distance from each other, leaving islands between them, and the district is called Cuama, our discoverers, finding five rivers in it, called them the rivers of Cuama.[6]

The first detailed description of the river and the communities that lived along its lower reaches was given by Francisco Monclaro, who accompanied the former viceroy, Francisco Barreto, on his ill-fated expedition to conquer the mines of Monomotapa in 1571–2. The Zambezi, he said, entered the sea through seven or eight streams, but only two of these were navigable: that which entered the sea at Quelimane (the Qua Qua) and the stream furthest to the south at Luabo. The Quelimane mouth only connected with the main stream for six months of the year, but the Luabo mouth was open all the year. The water of the river was saline ten or twelve leagues inland.

The Qua Qua river (called by Vasco da Gama the 'Rio dos Bons Sinais') provided a direct waterway to the Zambezi only during the flood season, when it became one of the Zambezi's outlets to the ocean. At other times, overland porterage for anything up to twenty miles was needed before the main stream could be reached. Even with these disadvantages, this tributary of the Zambezi was preferred to the other mouths of the delta, which were always difficult to navigate and changed their course from year to year, devouring any settlement built on their banks.

Access to the Qua Qua river from the sea was dangerous. According to Barretto,

Quelimane is the port and stopping place for the rivers of gold ... It is formed by a small arm of the famous river Zambezi. At its entrance there is a formidable bar in the shape of a half moon, which is uncovered at low water of spring tides, and at high tide there are three fathoms of water, and in places where there are rocks or sandbanks two and a half or perhaps two [fathoms]. Never till the present time have the careless Portuguese set up marks or buoys in the two channels in this bar.[7]

This description of the entrance to the Qua Qua is echoed by the Augustinian priest António da Conceiçâo, who was writing in the 1690s:

> There is a sandbank three or four leagues out to sea with two channels, one in the direction of Sofala and the other in the direction of Mozambique. However, because of the lack of pilots with experience of the bar, frequent mistakes are made. Of the four times that I came that way, I crossed it twice at one and a half fathoms and the other two times with four fathoms at half tide, which is the time that one should enter. For this reason only small boats and those requiring little depth seek out this port. However, it is certain that larger ships could enter if there was a pilot for the bar who placed buoys in the channels every year and who, on the approach of a ship, would go to meet it.[8]

Although the Qua Qua had a dangerous sand bar at its mouth, once inside it provided a safe anchorage, and one where a permanent settlement could be established.

The passage up the river of Francisco Barreto's flotilla in 1571 was described by Monclaro. The Portuguese, he said, used locally constructed boats called *luzios*, "smaller than a *pangayo* [dhow] and sewn together with coir. They have a cabin in the middle, with a gallery above, in which they place the cloth and other goods".[9] The Portuguese "proceeded up the river for sixteen days, and when the wind failed we were towed along".[10] As well as towing, the Portuguese used the established technique of sending an anchor ahead in a canoe and then hauling the boat upstream after it. They passed two large islands, Caia and Inhangoma, each ruled by its own *fumo*.

The country each side of the river he found to be "the most fertile I have ever seen, except the flat lands of India", and the Portuguese obtained plenty of food: "hens, capons and fish from the river". When they reached Sena, Monclaro heard rumours about the upper reaches of the river, that it was only the arm of another very large river that was so wide that the opposite shore could not be seen. Monclaro did not believe this story, but it is easy to see it as an indirect reference to Lake Malawi. He was also told that "silver mines are being discovered of which reports have already been received".[11]

João dos Santos agreed that the lower reaches of the river were very fertile:

When the Portuguese navigate this river they take shelter at night ... and navigate during the day time only ... When boats are proceeding along the river the cafres who inhabit the many villages on its banks approach in their little canoes laden with fruits of the land, rice, millet, vegetables, fresh and dried fish, and numerous fowls, which things they sell cheaply to the passengers, as these lands are very fertile and abundant.[12]

António Bocarro's 'Decade', which dates from the 1630s, provides further information:

the great empire of Monomotapa is crossed by an important and large river which the natives call the Zambezi, into which others flow in the space of the three hundred leagues which we have explored upwards from the mouth at present. It enters the ocean between Mozambique and Sofala, by four mouths flowing towards the southeast. The principal mouth is Quelimane, which is ninety leagues distant from Mozambique; the second is Cuama which is twenty-five leagues farther towards the south; the third is Luabo, which is five leagues lower down; and finally the fourth, which is also five leagues further to the south, is called Old Luabo. These arms, by which the great river enters the sea, form between them very large islands, exceedingly fertile in provisions, and one of them surrounded by the rivers and the sea is nearly sixty leagues in circumference. Each of the mouths of Quelimane, Cuama, and Luabo may be entered by vessels of a hundred tons, which are galliots and *pangaios*, laden with cloth and provisions. When they enter the river their cargoes are discharged into other vessels, very light and long, which are called *almadias*, and each of these can contain from twenty to twenty-five bales of cloth of twenty-five *corjas* each. These *almadias* navigate sixty leagues up the river to the settlement of Sena, where about thirty married and some single Portuguese live with their slaves, fighting men, who serve as sailors on the *almadias* and guard their masters and the merchandise which they carry inland.[13]

The Lower Zambezi runs from the Cahora Bassa rapids to the sea, a distance of approximately three hundred miles. In the nineteenth century, David Livingstone, Britain's most famous explorer of Africa, was surprised to find the river blocked at Cahora Bassa by 30 miles of rocky torrents and cataracts. These were, of course, well known to the African inhabitants of the valley and had been described by the Portuguese in the seventeenth century. The first clear description of Cahora Bassa can be found in the *Etiópia Oriental*:

> Going up the river, always to the west-north-west, about two hundred leagues are traversed before reaching the kingdom of Sacumbe ... at which place the river forms a rapid over some rocks, and thence it continues to be very rocky in the middle for the space of twenty leagues, as far as the kingdom of Chicova, where the silver mines are situated. The twenty leagues therefore from Sacumbe to Chicova are not navigable, by reason of the rapid current of the river, which rushes down breaking from rock to rock, but from the kingdom of Chicova onward it is navigable, no one knows how far.[14]

In order to open a new route along the river which would not pass through the Monomotapa's territory, Diogo Simões Madeira, then commander of the Portuguese forces, sent a small party consisting of one Portuguese and two Afro-Portuguese men to explore the route along the north bank through the Cahora Bassa mountains. The reports that subsequently reached António Bocarro in India enabled him to give the first detailed description of the gorge, including the names of all the African villages along the route. He concluded "that the river Zambesi was not navigable for twenty leagues ... because of the many rocks and stones both in the middle and at the sides, where the currents are so strong that they inspire awe in those who view them from afar". And he goes on to describe a place "where the river is crossed by a large rock from side to side, and the waters of this impetuous stream dash over it, and fall into the depths below and a noise can be heard at a great distance".[15]

Below Cahora Bassa, the river flows downstream through a wide valley which the river itself has carved out, flanked by the broken mountain ranges of the escarpment beyond which lie the central African plateaux. The last of the gorges, a gap in the Lupata mountains, is some 200 miles from the sea. Manuel Barretto described this last of the Zambezi gorges:

> Lupata is the name of the famous range of mountains which nature has formed across the river Zambesi in the great plains which traverses from Tete to the sea; but to give passage to the river nature has ingeniously opened a channel through the mountains, which looks as if it were the work of art. At the place where the river enters high and sharp mountain peaks are seen on either side, with an islet in the middle, which they call Mozambique, because they say it is in the same latitude as the island of Mozambique.[16]

João dos Santos states that the Africans called the mountain range, through which the Lupata gorge forces a passage, "the spine of the world".[17] In the gorge, the river is reduced to only 300 feet wide, and "the mountains hang over the river in an awe inspiring manner, seeming as though they were about to fall upon the boats passing underneath".

Beyond Lupata, the river is joined from the north by the Shire, which provides the Zambezi as it enters its delta with 40 per cent of its water. After this, the Zambezi enters a flat plain and spreads out over a wide bed. Before the building of the dams, this floodplain was inundated with the annual rise of the river, which deposited silt brought down from the interior. João dos Santos described this inundation of the land:

> The reason for this fertility is the overflowing of the river, which frequently inundates the fields lying along its banks, and more especially in the months of March and April, when other rivers and very large streams which empty themselves into it are full and increase its waters, by which inundations the lands are covered with ooze, which increases their fertility. In these two months the greatest floods of the river take place, though there is no rain in the lands at this time, nor snow that melts and runs down into it, which clearly proves that these waters come from a great distance and cause inundations at this place, as do those of the river Nile in the lands of Egypt.[18]

At the height of the rains, the river flowed some 2 miles wide, its main bed uncertain and hidden by the flood waters, but as the floods subsided the river became a maze of sand islands, pools and shallow streams. The main bed of the river was reduced to less than 100 yards wide.

Silt brought down from nearly 1,500 miles of the river's course created a huge delta which was a maze of waterways, lakes, marshes and mangrove forests. The river had to force its way through the silt of the delta, dividing into many different channels, which each year were redirected and re-formed by the annual floods. In the dry season, when the waters were low, there was often no direct access from the sea through the delta at all.

When eventually the waters of the Zambezi reach the sea, it is through dense mangrove swamps, undergrowth and mouths of streams disguised by sandbanks.

The peoples of the Zambezi valley

The Portuguese writers provide some detail about the African populations who lived along the river. They made a clear distinction between those who inhabited the lands north of the river, who they called 'Bororos', and those to the south who were called Botonga. According to Santos, "the sailors, in navigating, direct their course by those two names, steering now to Bororo, now to Botonga, as in large ships they steer to larboard or to starboard".[19]

The term 'Tonga' meant simply 'slave' or 'subject' and was a general pejorative term used by the Karanga to describe the subject populations of the Zambezi valley and the coastal lowlands. Although they paid tribute to the Karanga, they otherwise had little in common, as they spoke different languages, organised politically in different ways and were influenced by different spirit cults.

Up to the present, the term 'Tonga' has been used as a descriptive ethnic term for peoples as varied as the 'Valley Tonga' of Zambia, the 'Lakeside Tonga' of Malawi and the inhabitants of the hinterland of Inhambane. The term, which exists in one form or another in most Bantu languages, turns up in the most unexpected places—and is even used for the descendants of contract workers resident on the island of São Tomé in the Gulf of Guinea. It is not clear if the people themselves used this name or whether the Portuguese learned of it from their Karanga overlords.

The Tonga were agriculturalists who lived in small, lineage-based communities whose rulers were called *fumos*. There were no large Tonga states, and the *fumos* ruled either single villages or small groups of settlements. As Monclaro stated, "this river is all divided among *fumos*, and there is no great chief to whom they pay tribute, but they live as in a republic".[20] Among the Tonga, spirit cults were particularly influential. These were of two kinds: local spirits of the land, specific to localities and powerful in the summoning of rain and securing of the fertility of the soil, and spirits belonging to ancestors who inhabited the bodies of lions.

Spirits of both kinds spoke through mediums selected to be their mouthpiece and were always consulted about matters of interest to a particular lineage. These powerful spirits retained their hold over the people even when the land was conquered and occupied by invading Karanga or later by the Portuguese, and the influence of spirit mediums has remained very powerful up to the present.

The Portuguese believed that *fumos* were chosen for their wealth and that they were expected to use their property for the welfare of the community. The Jesuit António Gomes gives a colourful account of this selection process, as it was understood by an outside observer:

> They also elect their *fumos* and in these *muzindas* [large villages or towns] those who are elected have the first say in everything. They hold their office just as long as it takes to consume what they have. This is how they are elected. When a cafre is known to be rich, a *muzinda* sends him word that they want to honour him and make him one of their elders. He usually accepts and they go to fetch him from where he lives with many festivities. When he comes into the settlement, they give him houses in the construction of which they all take part, sit him by the door on a very elaborately carved *quite* which is a round three-legged stool and people of every condition, men, women, boys and girls come there and dance one at a time. Then old men recite praises to him and there is a lot of food and *pombe*, which is their wine, and in addition he gives cloth for the elders to wear, and jewellery for the women, and so it goes on until he is left with nothing. When he has nothing else to give, they make him a carnival king and throw mud at him and fruit from the forest such as apples and other [fruit], tied in bundles with straw.[21]

The Tonga may have lived in small communities, but this did not mean that they were not determined fighters when the occasion required. The Portuguese army under Francisco Barreto fought a number of hard battles with the followers of Chombe in the Lupata region, and there were numerous occasions in the next two centuries when the creole Portuguese met armed resistance from the Tonga population. Many of the Tonga, however, found that joining the armed forces of the Portuguese creoles was more rewarding than resistance, and the next chapter explores further the nature of warfare in the Lower Zambezi valley and its role in the life of the Tonga population.

One Tonga custom, which Christian missionaries found hard to accept, was the *gero*. According to Leroy Vail and Landeg White,

> the *gero* is the building in which, according to Sena custom, adolescent girls of a village live together immediately after initiation rights at the end of the dry season. At this time they receive young men in the *gero* for intercourse, and after the girl has become pregnant, marriage occurs.[22]

The *gero* changed over time into the *nomi*, an association of adolescents who sold their labour. It has mostly been investigated in the context of the twentieth century, but it seems clear that it already existed 300 years earlier. António Gomes described how "in order that they may have better opportunities [for marriage] the children, after they are eleven or twelve years old, have their huts separate from their parents, near to each other".[23]

As the Zambezi valley was not suitable for the breeding of cattle, hunting was a major source of protein, and Portuguese who chronicled life on the lower stretches of the river described the methods for hunting hippopotamuses, crocodiles and, of course, elephants, which were valued as much for their meat as for their tusks. Gomes gave a lively account of the enthusiasm with which a Tonga valley community joined in a successful elephant hunt.

> Then they send for the wives, the children and other people from their village. They build houses there and each one begins to cut into the elephant with his knife, some from the inside, others from the outside and sometimes they meet and cut one another, but they do

not leave until everything has been cleaned up. Some take the intestines, well or badly washed, and make sausages two or three *covados* long; they cut the meat in pieces and fry it in the fat, and fill the intestines with it to store for future use; they cut the meat into strips and dry it in the sun and tie it in bundles which they barter for other things. They break the bones and take out a fatty substance so white and nice that many people who are not cafres use it for making cakes and other such things.[24]

The Karanga

The other element in the African population with which the Portuguese came into contact south of the Zambezi were the Karanga. They were the ancestors of the modern Shona and in the sixteenth and seventeenth centuries were the ruling elites controlling the large states in the region immediately south of the river. When Portuguese records begin, the Karanga, who were cattle owners, were in the process of imposing their rule over the Tonga populations of the northern plateau, the Zambezi valley and the coastal lowlands. With the Karanga conquests in the northern part of the Zimbabwe plateau, alternative trade routes were being developed, and the Karanga made much use of the Zambezi for their contacts with the outside world. Fairs held either close to the river or inland near the gold mines attracted Muslim traders from the coast, and it seems that it was at this time that Sena and Tete became established as permanent trading settlements on the lower reaches of the Zambezi.

A Portuguese report, written as early as 1506, described in detail civil strife among the Karanga elite and mentioned the state ruled over by the Monomotapa, which was called "Ucalanga", and another state called "Torwa". As their knowledge grew, the Portuguese began to refer to the Monomotapa as an 'emperor' whose territory was called Mokaranga, and to identify four states whose rulers were descended from the sons of

Monomotapa and who had broken away from the original 'empire' to establish independent kingdoms.

The idea took root in the Portuguese imagination that there had at one time been an 'empire' of Monomotapa, which covered the whole north of the plateau and may at one time have included the south-west Butua/Torwa region, and much of the low veldt of the Zambezi valley and the sea coast. This was a period when the Portuguese had dealings with the large kingdom of Kongo in western Africa, and when the Castilians were discovering the empires of the Aztecs and Incas in Central and South America. This coloured their perceptions of south-eastern Africa and influenced the accounts they wrote of the region.

Whether or not there had ever been a single 'empire', by the middle of the sixteenth century there were a number of different states that had Karanga ruling dynasties. Some of these were large, like Mokaranga (ruled by the Monomotapa) and Torwa; others were medium-sized, like Teve, Manica and Barue; and many were quite small like Maungwe. David Beach, the historian of the Shona, thought that "the Shona founded [only] four states in nearly a thousand years", but he recognised over forty Karanga dynasties which ruled over smaller polities.

Beach thought that the boundaries of these polities, and the relations between them, were very fluid. They had come into existence over quite a long period, and they were formed through accommodation between the indigenous Tonga populations, with their influential spirit cults, and the Karanga ruling elites. Mokaranga, the core of the Monomotapa state, at its height in the early seventeenth century consisted of the gold-bearing regions in the north of modern Zimbabwe and two regions on the southern bank of the Zambezi between Tete and the Luangwa confluence, known as Chedima and Dande. It was here that the spirit mediums of the early Monomotapas were to be found in the nineteenth and twentieth centuries. Other smaller Karanga polities may at different times have paid tribute to the Monomotapa without ever being formally incorporated into the monarchy.

The Monomotapas never extended their rule beyond the river, and the Zambezi was always the northern frontier of their kingdom, a fact which apparently the king greatly resented, as António Gomes explained.

> I have written before about these two empires of Bororo and Monomotapa and how the boundary is the Zambezi, which the Monomotapa kings used to call *impando*, which is the same as rebel, and thus, when they come near it, it was their custom to come with eyes covered so that they could not see the rebel that prevented them from extending their empire.[25]

There is little in the writing of the Portuguese to indicate that slavery or the slave trade played any significant part in the Monomotapa state, but in the eighteenth century, when the kingdom had shrunk to the lands along the Zambezi, the Monomotapas began to recruit bodies of armed followers who became known as Vanhai. The Vanhai were in many respects similar to the *chicunda*, the armed followers and clients of the Portuguese creoles, but it seems they were locally recruited and were not slaves.

Further down the river there were rulers who were effectively independent of the Monomotapa, and when part of this region was formally handed over to the Portuguese it became apparent that the king had had little more than nominal control of any of the peoples between Tete and the sea. Karanga rule was, at best, a process of accommodation with the existing inhabitants brought about by intermarriage and the adoption of the local spirit cults. In time, the Shona language was adopted throughout the high veldt regions, but in the valley and the escarpment languages other than Shona prevailed, which illustrates better than anything else the limits of effective Karanga rule.

The rise of the Rosvi rulers of Butua at the end of the seventeenth century led to the Monomotapa state losing control of the gold-bearing regions of the high veldt, and from that time the kingdom was confined to the Zambezi valley. The Rosvi are probably best described as the elite followers of Changamire Dombo, whose rise during the 1680s culminated in the destruction of the Portuguese settlements on the Zimbabwe plateau between 1693 and 1695 and the end of the rule of the Monomotapa in that area. Changamire Dombo had originally taken over the state known as Butua, which lay south-west of the Sanyati river, one of the major tributaries of the Zambezi. Although he died in 1696, his followers extended their influence across the whole of the Zimbabwe plateau as far as the Manica highlands. Although the Rosvi were prepared to trade with the Portuguese at certain designated fairs throughout the eighteenth century, they refused to allow any Portuguese to enter their kingdom.

Bororo and the Macua

Bororo was the name given by the Portuguese to the land to the north of the Zambezi. This is a name that was later used more narrowly to describe the district immediately inland of Quelimane, with its inhabitants referred to as the Lolo. However, in the sixteenth century the Portuguese used the term to describe all the land on the north bank east of the Shire river. The people who inhabited this region were known as Macua, a widespread generic name which covered all the people who inhabited the lowlands from the Zambezi northwards, including those in the interior opposite Mozambique Island. The Macua were a matrilineal people who lived in small, lineage-based communities. The Portuguese described them as having teeth filed to a point and heavy facial tattoos. They were agriculturalists rather than cattle breeders, while those near the coast had an economy based on fishing.

Further up the Zambezi, and in the lands along the Shire river, there was an extensive cloth-weaving industry which utilised the cotton that grew wild in the region. João dos Santos described how

> on the banks of these rivers grow many cotton plants, in plantations which the cafres sow, cultivate and prune almost in the same way as vines. With the cotton they make pieces of cloth which they call *machiras*, with which they clothe themselves. These pieces are of the same size as a scarf.[26]

Machiras were much in demand among the people south of the river, and the Portuguese enthusiastically participated in this commerce.

The Portuguese had witnessed the Karanga imposing their overrule on the Tonga inhabitants of the lowlands south of the Zambezi. On the north bank, a very similar state-building process was underway. In the second half of the sixteenth century, after a prolonged period of drought, the region north of the Zambezi was invaded by armed groups organised, like the Imbangala of Angola, in war camps. The Portuguese had a variety of names for these people—Mumbos, Ambios, Cabires and Zimbas—and there may have been a number of different groups involved. Some of these war bands ranged further north to Cape Delgado, Kilwa and even as far as Mombasa and Melinde.

The Portuguese claimed that these people were cannibals and, although this may just have been an expression of Portuguese ignorance and moral panic, this is not necessarily the case. In Angola, the Imbangala are known to have used ritual cannibalism in the ceremonies that bound young men into the warrior caste, and it could well be that the nomadic groups which appeared on the northern shores of the Zambezi used the consumption of human flesh in a similar ritual way within their war camps.[27]

After a series of armed conflicts with the Portuguese in Sena and Tete, most of the newcomers settled down and established ruling dynasties which lorded it over the local population in much the same way that the Karanga had done south of the river. The Portuguese later gave the collective name of 'Marave' to the ruling elites, probably derived from the name of the capital of one of the rulers.

The lands subject to the ruler known as Lundu extended up the Shire river, where the important rain shrine of Mbona was located. The Shire was a highway for merchants who travelled to Lake Malawi trading in ivory and in the locally woven cotton cloth. Some 20 kilometres up the Shire was the impressive Mount Morumbala. The people who lived there were notoriously independent and in the seventeenth century provided a refuge for slaves escaping from the Portuguese, although they were not averse to earning money by selling them back to their former masters on occasion. Briefly, a creole warlord established his dominance over the mountain but this did not last, and the cre-oles of Sena continued to maintain a rather uneasy relationship with the people of the mountain.

Early in the seventeenth century, another warlord named Muzura established himself north of the river, and António Gomes gave an account of his rise to a position of power:

This empire was formerly divided among various kings and began [to be united] not long ago under a cafre who was said to be a slave of a Portuguese. However, as he had great enterprise, he ran away from his master, crossed into the lands of Bororo on the other side of the Zambezi, and came to a village. As he was a strong and brave man, he would go into the bush alone with only his assegai ... He killed one or two animals and brought whatever he could to the village and left the rest covered by a few branches. On arriving, he told them [the villagers] to go and fetch the meat he had left in the bush ... He did this a number of times so that some people went with him and he shared everything with them leaving nothing for himself, saying that, when he needed anything, he had his bow and assagais. He continued in this way for a few days, together with some young men who came with him. Then the *fumo* of that place thought to marry him to his daughter and had it carried into effect. There was a big party ... [and] after this party, he got more followers each day as he was very generous. At dawn he struck at a neighbouring village, killed the *fumo* and divided what he found equally with everybody, and the people of the place obeyed him. He found himself with more people and thus, by subjugating some and with others submitting themselves [to him], he became such a great lord that he ruled from the banks of the Zambezi to the Mozambique coast.[28]

Muzura's relationship with the Portuguese creoles remained difficult, and he was involved in the wars that broke out in the 1620s. The Portuguese continued to believe that Muzura's fighting men were cannibals. Pedro Barretto de Rezende, who was writing at the same time as Gomes, speaks of Africans from north of the Zambezi who were engaged to fight in the wars:

Their food is anything which they kill, from the smallest animal to the largest, and even men, women and children; thus whatever their spoil may be, they keep it as provisions until they kill something else. These eaters of human flesh are only the Bororos, and such are the greater number of those we employ.[29]

Gomes states that, in their wars south of the river, the Portuguese "went to king Mozura, whose rule extends over all Bororo and reaches as far as Mozambique, and asked him for 4,000 Marave cafres barbarous people accustomed to eating human flesh". He then describes the cannibalistic habits of these fighters in almost pornographic detail. Many of those who were 'eaten', Gomes alleged, were captives taken in warfare, and he claimed that slave women that the Portuguese bought from the Marave were being rescued from this fate. Male captives, however, were not sold to the Portuguese but were employed by the

Marave as fighters. Whatever the truth behind the Portuguese allegations, it is clear that there was a considerable slave trade in operation in the Marave kingdoms, and that allegations of cannibalism were employed by the Portuguese to justify their purchases of war captives.

However, Gomes also describes how Muzura was scrupulously fair in his commercial dealings with the Portuguese and how he tried to persuade them to build a boat so that Lake Malawi could be properly explored. Muzura disappears from the record by the middle years of the seventeenth century, when reference starts to be made to Kalonga as the paramount ruler of the Marave, whose capital lay in the interior near Lake Malawi.

The region from the right bank of the Shire to the left bank of the Luangwa was dominated by Undi. The Portuguese traded ivory with Undi's kingdom during the seventeenth century, and in 1616 a Portuguese trader left a record of a journey he made through Undi's territory en route for Kilwa.

Relations changed in the eighteenth century when alluvial gold was discovered on the left bank of the Zambezi opposite Tete. The gold attracted creole adventurers, and gradually a pattern of relations was established similar to those which had been established south of the river in the seventeenth century. Portuguese creoles made arrangements with African rulers to establish mining camps and by the middle years of the eighteenth century were negotiating grants of land that were turned into *prazos* (land titles recognised by the Portuguese government). Creole settlements were now established from the region immediately opposite Tete westwards as far as the Luangwa. Undi either made no attempt to prevent this alienation of land or was too weak to do so.[30]

The ruling Marave dynasties conformed very much to the type of Zambezian state described in the first chapter. The kingdoms were dominated by two ruling clans, the Phiri and Banda, and

Marave rule consisted largely of taking tribute from subordinate populations and attempting to control the long-distance trade routes. The rulers reached an accommodation with the dominant spirit and rainmaking cults, notably with the rain shrine of Mbona. The Marave kingdoms were very decentralised, and the minor rulers whose lands bordered the Zambezi, while recognising Marave overlordship, maintained independent relations with the Portuguese creoles. According to Portuguese sources, not only were the inhabitants of Mount Morumbala effectively independent: but near Chicoa a ruler called Sacumbe was also, in effect, independent of Undi.

The Zambezian silver mines

One of the strangest stories in the history of the Zambezi revolves around the Portuguese conviction that there were silver mines located just upstream of the Cahora Bassa rapids. The search for these mines would dominate Portuguese relations with the Monomotapa for much of the seventeenth century, and numerous expeditions were sent to find and take possession of them. Yet there are no silver deposits in eastern Africa, and this remains an almost inexplicable example of self-delusion passed down through three or four generations.[31]

The Portuguese first started to talk about silver mines when Francisco Barreto's army was sent to East Africa in 1569. At approximately the same time, Paulo Dias was granted a captaincy in Angola and rumours began to circulate about a mountain of silver called Cambambe in the west African interior. Barreto's successor, Vasco Fernandes Homem, heard that the Zambezian silver mines were located upstream of Tete near Chicoa. He sent a strong expedition, but no mines were found, "for no Cafre dared to point out the exact situation of the mines, as they were in great fear that the Portuguese, after discovering them, would take their lands from them".[32] Eventually, some Africans buried two lumps of silver ore weighing four or five pounds each at a location that they subsequently revealed to the Portuguese. The Africans then vanished, and the Portuguese dug in vain for the mine they thought they had been shown. The search ended in disaster when the soldiers sent to Chicoa were all massacred.

In this account are all the elements that were to characterise the Portuguese search for the mines: the Portuguese start with the belief that there are mines in or near Chicoa; they send an expedition; the Africans refuse to show them where the mines are and lead them on false trails; eventually, the Portuguese obtain samples of ore, which yield fine silver, but find no mines; the Portuguese retreat, baffled. This pattern would repeat itself again and again over the course of the next century and a half.

It was not until after the wars of 1629–32 in the interior that the Lisbon authorities at last sent out a team of expert silver miners under the command of Andres de Vides y Albarado. Albarado reported that the mines did indeed exist and were very rich.[33] However, when he visited Chicoa himself, he had exactly the same experiences as his predecessors. Various people were produced who were alleged to know the location of the mines. One inconveniently disappeared. Another claimed he had to dream where the mines were. Meanwhile, all the places where the miners dug yielded no silver.

When António da Conceição wrote his *Treatise on the Rivers of Cuama* in 1696, he stated that once again silver mines had been discovered, and he was entirely confident that the silver these would yield would not only pay for the expenses of the government in east Africa but would also help restore the fortunes of the Estado da India.

So what, one might well ask, was going on? Why were the mines so frequently 'discovered' and yet somehow never yielded any returns, or could never be precisely located?

Reports that the silver ore discovered was very rich and even "almost pure silver" makes it very unlikely that genuine discoveries of silver-bearing ground had been made. This was certainly suspected by many contemporaries. António Bocarro, writing in 1634, said, "it has been ascertained that these lands are not of a nature to contain silver mines,"[34] while Manuel Barretto in 1667 wrote of "the pretended mines of Chicova ... where Dom Estevão de Ataide found silver buried in great quantities, but not formed there". Moreover, the only time we know of that experienced miners investigated the possible presence of silver deposits, nothing was found. However, this scepticism did little to discredit the belief that silver was there, and there in quantity. The evidence for this was the frequent discovery of samples; the manufacture of silver objects for use in churches, the houses of residents and the court of Monomotapa; and the evidence that soldiers were sometimes paid with this silver.

It has been said that the genius of successful fraudsters is to know exactly what the public most wants to believe at any moment. Following the discovery by the Spanish of Potosí (the mountain of silver in Bolivia) and the mines in Mexico in the 1540s and 1550s, the Portuguese became obsessed with finding similar mines in Africa, which they already knew to be rich in gold.

However, a successful fraud needs fraudsters as well as gullible victims. It was believed that silver discoveries would be rewarded with honours, grants, the sending of soldiers and trade goods and even advances of money. António Gomes recorded that when Diogo Simões Madeira first reported his finds of silver, "he was called Excellency by some, Your Honour by others, thinking of him already a Count or Marquis."[35] It was also in the Africans' interest to pretend they knew where the silver was, since they often received rewards and gifts on the promise of revealing the mines. Monomotapa Mukombwe himself wrote to the king of

Portugal saying that two Africans had come to him claiming to know where the mines were, "and I spent some cloth and cows on them only to find out where it might be and after they had taken that from me, they left without saying where it was and went to cheat the Portuguese."[36] According to Francisco de Souza, who wrote in 1710, an African called Manuel persuaded the Monomotapa to make him a chief, after which he said he would reveal the mines.[37]

How was the fraud carried out? It is clear that samples of silver, allegedly assayed and smelted in the Rivers, did from time to time reach Goa and Lisbon, but these were almost certainly fashioned from the silver *patacas* (Spanish coins) which were common on the coast and formed the currency of international commerce in the Indian Ocean, or from other silver objects. The same is probably true of the silver items found in the houses of the Portuguese and worn as jewellery at the court of the Monomotapa. António Gomes heard a story about the Peruvian miner Andres de Vides y Albarado. He had a smelter with him and together they "began to make a big fire and in the end they took about two silver *patacas*. A few months later D. Andres and the smelter had a fight, and we learnt that the silver came from a fork of D. Andres".[38]

3

THE CREOLE STATE ON THE LOWER ZAMBEZI

The best-known account of the Portuguese community on the Zambezi is undoubtedly the *Etiópia Oriental* written by the Dominican friar João dos Santos and published in 1609. This and a number of other important accounts were translated and published by the South African historian G.M. Theal at the end of the nineteenth century. However, perhaps the most interesting and certainly the most attractive of these accounts was not known to Theal. It was written in 1648 by the Jesuit António Gomes, and, although the Portuguese text was published in 1959, no English translation was available and it is still little known. The description of the creole society in this chapter will draw heavily on Gomes's *Journey*.

The term 'creole' is used deliberately because the society that came into existence on the Zambezi was never a European colony like Brazil with its slave-run sugar plantations or New England with its white settler families and their genocidal behaviour towards the native Americans. All attempts to found colonies of this sort in eastern Africa failed, and instead a society came into being based upon institutions, ideas and practices derived from the interaction of European and East Asian traders with the African societies of the region. What emerged was not a European colony but an Afro-Portuguese community that came to resemble in many respects the type of Zambezian state that dominated the plateaux and the upper river.

The emergence of a creole society

The Portuguese had first visited eastern Africa in 1498, and thereafter annual fleets from Portugal made stops at various ports on the coast. By 1506, permanent bases had been established at Mozambique Island and Sofala where, it was hoped, the gold trade could be controlled. Gradually, the Portuguese began to acquire knowledge about the interior. In 1506, a report written by Diogo de Alcaçovas, based on information received at the Portuguese factory at Sofala, gave some idea of the developments associated with the Karanga conquests. Further information reached the Portuguese when one of their number, a *degredado* (convict) called António Fernandes, made two journeys into the interior and visited some of the communities on the Lower Zambezi. In 1513, the Portuguese sent a caravel to investigate the delta region, but the mission ended badly when the captain and trading factor were invited ashore and murdered.

However, as the Jesuit Francisco Monclaro was later to explain, "the existence of this river of Cuama [the Zambezi] at the time of the discovery of Sofala was kept secret by the Moors of Sofala and the coast, who made it very difficult to reach it until the time of one Gaspar da Veiga who found out what we now know of it."[1] It seems that it was only in the 1530s that a permanent Portuguese settlement was made at Quelimane on the Qua Qua river at the ocean terminus of the Zambezi trade route, at which point Portuguese traders began to make regular journeys to the fairs.

The community that grew up was similar to the *lançado* community in Guinea. Individual Portuguese established good relations with African rulers and, like their counterparts in Guine, they made local marriages. Some became well known at the court of the Monomotapa and, when the Jesuit mission of Gonçalo da Silveira reached the trading town of Sena in 1560, he found a creole community already established. There were

> ten or fifteen Portuguese settlers, with some Christians from India ... The greater number of the Christians there were living in concubinage and the Father induced most of them to marry ... He baptised the Portuguese slaves and the members of their families, who numbered about five hundred souls, a little more or less.[2]

Familiar with the Portuguese who had arrived at his court, the Monomotapa sent Silveira "people to serve him" and asked how many wives he wanted. The community of interest and cultural interchange between the local African society and the creole Portuguese was already apparent. When Monclaro arrived a decade later, he observed that the Portuguese traders of Sena lived alongside the Islamic merchants, "mixed as if they belonged to one creed".[3] A similar creole society was emerging also around the fortress and trading post of Sofala. The Portuguese had followings of African servants, similar to the *grumetes* of Guine, who served them in a variety of capacities. Some Portuguese who resided at the gold-trading fairs were apparently accorded a special status by the Monomotapa which allowed them to act as judges in disputes, even those involving Africans.

The formation of a creole society in the settlements along the Zambezi was not entirely peaceful. In 1560, Gonçalo da Silveira tried to achieve a dramatic conversion of the Monomotapa, as had happened with the king of Kongo. However, this led to his murder by hostile factions at the court. A decade later, the Portuguese sent an army with the dual mission of conquering the mines and avenging the death of Silveira. If this was an attempt to replicate the dramatic conquests that the Spanish had made in the New World, it failed, as most of the soldiers died without getting anywhere near the Monomotapa. However, motivated by Portugal's deep suspicion and hostility towards all Muslims, the soldiers murdered most of the Muslim community in the Zambezi towns they moved through. The remnant of the expedition was finally withdrawn, but in the meantime two official captaincies had been created at Sena and Tete and, through negotiation, Monomotapa had granted the captain of Tete the possession of some territory ruled by Tonga *fumos* which had been tributary to him.

This proved to be a significant enlargement of the territory controlled by the creole community, and it greatly increased its military capacity. The Portuguese were now able to become major participants in the politics of the region. João dos Santos explains how the Tonga, who now lived under Portuguese rule, came to form part of the work force and army of the creole community.

> Whenever the captain of Tete requires the assistance of these *cafres*, either for war or the service of the fort, or some other necessary work for the public good of his jurisdiction, he sends a message to all these eleven chiefs, who come forthwith with their men armed with bows, arrows, assegais, hoes, axes, and everything else that is required, according to the service for which they are summoned. Being arranged in order, each captain with his men, drums, trumpets, and banners, they enter the town of Tete and present themselves before the captain of the fort; and among them all they number more than two thousand *cafre* warriors, most valiant and warlike men. Upon these the captain of Tete can always rely when he requires them for any purpose.[4]

Santos explains more about this African army:

> These *cafre* vassals of Tete are very much addicted to war, and if it depended upon them they would always be fighting, for the sake of the spoil which they obtain; and they say they would rather fight than dig, as those who die in battle end their labour and the survivors become rich with the spoils. For this reason, they respond

joyfully whenever the captain of Tete summons them to take part in war.[5]

Santos goes on to explain what these spoils were. After one such war against the Mumbos north of the Zambezi, the captain of Tete "returned with his men to Tete, taking with him as captives all the women of the enemy in the place".[6] Female captives were much in demand. In the largely agricultural communities of the Zambezi valley, men were continually trying to increase their lineages as well as their productive resources. The preferred way to do this was by acquiring women through capture in warfare, women who could be incorporated as working wives and whose children would then become part of the lineage. The Portuguese records suggest that this was an established practice from which the creole Portuguese were able to benefit.

António Bocarro gives an account of Diogo Simões Madeira's attack on the independent Tonga ruler, Chombe, early in the seventeenth century: "Reaching a village of Chombe's ... our cafres attacked and destroyed it carrying off many black women and much spoil."[7] Chombe for his part had been able to buy firearms from the Portuguese at Sena "in exchange for negresses, millet and other merchandise".[8] Later, when Madeira fell out of favour, Bocarro recounts how a judge sent to the Rivers "attacked the houses and settlement of the slaves of Diogo Simões ... and made prisoners of many black girls and women belonging to Diogo Simões".[9]

Meanwhile, the Portuguese began to make more frequent use of the Luabo mouth at the southern end of the delta. According to a report written in 1667, "Thirty leagues below Quelimane most of the water of the Zambezi is discharged by many mouths, some of them admitting caravels and small vessels. This port and river is called Cuama or Luabo."[10] At Luabo, a typical creole Portuguese settlement had grown up.

Pedro Barretto de Rezende, writing in the 1630s, explains how in the Portuguese territory of Luabo

> there are many *cafre* warriors subjects of his Majesty. Every time they are summoned, by giving a little cloth to the chiefs only, which is sufficient for their dress and also to their captains and some of their sons, they will go to war, or be ready to do whatever they are told, as long as the war lasts ... when the time of their harvest comes, if leave to depart is not given to them, they go without it.[11]

The creole towns

The three river ports on the Lower Zambezi, Quelimane, Sena and Tete, had been founded by Muslim traders towards the end of the fifteenth century. When in the 1570s the Portuguese expelled most of the Muslims and installed themselves in these settlements, they became nuclei around which a creole society was formed. This society was made up of Portuguese and their families, the African population of the valley that was brought under Portuguese control and influence, and the growing population of slaves and clients who attached themselves to the Portuguese. The 'Portuguese' themselves were a very diverse community and included Indians and people from all parts of the Estado da India. Over time, this community came to include an increasing number of people of mixed heritage who combined an inherited African culture with their status as *moradores* (citizens) within the Portuguese world.

Quelimane was situated on the Qua Qua river about twenty miles from its mouth and its dangerous bar. It was there that ocean-going vessels entering the river transferred their cargoes into the smaller river boats. Quelimane itself was made up of the house. of some Portuguese settlers and a church served by the Jesuits. Gomes served this church for some years, long enough for him to learn the Macua language. He explains something of its history and, in his view, its significance.

It is a small settlement with a few Portuguese and many cafres, most of them slaves (*captivos*) of the Portuguese. There is a Residence of our Society there, with a priest who takes care of the spiritual life of those people and is also a great help to travellers who, when they experience air and a climate which is new to them, often become ill. Although the priest is poor, he helps them with medicines and other things which at sea they often lack ... I wish to God that somebody would inform His Majesty of how advantageous it would be for some of the larger ports [on this coast] to have a Church and a settlement because, as soon as there are four Portuguese houses, the cafres start to arrive and become domesticated. Our sailors would find shelter, and those who wanted to stay could trade in ivory, ambergris, turtle shell and many other things which the land produces.[12]

By the eighteenth century, a mud fort, known as a *chuambo*, had been built, though plans for fortifications near the mouth of the river had been abandoned. The African population who lived around Quelimane became known as Chuabo, the people of the fort. The captain of Mozambique appointed a captain to be in charge of the town which, until the middle of the century, consisted of African huts and a few houses belonging to the Portuguese creoles who lived there. It was only towards the end of the century that municipal buildings were constructed. Even then, the port offered few if any services for incoming ships; there were not even any buoys marking the channel across the bar where ships continued to run aground.

Sena was situated 60 leagues upriver. By the middle of the seventeenth century, it had grown into a considerable town. A mud fort had been built on a small eminence within the town by Francisco Baretto in 1573. According to Gomes:

Sena is the capital of this Empire and the fair from which all the other fairs get their stock. It has a cathedral (*Sé*), a *Misericórdia*, a House belonging to us [Jesuits] and another of the religious of St Dominic. The houses are all of mud, very nice and spacious inside and are roofed with straw, with only a few having tiles. The residents think thatch is better because, as the heat in summer is great, it is retained by tiles and makes the houses very hot. Thatch does not retain the heat so much and, so that they will not lose their precious possessions through fire, they keep them in the lower part of the house and the upper floors are built of rubble two palms thick and on thick poles to stop the fire penetrating below. Here at the Sena House, there is a school to teach reading and writing and a chapel master who teaches music to the children of the Portuguese and some others of all races, the children of Chinese, Javanese, Malabares, Singhalese etc. and to some of the natives, mulattos rather than *cafres*.[13]

The Augustinian, António da Conceição, described the town as he saw it in the 1690s:

The settlement of Sena ... consists of more or less thirty houses belonging to residents of importance, as well as others of less importance. This settlement is the head of all the rest and at one time was a great customs house for gold and ivory, which came from settlements up river. Its citizens displayed great luxury, not so much in their dress as in their entourage of cafres, and even in my time there they always lived well, though admitting that this was not a shadow of what happened in the past. From here we used to obtain the bulk of our armies and all the other settlements together could only assemble as many people as this one alone. The houses in this settlement are made of mud bricks and are covered with straw. They could be made of stone and mortar and roofed with tiles but some people say that straw is more healthy. They are built closer together than those of Quelimane because they are only separated by their walled gardens and streets which they barricaded when they were threatened by our enemy Changamira last year in 1695 ... The important inhabitants of Sena usually make their living by trading to Mokaranga and Anvuas [on the Middle Zambezi] where some go in person and others send their servants or slaves. I say 'usually' because some do business by buying and selling in this settlement. Those who have crown lands [*prazos*] receive considerable benefit from them but no one can maintain the status he has simply from his rents, without trading. One should not think that maintaining this status is superfluous but rather that it is very necessary in order to make us respected in Cafraria.[14]

Most of the town was made up of the huts of African workers employed by the Portuguese. At its height, there may have been 70 houses of the Portuguese creoles and huts for 3,000 of their African dependents. However, the town was very unhealthy due to its low-lying situation, contributed to substantially by the custom of sinking pits in the vicinity to obtain clay for making bricks. The pits filled with water and bred every kind of disease. In 1767, the capital of the Zambezi settlements was moved to Tete. Following this move, although Sena remained a place for landing and warehousing trade goods coming upriver from Quelimane, its importance declined. By the early nineteenth century, only a few houses, a fort, some churches in very bad repair and a scattered population were left. All that remained to commemorate the town's former importance was the stone portal to the fort that had been erected in 1702.

At Sena, trading caravans were organised for the Manica gold fairs, and canoes went to trade for locally made cloth (*machiras*) up the Shire river. In the seventeenth century, there were three or four fairs and gold mines in Manica with a resident Portuguese population. However, Manica was brought under the control of the Rosvi in 1696 after the successful wars of Changamire expelled the Portuguese from their lands on the Zimbabwe plateau. After this, the Portuguese presence in Manica was limited to the single fair at Massekessi.

If Sena was the point of departure for traders heading for Manica or the Shire, Tete, which had also been a Muslim trading settlement, was the base for traders bound for the fairs in Mokaranga. Unlike Sena, it was situated on rocky ground by the banks of the Zambezi, a few miles upriver from the Ruenya confluence. In the seventeenth century, it had been surrounded by a wall with bastions, and this was renewed and rebuilt from time to time. With the expulsion of the Portuguese from Mokaranga in the 1690s, the town went into decline, but it revived with the opening of new gold fairs north of the river and with the expansion of trade further up the Zambezi at the Luangwa confluence. In 1767, Tete was made capital of the Rivers, and government buildings were erected so that it assumed more of the character of a European town: with a hospital, a building for the town council, a prison and a fort with barracks for soldiers. Whereas Sena declined almost to the point of disappearance, Tete would eventually grow to be the most important town on the Lower Zambezi, and in 1973 it would be the site of the first road bridge across the river

The *prazos*

The most distinctive feature of creole society on the Lower Zambezi was the institution of the *prazo*, which was to survive in one form or another until the 1930s. As an institution and a legal concept, the *prazo* had its origin in medieval Portugal where Crown land that became vacant through depopulation could be leased for a number of 'lives' in return for a quit rent and for the lessee assuming obligations to cultivate the land. The word '*prazo*' was derived from a Portuguese word used to describe the period of time of the lease. In the Estado da India, the idea of the *prazo* developed in a wholly different way. Here there was no depopulation, but the Crown needed to find a way of administering and controlling territory that came under its control. Indian and Sri Lankan territory with its resident population was allocated to individual Portuguese who had the right to claim rents and services from the population and in return undertook to administer the territory and provide workers and soldiers for the defence of the Estado da India.

The institution of the *prazo* was adapted for use in Africa. Land, and the population living on it, was leased to individual Portuguese on limited tenures, which were usually three lives. A three-life tenure could obviously vary considerably in length but was supposed to give an element of continuity while at the same time preventing the emergence of a dominant feudal class outside the Crown's control. The *senhores* of the *prazos* could tax and command the services of the African population while at the same time being obliged to provide labour and an armed force for the government, pay a quit rent and perform other duties. A *tombo* or register of *prazos* exists dating back to 1637 and shows the lands (*terras*) that had been formally granted. Seven were held by the religious orders, fifty-nine by men, thirteen by women and two by African *fumos*—a total of eighty-one.[15]

However, the Zambezi *prazos* acquired a distinctive character when the Portuguese Crown, through the viceroy in Goa, provided that they would be awarded to women on the condition that they marry Portuguese men. This was to apply also to inheritance in the second and third lives. The Portuguese Crown had for a long time adopted the practice of granting offices to women, usually as a reward for the service of their fathers, on the understanding that this would be a dowry to enable them to marry Portuguese men approved by the Crown. These policies were intended on the one hand to meet the expectations of long-serving soldiers and administrators for rewards for their service, and at the same time to give a boost to the Portuguese community in the outlying parts of the empire.

In Zambezia the '*donas*', the women to whom a *prazo* was granted or who had inherited one from her mother, acquired a unique status, reflecting the pattern of creole culture that had grown up elsewhere in upper Guinea, the Atlantic islands and

Angola where powerful women often dominated creole society, owning property and ships and organising commercial activities. Meanwhile, husbands were often absentees, or died in royal service, enabling their wives to make second and third marriages and to accumulate wealth through inheritance.

Matrilineal descent was, of course, well understood in African societies north of the Zambezi, and the *prazo* inheritance system had many of the characteristics of a matrilineal society. This helped Portuguese creoles to adapt to the norms of the surrounding African cultures.

The land which was leased as *prazos* extended from the river Licungo, north of Quelimane, south to Sofala with outlying *prazos* at Mambone near the Sabi mouth. A detailed list of all the *prazos* with their owners and products was compiled by António Pinto de Miranda in 1766.[16] A group of fourteen *prazos* existed in the captaincy of Quelimane; another group depended on the Sofala captaincy, but the largest group were to be found in the delta and along the southern bank of the Zambezi. The Sena captaincy extended up to the Ruenya river and included the Lupata mountains. There were twenty-six *prazos* in the Sena captaincy. Another group of fifty-three *prazos* existed around Tete, many of them very small in extent, and later in the eighteenth century *prazos* were granted in land north of the river where new gold deposits were being exploited. There were thirty-five *prazos* in this group. The Querimba Islands on the northern part of the coast extending up to Cabo Delgado and some land in and around Mozambique Island were also granted as *prazos*, though these were quite different from the large and populous semi-feudal holdings in the Zambezi valley.

The creole society of the Lower Zambezi

By the middle years of the seventeenth century, the creole society of the Zambezi valley had become fully established and had assumed some of the characteristics of a typical Zambezian state. This society had three distinct classes, perhaps even castes. The dominant class were the *muzungus*. This African term was used to describe a rather diverse group consisting of European-born Portuguese, few in number but often holding important official positions; Indians from the Portuguese Indian territories who were often referred to as Canarins; and individuals from places like Macao, Thailand, Java and Sri Lanka. A significant group were people of mixed racial origin, and there were Germans and Italians among the missionary priests. The *muzungus* held administrative and military posts, leased the *prazos* and organised the trading expeditions to interior fairs. Through intermarriage, many of them, even those born in Zambezia, belonged to family networks linking them back to Mozambique Island, India and even Portugal itself. Though not all were wealthy, the holders of the *prazos* formed a distinct social elite. As with the creole societies in western Africa, disease dealt harshly with new arrivals from Europe, as it had with Francisco Barreto's army in the 1570s. However, people coming from India, and still more those born in the country, were more likely to have some immunity, a factor which over the long term gave a survival advantage to those from the ethnically mixed population.

A woman who inherited or was granted a *prazo* would look to make a marriage which enhanced her position, often with one of the Crown's officials, a captain, factor or judge, enabling her to access prestige goods and firearms and to secure for her family offices, titles and status within the society of the Rivers.

Typically, the *muzungu* elite owned country properties which were known as *luanes*. These would have residences surrounded by deep verandas, built in a style which became typical of the lands along the Zambezi. They were situated on the *prazos* and were surrounded by whole villages of their dependents. But the *prazo senhores* and *senhoras* also had houses in the towns, again large residences surrounded by compounds containing the huts of their entourage.

All the *muzungus* adhered to Christianity and sporadically attended one of the relatively few churches built in the towns or on missionary-owned *prazos* like Caia or Marangue. Their African entourage was also nominally Christian. António Gomes had written with deep feeling about the conversion of the African population.

> These are the results of having churches in these wildernesses. If only His Majesty the king of Portugal could see one of the cafre women pass the door of the church and make a curtsey before going on her way and see the children who come to school and to religious instruction, who in the old days used to invoke Mohamed and now sing prayers along the roads, and if he could hear how their mouths invoke the sacred name of Jesus and Mary, and come on Saturdays and holy days to decorate their church, loaded with branches on their backs and flowers ... If His Majesty could see this, he would have his Ministers be more generous towards the Church.[17]

However, the leading *prazo* elite also assumed ritual roles within African society, presiding over fertility ceremonies connected with sowing and harvest, and sharing many of the beliefs of their subjects in the ever-present potency of the spiritual world. In some cases, when a rich creole *muzungu* died, a medium would be designated to communicate with his spirit in the after-world.

António Gomes was very critical of the Portuguese creoles. He thought the *prazo* system was preventing the Portuguese population from growing, and he became an advocate of a policy of settling the Zambezi region with Indians.

> These lands are divided into several domains (*senhorios*) and each one took [possession] of what he wanted and all they [the African inhabitants] produce is food, pumpkins etc. Each person brings a little of all that it produces to his lord and some have a little ivory from some

elephant that dies. Because this amounts to so little, no owner will allow anybody else to live on his land. He says that the land belongs to him and people can go and live somewhere else. Strangers come from India and do not find a place to live, so they go inland where the gold mines are. They become traders and the Portuguese [become] farmers ... They then complain that the people from India spoil their lands but do not complain of themselves who are the cause of all the trouble. I saw parts of the bush that had been turned into wheat fields, orange groves, palm-tree plantations and orchards of other fruit trees, and nice vegetable gardens, but with "I do not want you on my land", all this turned again into bush ... One house is enough for a *casado* from India [who will] in no time start a big village, both with his own people and with the cafres who arrive to serve him. All this causes great sorrow to those who see these things and cannot set them to rights when the remedy is so easy, and this [country] could be well populated but, on the contrary, is becoming depopulated.[18]

The creole society of the Zambezi was similar in many respects to that of upper Guinea where rich creoles had their own towns on the Guinea rivers and lived by trading with the neighbouring African kingdoms and forming alliances through marriage with societies that were predominantly matrilineal. The creoles gathered around themselves groups of clients, slaves and servants who adopted some aspects of lusophone culture while the creoles themselves adapted to their African environment and came to share in the cultural norms and religious beliefs of the African populations. The creoles looked in two directions: to the centres of Portuguese culture and power for international trade links and validation of their status within the wider Portuguese world, and to Africa for their everyday needs and the day-to-day underpinning of their social relations and local sources of wealth and status on which their position depended.

Each Portuguese creole community had its own character. Where the Guinean creoles were linked to the Atlantic Islands and through them to Brazil, the Angolan creoles were defined by the dominance of the slave trade. In Mozambique it was to Goa and the Estado da India that the creoles looked for their contacts with a wider world. Indian influences were strong and those of Europe and Brazil correspondingly weaker.

The *muzungu* community of the the lower Zambezi was never large. Various estimates of its size were made from time to time. Figures published in 1806 by Vilas Boas Truão gave a total of 502, with 198 adult males and 141 females.[19] Moreover, it had a different economic foundation. Unlike the creole societies in western Africa, the predominant commerce of Zambezia was, until the end of the eighteenth century, gold and ivory rather than slaves. It is nearly impossible to estimate the value of the gold and ivory that was exported over a period of nearly three hundred years. However, Vitorino Magalhães Godinho gave figures ranging from 574 kgs of gold in 1585 to 1,487 kgs in 1667, but as the trade of Zambezia was a monopoly of the captains of Mozambique such figures were little more than guesswork on the part of writers.[20] However, if these figures for the gold trade were even close, it would have meant that in 1667 a tonne and a half of gold was traded by the Portuguese. Figures for the trade at Zumbo around 1750 suggest that 9,900 ounces of gold were traded, an amount equivalent to a third of a tonne. In the seventeenth century the Portuguese creoles had been actively involved in this trade themselves but in the eighteenth century trading was increasingly undertaken by African agents called *mussambazes*.

Missionaries and the creole society

The missionary priests, mostly of the Dominican and Jesuit Orders, usually came from Europe, sometimes via Portuguese India. There were also priests of Indian origin from Goa. Many of the accounts of the creole society, particularly in the seventeenth century, were written by priests. António Gomes's account in particular emphasises the role of the missionaries in mediating the African and Christian worlds. Three examples show how the Jesuit understanding of conversion blended with the cultural norms and patterns of belief of the African population.

During his residence in Zambezia, Gomes served the church at Quelimane:

> When I was serving this church, the Devil got into a person's body and he became so violent that he broke to pieces everything he touched. I went to the house where he was and they warned me not to go near him as he would tear my clothes. I put on my surplice and stole in order to drive it [the devil] out and told it that the surplice was used in the church of Nossa Senhora do Livramento. It then became so weak that from that time it could not do anything and Nossa Senhora do Livramento immediately drove it out and left the person free and giving thanks to Our Lady. Since then there has been great devotion to Nossa Senhora do Livramento.[21]

In the course of Gomes's narrative, there are a number of accounts of spirit possession and appearance of the dead to intervene in some situation affecting the living. Although these happenings are described in terms of Catholic beliefs, it is clear that they fit comfortably with African experiences of spirit possession and the continuing role of the ancestors in everyday life.

> The *senhor* of the Luabo region was in a house surrounded by a palisade, about a musket shot from the church. Round about were a lot of cafres, some living inside [the enclosure] and others in small huts round about. In the middle of the night, three knocks were heard at the door. He and his servants went to see what it was but neither those inside nor those outside the door of the house found anyone there. The next day there was more knocking and the guard posted there heard it but did not see anyone ... He said he thought it might be one of his servants, who had died on the Luabo bar, coming back for some Masses ... There was a boy who cooked for them and one day, as he was serving the plate of one of the survivors from a caul-

dron, he died, the spoon in one hand and the plate in the other. As it was so far from the church, it was ordered that he should be buried there and a cross was placed [on his grave]. The priest was entrusted to say a few Masses for him but must have forgotten to do it. I told him to watch to see if someone came again that night knocking three times in the same way. They were to send a message to me before Mass and I said Mass [for the boy] as planned and did the same all that week and there was no more knocking at the door.[22]

Conversion might also result from the intervention of the other world.

A Muslim *caciz*, who was in prison at Sena by order of the priest, said that in the cell where he was kept (which was a dark building) he had seen a priest who had said to him, "Now is the time? What are you going to do?" The priest was wearing a cassock and stole and we think he must have been the great Apostle of Africa and Holy Martyr, D. Gonçalo da Silveira.[23]

The direct interference of a dead man whom the Jesuits already considered a saint would have seemed quite appropriate to any Catholic in the seventeenth century.

The priest at the time was father Mateus Gomes Ferreira ... With much zeal he baptised him as soon as he could and, after he had been baptised, he then went to Luabo, where he lived, and had his wife, children, sons-in-law and daughters-in-law baptised as well ... As he had two wives, the other one was married to another important Muslim, Bernardo de Sá. Francisco Gomes [the former *caciz*] ... had many families of slave women who were married to his male slaves and they were all baptised with great pleasure and brought along their sons and daughters and, until the present, they all take pride in doing this. And some [men] who were not married, later married the grown up daughters of the others. Other cafres would come to church with them and see them take each others' hands [in marriage] and [said] they were very happy that "these *cacizes* give us women to marry" ... And as Francisco Gomes was a rich man, he sent his wife to church in great style in a palanquin with a carpet and his daughters in the same way. And those of his female relations who did not have carpets travelled with very finely decorated straw mats.[24]

That the conversion of a leading male figure should have been followed by the conversion of his extended family and his slaves would have fitted the African understanding of a person not as a 'free-standing' individual but as a member of a lineage which conferred on him his identity.

Some of the priests tried to fight against what they saw as the immorality and licentiousness of creole society, complaining that marriage vows were treated with a scandalous lack of seriousness. But others made no bones about joining creole society, the most famous being the Domincan Frei Pedro da Trindade, who was alleged to have had 30 'wives' and whose 25-year career as priest at Zumbo led to his acquiring a cult status among the African population, as will be described in a subsequent chapter.

António Gomes saw the problem in terms of finding suitable wives for the settlers to marry.

In this wilderness, there are many people from Portugal and India who are rich and have a lot of slaves, cattle etc., and because they cannot find a wife, they live as God alone knows, while in India there are so many poor orphan girls, both the daughters of Portuguese and of native people, that at small expense a lot could be done for the service of our Lord and the public good. What is more, if those men were made to choose between marrying and having to leave the Rivers, many would choose to marry and pay to have an orphan girl sent over from India ... Speaking generally of the Portuguese, many of them are widowers or former soldiers, rich and with much property. I asked many of them why they were not married and they said, "With whom?" They themselves want to get married in order to have some relaxation and someone to look after their affairs. In this way good would result and many problems would be solved: [for example] the problem of early deaths, because the native people are strong and their women are poisonous to strangers who have illicit intimacy with them. Their blood becomes infected within a few hours and death comes to many people caused by this disease which the natives call *antaca*.[25]

Slaves and clients

Soon after their arrival in eastern Africa, the Portuguese began to acquire slaves to provide a workforce for the forts and fleets of the Estado da India, but they also acquired followers who were not chattel slaves at all and are best understood as 'clients'. These clients, similar in so many ways to the *grumetes* of Upper Guinea, were a kind of personal following employed by the leading creoles in all sorts of tasks, from the most menial to missions of great importance.

At one level these clients formed a military force in the service of the leading creoles, a kind of private army which was employed in the seventeenth century to conquer African territory which would then be turned into *prazos*. The Portuguese presence in Zambezia rested ultimately on these private armies whose first loyalty was to their creole overlords, not to any distant Portuguese king. They could be unruly and were often used as instruments of private vendettas and internal power struggles within the creole community.

The clients of the *muzungus* were also employed as hunters, canoemen and carriers. The Zambezi boatmen had their own particular traditions and esprit de corps, and António Gomes gives a colourful description of travelling up the Zambezi in their company:

They sing all day to the accompaniment of a bell and some little drums. The *mestre da capella* is the helmsman and their music is very tuneful. They do not sail faster than what has become the custom ... They start at six o'clock [in the morning], and at five or six in the afternoon they stop and twenty or thirty boats all gather together for the night. It takes them fifteen to twenty days from Quelimane to Sena and it always seems slow to the Portuguese merchants who come for the first time. If the boat they are in is not in front of the others, they worry and shout at the cafres. These calmly say, "Muzungo, go to sleep and rest" and with such quiet answers they worry even more. One man, who was the chief captain of a fleet and was there for the first time, grew worried and angry and, no matter how much I told him during the voyage not to worry, he never paid any attention and the cafres just kept going on as leisurely as ever. After he had shouted a lot, he said in great anger, "By the Holy Gospel, I am going to take a cutlass and split your heads". The cafres changed the song they were singing and the helmsman started with "Hear, Hear, Hear! Holy Gospel! Chief Captain. Pick up? Cutlass? Split Head? Holy Gospel! Hear? Hear?" and this was made twice as long with the pauses. I was in another boat, he looked at me and laughed and from there to Sena he did not argue with them again, and they went on singing that same song every day. There are at least twenty-five men in each of these boats; one in the prow, another at the helm, twenty-four or twenty rowers, apart from the drummers and a youngster who sits on top of the shelter to warn the man at the helm because the man in front cannot see the one in the stern and he is the man who finds the way. These men are slaves of the Portuguese of Sena, already trained and domesticated and the best fighters there are there.[26]

Women were employed digging in the mines and the fields, and as household servants. These 'slaves' of the Portuguese were organised in a complex hierarchy. At the top were important figures known as *mucazambos*, who were in charge of organised groups, and the *mussambazes* who led the trading expeditions into the interior. These were highly trusted individuals. As Pedro Barretto de Rezende commented in the 1630s,

> All the trade and merchandise of the Portuguese in these extensive territories passes through the hands of cafres either their captives or

individuals known to them, to whom they entrust large quantities of the goods most esteemed and valuable among them which they carry for many leagues into the interior and barter for gold and ivory returning punctually with all the gain with so much truth and loyalty ... [that] puts to shame the more esteemed nations of the earth.[27]

These clients were also entrusted with imposing the authority of the *senhor* over the African population of the *prazos* and collecting tribute from them.

By the eighteenth century, the ordinary clients of the Portuguese were being referred to as *chicunda*. The *chicunda* had their own villages, in which they married and had slaves of their own. They were on the way to becoming an ethnic group with their own dialect, distinct from that of the other inhabitants of the Zambezi valley. The Portuguese governor of the Rivers, Vilas Boas Truão, estimated in 1806 that there were 10,960 slaves in Zambezia with an equal number who had become absentees. These were round numbers, but there exists a detailed list of the slaves of two of the largest *prazos*, Cheringoma and Gorongosa, which had a total of 946 and 895 slaves respectively. Listed were some of their special skills. Gorongosa, for example, had sixteen goldsmiths, thirty-one fishermen and five blacksmiths. The goldsmiths are a reminder that the Zambezi craftsmen were famous for the manufacture of gold filligree jewellery and remained so into the twentieth century.

Some of the slaves and clients of the Portuguese were prisoners taken in warfare, but most joined the following of a *senhor* for other reasons. Contemporaries listed the prevalence of famine in the free populations, or the destruction of communities in warfare that led individuals to find some other community to which to attach themselves. Some also appear to have been given to the Portuguese as a form of debt repayment or as gifts from some African ruler.

Gomes describes how debt might turn an African into a dependent of a Portuguese.

> The Portuguese sell on credit to the cafres and a cafre will not think of the future. He only cares about the present. As long as he has got something to spend, he will not leave the house and when payment is due he cannot meet it. The trader then sends along twenty or thirty cafres to collect it and thus, if he still has anything left after such guests have been there, his house will be empty. When he comes before the trader, he tells him he cannot pay [his debt], that he will be the trader's slave and, with the same facility, he goes to look for his wife and children and becomes a house slave, and starts behaving the same as the others.[28]

When an individual sought to join the entourage of one of the *senhores* there were rituals to be observed. A.C.P. Gamitto, who was a member of an expedition to Kazembe's Lunda in the 1830s, described the ceremony whereby someone became the slave or client of a Portuguese *senhor*. The procedure was known as 'breaking the *mitete*':

> it is customary to give protection to any negro, freeman or slave, who is fleeing from a persecutor, or from someone to whom he does not want to act as a slave, or from some powerful man; or again if he is in danger of dying from hunger. To get this protection all he needs to do is to break some utensil, or tear a cloth, however small, belonging to the person from who he desires help. This is done without a word being spoken. The new owner asks him why he is seeking refuge with him, whether he is a slave or free and why he broke the *Mitete*. Then the old owner or persecutor can only get him back by paying a ransom.[29]

There was also a tacit understanding that becoming the 'slave' of a *senhor* meant that he could not be sold abroad into slavery, an aspect of the relationship that became of particular importance in the nineteenth century, when the slave trade in eastern Africa grew in volume.

The way in which individual Africans attached themselves to Portuguese creoles and became their clients reflected a practice that was customary in many parts of Africa in which leaders of strong communities would attract outsiders to settle under their authority, and successful hunters or warlords would build followings and establish viable communities under their protection.

The extent to which these 'slaves' of the Portuguese acquired an element of Portuguese culture is open to question. They were not, like the slaves in the Cape Verde Islands or Brazil, living in a predominantly Portuguese environment. On the contrary, the creole community of the Zambezi was embedded in an African world. On each side of the valley were African states whose lands reached the river at various points, and even the *prazos* under Portuguese control had large populations of free Africans living in traditional, lineage-based villages. Many Portuguese who visited Zambezia during the seventeenth and eighteenth centuries thought that it had the potential to be another Brazil. However, extensive as the Portuguese-controlled territory was, the fact that it was surrounded and interspersed with independent African communities created a fundamentally different environment from that in Brazil.

Colonos—the free African inhabitants

By the middle of the seventeenth century, the Portuguese controlled most of the south bank of the Zambezi as far as the Cahora Bassa rapids. However, the north bank from the Shire confluence upstream was in the hands of independent African communities which acknowledged the overlordship of the Marave kings, Lundu, Undi and Kalonga. The Portuguese had frequently been at war with these states in the early seventeenth century, but by the eighteenth they were, for the most part, trading peacefully with them for ivory.

As the *prazos* had expanded, large African populations had come under Portuguese control. The lands ceded to the Portuguese around Tete at the time of the Barreto expedition in the 1570s brought a sizeable population under the control of the captain of Tete. He was able to call on them to provide fighters, and, as already noted, they were rewarded with the booty taken in warfare. The captain assumed some of the ritual functions of an African ruler and performed ceremonies connected with the sowing and harvest. As Santos explained, "the cafres show the same obedience to the captain of Tete as if he was their king, and thus they undertake nothing in their lands without his permission, such as planting the ground or gathering the harvests".[30]

As the reach of the *prazos* extended, more and more African communities came under the control of creole *senhores*. These free inhabitants were known as *colonos*, and they owed a kind of feudal obedience to their overlords which conformed to the sort of obligations that were traditionally owed to paramount rulers. The *colonos* could be summoned to provide a fighting force or labour service, although in practice much of this was usually performed by the clients of the *senhores*. Most important was the payment of tribute, either in gold or more usually in produce of some kind.

Portuguese Zambezia was not always peaceful. A *senhor* or *senhora* perceived to be weak would find that the *colono* population refused obedience and the *prazo* became effectively independent. On the death of a *senhor*, there was a period of anarchy during which law and order was suspended and the community was made to weep for the dead. This custom was known as *choriro* and involved an orgy of looting and general mayhem.

Gradually, the African populations which became resident around the Portuguese towns assumed their own separate ethnic identities. Whereas at one time all had been called by the generic name of Tonga, now they became known as Chuabo after the

African name for the stockade at Quelimane, Asena after the town of Sena or Nyungue after the African name for Tete.

The Portuguese creole community did little to alter the traditional way of life of the African population, and the few mission priests made no effort at mass conversion, largely confining themselves to serving the creole community. The *senhores* and *senhoras* assumed the role of traditional African rulers over the 'small society' of the *colonos*. They were active in approving the selection of *fumos*, who were then formally instituted by the *senhor* in ceremonies described as a 'marriage' between the *senhor* and the *fumo*. Elaborate ritual surrounded the coming of a new *senhor* and the burial of one who died. In all these the *colonos* took part. In many cases, the spirit of a dead *senhor* subsequently spoke to the *colonos* through the voice of a medium. However, the relationship was dominated above all by the customary tribute paid by the *colonos* to the *prazo senhor*. Eighteenth-century records show the nature of this tribute, which was known as *missonco*. In 1783, payments made on the *prazo* of Gorongosa, one of the largest of the *prazos*, were made in gold, *machiras*, ivory, honey, wax, oil, chickens, *manilhas*, salt, wooden mortars, shells (*pandes*) and sugar.

The most striking feature of the relationship was the lack of any transference of technology between the creole community and the African *colonos*. Francisco Barreto had brought wagons, oxen, camels and horses with him, but the disease-ridden environment, coupled with the lack of roads, soon ended this experiment. Thereafter, the Portuguese were content to employ African technology. Mining was done in the traditional way: no machinery, no pumps, no wheelbarrows. Weaving and spinning used narrow African looms and spindle whorls; pottery was formed by hand, not on pottery wheels. Most boats on the Zambezi were traditional African dugout canoes. There were no sugar mills, and corn was ground with the traditional African pestle and mortar. As elsewhere in Africa, the only European technology that was adopted was the gun. Firearms gave the creoles a certain advantage when it came to warfare, though independent African societies also adopted firearms when they could get them.

It has often been claimed that slave societies are almost by definition non-technological. All tasks that need to be done are done by slaves, and all problems are overcome by slave labour. The use of slaves not only seems to be the simplest and most direct way of obtaining and applying energy, but their acquisition by force or by purchase seems the most rewarding way of investing capital. This in time becomes a habit of mind, and the alternative of developing machines to perform certain tasks does not become part of the mental universe.

4

THE MIDDLE ZAMBEZI

CAHORA BASSA TO VICTORIA FALLS

The Middle Zambezi conventionally extends from the Victoria Falls to the Cahora Bassa rapids but, until the frontiers of Central Africa were drawn in 1891, it was the least-known stretch of the river. To understand its history, a further division is needed. Approximately halfway between Cahora Bassa and the Victoria Falls is the Kariba gorge, another massive impediment to navigation and free movement of commerce. It also acts as an ethnic frontier separating the Lower Zambezi populations from the Tonga and Toka of the middle reaches of the river. The Middle Zambezi is bounded by the mountains of the escarpment, and people who inhabited this part of the valley were all categorised in colonial times as Tonga.

On the south bank, the land from Cahora Bassa at least as far as the Sanyati had been part of the Karanga monarchy of Monomotapa, which extended over much of the Zimbabwe plateau as well as the valley. The Monomotapa state lasted from the end of the fifteenth century until the rise of the Rosvi at the end of the seventeenth century confined the Monomotapa's rule to the two provinces of Dande and Chedima which extended along the southern bank of the Zambezi between the Cahora Bassa gorge and the Luangwa confluence. The rest of the southern shore as far as the Sanyati river and possibly beyond was controlled by the Rosvi state of Changamire. North of the river, the Marave kingdom of Undi exerted a rather informal rule over the country as far as the Luangwa.

The north bank between the Luangwa and Kariba does not appear to have formed a permanent part of any large state system, though the excavations at Ingombe Ilede indicate that it was closely integrated into the long-distance trade that linked the regions north and south of the river.

A trade route had always existed from the Lower Zambezi towns up the river beyond the Cabora Bassa rapids. The route ran on the right bank of the river, and goods had to be carried by porters and relaunched into canoes upstream of the rapids. This route had also been followed by the Portuguese expeditions sent to find the elusive silver mines at Chicoa. Homem's expedition had suffered a major setback there when the soldiers he had sent to prospect for silver were massacred. A generation later the creole warlord, Diogo Simões Madeira, had built a fortress at Chicoa. This was also abandoned for lack of any official support, but not before Madeira had tried to open up a new route on the left bank of the Zambezi as well.

Beyond the rapids the Zambezi was navigable, and traders went up the river trading principally in ivory and copper. According to the Augustinian priest, António da Conceição,

> From the district of the silver mines [i.e., Chicoa beyond the Cahora Bassa gorge] the road leads to the Anvuas along the banks of the Zambezi for the space of thirty days after which they [the traders] cross it and travel eastwards inland for eight days to arrive at a place called Uroana where the greater part of the trade is carried on. Others go further up the Zambezi for four days and carry on their

trade near to it in a land called Umburuma. Others go still further six or eight days to reach Angoza and others eventually reach Mozimo by travelling a further ten or twelve days, always by the river or near to it. These lands all belong to different chiefs and a lot of cafres live there. All go naked and only on their legs do the women wear some rings made of copper of which there is a quantity there. And round their necks and waist they wear what are here called Balagate beads which are large, badly made beads.[1]

The Amuvas or Anvuas had already been described in 1667 by Manuel Barretto as "formidable to Marave for their numbers and their courage" and their land as rich in ivory.[2] Mburuma is easily identifiable as the Cewa ruler of the country near the Luangwa confluence. The other places cannot be identified, but the distances travelled seem to indicate that the Portuguese were trading at least as far as Kariba.

They bring a lot of ivory, which can amount to two hundred *bares* a year, and a lot of copper. In Mozimo there is also gold but the Portuguese do not take the trouble to obtain it because of the enormous profits they make from ivory. This is so great that a settler in these rivers only has to make two or three successful expeditions and he can, as they say here, lift his head, and he will have enough on which to live for some years without worries. We do not have any settlement in Anvuas but nevertheless our people come and go with confidence because they carry muskets, which the natives fear greatly. Some call them swords of fire and others lightning. However, where their goods are in most danger is on the river because in many parts it is very impetuous, which is the reason why some boats are lost and with them the ivory that they carry ... There is no certain information about the Zambezi river upstream from Mozimo.[3]

Zumbo—creole society expands up the river

Early in the eighteenth century, some Indian traders who had been expelled from Karangaland, when the fairs were destroyed by Changamire Dombo in 1693, built a trading station on the island of Chitacatira about 6 miles below the confluence of the Zambezi and Luangwa. They had probably been encouraged to settle there by the Rosvi, who now controlled the southern plateau and wanted to re-establish commercial links with the Portuguese but without allowing them to enter the Rozvi kingdom. This fair, which later became known as Zumbo, was sited where long-distance trade routes from the southern high veldt, the Luangwa and the upper Zambezi converged.

However, it was the arrival of the Dominican priest Frei Pedro da Trindade sometime around 1726 that enabled the early settlement to grow in importance. He negotiated the cession to the Portuguese of lands along the Luangwa and on the southern bank of the Zambezi, which then became recognised as sovereign Portuguese territory. The legend of the founding of the town of Zumbo was later related by Albino Manuel Pacheco in 1862.

> When there was a devastating famine in the lands of Senga, next to this place, he [Frei Pedro] sent a message that all those who desired to escape this terrible punishment should come to help him build the walls of the church and the convent, and he would then feed them plentifully as his storehouses were well provided. No one could refuse an appeal coming from the mouth of such a man, and the work at once went ahead ... From this action he acquired the name *Comanhundo*, given him by the natives, in memory of his having delivered them from hunger by working with a hammer; and his name is still held here in great veneration, to the point of it being considered gospel truth that his spirit roams in the incarnation of a lion like one of the immortals.[4]

Frei Pedro remained as the priest at Zumbo for 25 years, dying around 1751. He was remembered as a powerful and charismatic figure who was successful in mining gold north of the Zambezi. He also discovered an antidote to snakebite which was named after him (although when the explorers Capello and Ivens were in

Zumbo they were told that it was a cure for rheumatism), built up a large following of 1,600 slaves (and, it was cynically alleged, 30 concubines) and raised Zumbo to become the largest and most prosperous Portuguese settlement in the Zambezi valley.

In 1735, Zumbo had a Christian population of 270, which had risen to 478 (80 of them white Portuguese) by 1749. In 1750, it was alleged that the gold traded at Zumbo was between 500–600 *pastas* a year. If true, this would have been the equivalent of 8,250 to 9,900 ounces of gold, some mined near Zumbo by the Portuguese but most of it probably coming from gold mines in the region of modern Zimbabwe controlled by the Rosvi, for the trade of Zumbo with the Rozvi was said to amount to 2,000–3,000 packets of beads and 400–500 *bares* of cloth annually.[5]

On his death, Frei Pedro's *mhondoro* spirit continued to inhabit the body of a lion and to speak through a medium. Indeed, Pacheco records that he himself received advice from Frei Pedro's *mhondoro*. By the end of the nineteenth century, however, the cult of Frei Pedro was clearly in decline. Augusto Mesquita e Solla, writing in 1907, describes his attempt to find the grave of Frei Pedro.

> I set out [from Zumbo] with the present commandant *alferes* Azevedo and with the trader Eduardo Fialho Galliano and some natives for a range of hills ... some five kilometres distant from the town. After we had walked for some time searching amongst the thorn bushes and clambering up steep slopes thanks to our bad guides, who were young boys since we had not been able to find any old men, we reached a place where in a small clearing there was a miniature hut of the kind which is built in places designated for the *mourimo* cult. There was the customary clay pot, bird feathers and, nearby, ears of corn tied with shoots from the bushes but already lacking any grain because they had been there a long time. Above the small roof we saw an old skull of a chicken or some other similar bird. Our makeshift guide said to us only, "It's there". We wanted to

dig to see if there was the grave of *comanhundo*, the old priest who had lived and died here and from whom they begged rain and other things which they lacked. But he [our guide] replied that it is here that people came to "summon *muzima*" and that he and the others who accompanied us knew nothing more. Later we found out that no one had carried out ceremonies there for many years and that this year, when *mapira* had failed, the natives had been overcome with remorse attributing the lack of food which afflicted them to this neglect of the ancient ceremony which was a consequence of not having gone there to ask for rain.[6]

Frei Pedro was succeeded by Frei Manuel do Nascimento from Brazil, who tried to persuade the governor of Mozambique that the mines around Zumbo could be as rich as those of Brazil and that a full scale settlement should be attempted. In 1764, Zumbo was raised to the status of a town with a municipal council (*Senado da Câmara*). However, this represented the summit of its fortunes. The 1760s were years of drought and famine, and the route taken by merchants bringing trade goods up the river from Tete was subject to frequent raids and exactions from the *vanhai* soldiers of Monomotapa. Gold output from the Portuguese-controlled mines north of the river also went into decline and the famine led to disturbances in the Rozvi kingdom, which ceased to be able to offer protection to Zumbo. However, when peace was restored in 1769, Rozvi soldiers were sent to reopen the roads to the fair which began to recover.[7]

Pacheco's account of the final abandonment of Zumbo lays the responsibility on the then *capitão-mor* Alexandre da Costa, and is a cautionary tale about diplomatic relations in Africa. Costa had bad relations with other Portuguese at the fair and summoned help from the *vanhai* who duly sacked and burned the town. According to Mudenge, the burning of Zumbo occurred in 1779, but once again the Rozvi came to the rescue and the final move across the river to Mucariva only took place in 1788. The decline that Zumbo had experienced since the early 1760s is vividly described in an account of the state of the town written by Jerónimo José Nogueira de Andrade just before the move to Mucariva:[8]

> Here there is no fortress, nor any garrison, and I might say that there is no town, since there is no cultivation nor any established inhabitants (*moradores*). All, or almost all, of them are itinerant peddlers (*commisários volantes*) and Canarins of small reputation: their number scarcely amounts to eight or ten and these few men constitute the whole of the Senate, the nobility, the people and the Justices of the Town—or rather this wretched and depopulated settlement of huts scattered in the bush.

Then, in a much-quoted passage, he describes how

> in a nocturnal conclave at which a bottle of cashew spirit presides, there are concocted judicial decisions, intrigues against the commandant of the town and other disorders highly prejudicial to the settlement in that country.

The disorder, he said, is the result of robberies and hostilities by the local African population, "often carried out at the request of these same *moradores*".

After 1788, the Portuguese abandoned Zumbo on the left bank of the Luangwa and settled at Mucariva located on the opposite bank, on a peninsula of land formed by the Luangwa and the Zambezi. However, although established with the consent of the local ruler Mburuma, Mucariva was very vulnerable. The Portuguese had no sovereign rights in the area, and it appears that Mburuma did not want a permanent settlement in his country, as he attacked Mucariva in 1793. It was then that steps were taken to put the Portuguese *feira* on a firmer footing. José Pedro Diniz, who became *capitão-mor* in 1792, established a permanent garrison and began to fortify the new town. At his own expense, he had a wall built around the landward side of the settlement and recruited a body of soldiers from the local population.

The next major twist to the narrative of Feira/Mucariva was the siege and eventual destruction of the *feira* by Mburuma in 1804. Pacheco gives a very detailed and colourful account of this event, in which he places the blame firmly on Diniz. In so doing, he shines a vivid light on what might happen when relationships between the Portuguese creoles and the local African rulers broke down:

> The *mambo* Guende, the sixth Buruma in order of succession, lived with the Ninamuane Nhamangodo, his mother, in the place called Mandombe ... distant more or less three kilometres from Feira. There he bred some cattle, six head of which had been given to the *capitão-mor* to celebrate his nomination, among which was one that was pregnant. Near to the birth, the pregnant cow escaped into the bush and, hearing about this loss, the said *capitão-mor* sent a message to that princess that she should send it back, as he was convinced that it must have returned to Mburuma's herd ... Ignorant of what had happened, the princess replied to him that she knew nothing of the cow nor had any information about it. Not satisfied with this reply, the *capitão-mor* went in person to her residence and insisted in harsh terms that she should restore it to him. Receiving the same reply, he threatened her and, passing from threats to actions, beat her sorely with a *chicote*. Hurt, and above all offended, by the insult, she recounted this disagreeable occurrence to her son who was absent at another village in the interior ... In the middle of all this the cow in question, without being led, returned to the *capitão-mor*'s corral accompanied by a beautiful calf. When he heard about this, the *mambo* immediately insisted that the *capitão-mor* give his mother the satisfaction due to her, seeing that her innocence had been proved.

At this point the unfortunate affair might have been settled. However, Diniz made matters worse by threatening Mburuma:

> The Buruma's hopes were thus damaged and ... he turned to the ultimate recourse ... ordering an attack on the *feira* whose strength

he had first sounded out. Aided by the forces of other neighbour-ing *mambos*, which he had previously requested, he entered [the *feira*] on the sides that had no walls, taking advantage also of a rainy day, which made it impossible for the garrison to use its firearms or the gun ... which it possessed. In this way it [the garrison] was completely routed without offering the slightest resistance. In disorder and tumult the whole population took refuge in the territory of the old town [Zumbo] and on the island of Chitacatira, leaving behind them a great trail of blood and corpses not so much caused by the weapons of the enemy as by drowning in the Zambezi and Luangwa. The attack was followed by fire and in the confusion of flames and smoke everything disappeared except the church and the priest's house, for the priest, Frei António and the sacristan had stood guard over them so that they would not fall victim to the flames.[9]

Pacheco commented, "in the light of this example it should not cause any astonishment today that Troy was reduced to ashes because of the rape of Helen."

In 1813, the decision was taken in Mozambique to withdraw from the Mucariva settlement, and plans were drawn up to establish a new trading fair further up the Luangwa at Marambo. These were finally acted on in 1827, though this new settlement did not last very long.

The decision finally to abandon Feira/Mucariva in 1836 was ascribed by Pacheco to the costs of protecting traders trying to come up the Zambezi and to the arrival of the Nguni, creating conditions that made the continuation of the *feira* impossible.

When the frontiers of Mozambique and British Central Africa were drawn in 1891, the Luangwa became a frontier dividing the colonies. Mucariva remained in the British colony and was reoccupied under the name of Feira, while Zumbo across the river remained Portuguese.

THE ZAMBEZI

Albino Manuel Pacheco's account of the people of the Middle Zambezi

In 1861, while Livingstone and his companions were quarrelling with each other and steaming up and down the Zambezi and the Shire, searching in vain for a river passage which would take the steamers of the modern world into the African interior, a former slaver, Albino Manuel Pacheco, had been sent by the Portuguese authorities to travel up the river and re-establish the Portuguese settlement of Zumbo at the confluence of the Luangwa. Pacheco was a man of some education (acquired in Brazil), and as his force advanced along the southern bank of the river, skirting the Cahora Bassa mountains, he recorded in his diary a unique and fascinating description of the African peoples who lived along the river upstream of Tete, and of the complex relations that existed between the creole Portuguese and the independent African communities, as well as some of the history and traditions of the old Monomotapa empire.[10]

On 12 December 1861, Pacheco left Tete "only with difficulty recovering from a not very distant past which renders the names of Chissaca and Nhaude eternally hateful",—events which will be described in Chapter 6. For 7 days he proceeded slowly up the Zambezi, describing the Portuguese-owned estates on both sides of the river, noting the well-cultivated fields and sugar cane plantation of Matundo "where experiments already begin to give good results". At the beginning of the Cahora Bassa gorge, he

> set foot in the land of Chedima where the Muanamotapua rules ... It is an immense territory ... but the weakness of its ruler and the inconstancy of the natives have resulted in its being divided and cut up in such a way that it is no more than a shadow of what it once was.

Passing through the mountains, Pacheco encountered a population who called themselves Vadema, who were the primitive lords of Chedima. Cannibals in former times, they are today tractable in consequence of a horrible punishment inflicted on them by pondoro [*mhondoro*] Degue who, in order to put an end to such depraved tastes, made them eat all the bodies of those they had killed in defeating them.[11]

Livingstone's colleague, John Kirk, and Pacheco both complained that the Portuguese gave way too easily to demands for payment made by Africans who inhabited the line of the march, and Pacheco describes an incident when a local ruler demanded compensation from the headman of his carriers for having had an adulterous relationship with the ruler's wife. Pacheco explains the 'scam':

> Finding himself in a place near the road to Zumbo where travellers and merchants ... usually stop, the old rascal ... sends a black woman, one of his slaves, to visit them (calling her his wife although she is not) ... Either by natural instinct or by design this virago immediately strikes up a relationship with some of the carriers ... she allows herself to be seduced ... and in this way lays a snare for the poor master, who has to resolve the matter by paying to save himself and his property.

According to Pacheco, the compensation demanded in his case was "12 pieces of cotton cloth of 30 yards each, a black girl of 12 or 14 years, a barrel of powder of 25 pounds, three packets of beads, a demijohn of brandy"—an expensive way of washing away the stain on the ruler's honour![12]

By 1861, the large tribute-taking states that had dominated the Lower Zambezi region since the sixteenth century had largely disintegrated. The Marave 'empire' on the north bank had broken up. Undi's kingdom had been partly dismembered by the creole warlords, the Pereiras of Macanga, and Pacheco described the small ethnic groups—the Pimbes, Senga and Lenje—that had at one time been corralled under Undi's rule as now enjoying a precarious independence.

Pacheco's narrative is especially significant as it describes the final stage of the decay of the old Monomotapa monarchy that had played such an important part for at least three centuries in the history of the Zambezi. Chedima on the south bank was still nominally ruled by the Monomotapa. By this time, the Monomotapa title was claimed by two rival dynasties which, according to a tradition explained by Pacheco, alternated in possessing it. In practice, the succession was usually disputed and, even when a new Monomotapa had been installed, "Chedima is divided into lordships, governed by princes of the first rank (close relations of the Muanamotapa) which they rule as absolute lords, owing only a nominal, almost derisory, obedience to this emperor."

The decline of the old Karanga and Marave states had one feature in common: they were both relentlessly raided by the Nguni, against whom they had no defence. The Ndebele in the south and Mpesene's Nguni in the north had driven off the cattle that the people had once owned and now raided them periodically for slaves. When he passed through Dande, which had also been a province of the Monomotapa's Karanga kingdom, Pacheco commented that it was "less populated than Chedima, it is for this reason less cultivated. Both territories have been invaded by the Landins [Nguni] and the greater part of the population has been dispersed, which is why these vast plains and fertile valleys are virtually abandoned". He adds, "they do not have any cattle at all. At one time they had large numbers but they have all been stolen by the Landins".[13]

On 18 January, Pacheco visited a *mambo* called Candie who was surrounded by his *vanhai*. The *vanhai*, originally Monomotapa's soldiers, are referred to by many travellers in Zambezia, who usually identify them as an distinct ethnic group. Pacheco called them parasites "glued to his person like oysters to a rock and always ready at his slightest order to commit any excess that might come into their heads".

Subsequently, Pacheco had occasion to refer to the *mambo* Gire, the heir to the Monomotapa title, who lived among the Pimbes on the opposite bank of the Zambezi:

> but nevertheless [he] has houses and cultivated land in the territory of his future empire ... Although the present Muanamotapua is an octogenarian, he is so attached to life that only by decrees from on high will he be freed from his shackles. Such delay frets and irritates his successor but he consoles himself with his hopes, and is resigned to his fate until the day of his glory arrives.[14]

The Vadema inhabitants of Chedima "give great respect to the old because they are afraid of being bewitched by them since they say they could not have reached such an age unless they were magicians". Vadema children, he was told, receive the "name derived from the first object on which the mother gazes after the birth". According to the Vadema:

> God made humans of one colour, which was black ... all the people separated themselves and in order to reach the place that was designated for each one they were forced to cross a great river to purify themselves; however, their African forefathers were very lazy, they allowed themselves to sleep too long and when they awoke the others had got ahead of them and, finding the river had a great deal of water, they had washed themselves in it and had become white. However, when they [the Africans] reached the river, they found it almost dry, or with only a little water and in trying to cross it they fell down, getting only the soles of their feet and the palms of their hands damp, so these were the only parts of their bodies which have remained white.[15]

One of the most important aspects of Pacheco's journey was his meeting with Nebedza, the medium through whom Matope, the second Monomotapa, spoke. The Nebedza was to play a huge part in the history of modern Zimbabwe, providing a focus for Shona resistance both in 1895–6 and in the war of independence in the 1970s. Pacheco gives the earliest detailed account of

Nebedza and his role in the lives of the people of the valley: "Considered to have power that is both invisible and prophetic ... he is consulted by everyone and the natives hold his prophecies to be sacred." He had a very wide following which extended downriver as far as Tete, where "the lower classes of that town placed unlimited confidence in him".

Pacheco provides details of the obsequies of a dead *mambo*. These customs were known as *choriro* or *kolira*.

> On the death of a *mambo* the whole population of the district comes together in the settlement for a period of eight days ... dressed in the most indecent way possible, to mourn the terrible loss which they have just suffered. At the same time they behave in a frenzied man- ner, killing, wounding and robbing everyone who passes through the land where the death occurred until a new chief is proclaimed.

This was a custom also practised on the *prazos* when a *senhor* died. Pacheco recommended that "the trader or traveller should at once order the heads of his slaves to shaved, fire some shots in the cemetery where the body of the dead one is buried and give some trade cloth to serve as a shroud for the mourning of the relatives."

The dead man's wives apparently "remain at the tomb to watch for his resurrection, which they eagerly expect". This is accomplished when it is announced that his spirit has entered the body of a lion and can be consulted by a medium.

Eventually, Pacheco arrived at the old *feira* of Zumbo, and the reoccupation was completed with formalities which involved the local African rulers as well the Portuguese.

> I sent to inform Buruma of my arrival and the reason which had brought me to this place and, in the name of the governor of the district, I requested that he should come to hand over the territory which, by orders from above had been placed under his administra- tion since 1836 ... I waited for some days for my notification to have an effect, for I had omitted to send a present or to pay the respects

which were due to the said *régulo* since I was entirely ignorant of this formality. Once this important lacuna had been filled the aforementioned Buruma, accompanied by a numerous suite, appeared on the afternoon of 24 March, showing in his face that he expected to receive a considerable reward for his trouble ...[16]

The Portuguese then formally raised the flag over the ruins of the old fort at Zumbo.

On the 25th of the same month, at ten o'clock in the morning, I went to the site of the old *feira* and on the bastion of São José where on my arrival the national flag was already flying and the detachment formed up, I led the cheers for the following: His Majesty the King of Portugal and all the Portuguese royal family; the glory of Portugal and its dominions; the prosperity of Zumbo; his excellency the governor general of the province and the governor of the district. These were enthusiastically returned by the troops and the people. I declared that, in the name of His Majesty and by the order of the said governor of the district, I came to reoccupy the territory of Zumbo, and all the lands dependent on it.

He prepared a declaration which set out the terms on which Portugal was now reoccupying the old town:

to constitute a perpetual record that today and for the future this *feira* was newly established as a place where all Portuguese could freely carry on their commerce, agriculture and the useful arts, for which ... I promised full protection and security, which was extended to the above mentioned *régulos* while they remained our friend and ally. When this act was completed, the detachment fired three volleys as a sign of rejoicing and marched off to their quarters where, after a meal, Buruma's *narenjes* [an ethnic group known as Lenje] and the elders of his kingdom danced and sang after their fashion until late into the night. The songs were all allegorical and expressed the hope that there would be an end to the sufferings which for so long they had borne and that a new era of good fortune for the *feira* had begun, not omitting an invocation to Frei Pedro to be a guide for the new *capitão-mor* in his thorny and difficult undertaking.[17]

After Pacheco had reoccupied Zumbo, the whole stretch of the river from Cahora Bassa to the Luangwa passed finally under Portuguese control, while the lands on each bank were occupied by creole warlords who built their *aringas* (strongholds) along the river and settled their *chicunda* followers.

The Batoka plateau and the valley Tonga

Draw a line from the junction of the Chobe and the Upper Zambezi running north-east to the great bend of the Kafue, then follow the Kafue south-east to its junction with the Zambezi, and the vast tract of country enclosed by this line was in the nineteenth century inhabited by a population identifying themselves by different names but all belonging to the Tonga linguistic group. This region is made up of high plateau land and the rocky escarpment and valley floor of the Zambezi river. The Tonga-speaking population were also found south of the Zambezi, again occupying the valley floor and the escarpment. The river is broken 50 miles below the Chobe confluence by the Victoria Falls and the zigzag of the Batoka gorge. Beyond that, the river flows through 230 miles of the Gwembe valley, which, since 1960, has been drowned by Lake Kariba. The valley consisted of a relatively narrow floodplain along each side of the river which was around ten miles wide bordered by 50 or so miles of broken escarpment. The valley ends with the Kariba gorge where the river once again cuts its way through mountain barriers, below which the Kafue joins the Zambezi, effectively the limit of Tonga settlement.

Elizabeth Colson, who published numerous studies of both the valley and plateau Tonga, described the history of this region: "Early in the nineteenth century, the Tonga seem to have been a peaceful agricultural people living in small hamlets scattered across the plateau. They had herds of the small Ila cattle and large fields of maize, millet, kaffir-corn and ground nuts." There were no large state systems among the Tonga but only small groups of villages, while "the matrilineal clans were dispersed throughout the country, and did not form the nuclei of political and local organisation".[18]

From 1820 onwards, the region began to be regularly raided by war parties coming from the large kingdoms of the plateau, seeking cattle, ivory and slaves. The Tonga were very vulnerable as they lacked any central organisation, and their main response was to retreat where possible into inaccessible mountainous areas or remoter parts of the plateau. In the 1830s, Sebituane's Makololo, nomadic and organised for war, arrived at the Chobe confluence from the south. Threatened by enemies at their rear, they crossed the Zambezi and moved north and eastwards, eventually reaching the Kafue. In the process, they gained a good geographical knowledge of the Zambezi valley and the region of the Falls.

The Makololo did not settle among the Tonga but, according to Livingstone, they "obtained so many cattle, that they could not take any note of the herds of sheep and goats".[19] Instead, they moved back up the river, recrossed the Zambezi and settled in the triangle between the Chobe and the Zambezi where they established their capital at Linyanti. From there, their soldiers conquered the Barotse valley and forced the Lozi ruling family into exile. With the establishment of this Makololo state in the 1840s, the Tonga of the region between the Kafue and the Zambezi remained tributary, and Makololo representatives of the king were to be found in the country as far as the Victoria Falls, which seems to have been the limits of Makololo influence.

The Tonga of this region were more usually known as Batoka and were sandwiched precariously between the Makololo and the newly-formed Ndebele kingdom, which had established itself on the plateau land south-east of the Zambezi around 1840. When Livingstone first travelled on the Upper Zambezi in 1853, he described an incident that illustrated the unfortunate position of the Tonga:

A number of women and girls were brought in today from a tribe living adjacent to Mosilikatse [the Ndebele king]. Their husbands were engaged in making canoes for the Matibele, and it is believed that an attack on the Makololo by their means is contemplated. It was considered good policy to break up these canoes and capture the wives and children of these men, and they were accordingly distributed among the people of Sekeletu. The canoe makers were between two fires, if they obey one chief they displease the other. Such captures are of constant occurrence throughout the whole country ... Witnessed the sickening spectacle of a number of spears brought in from a Batoka village which was situated between Mosilikatse and the Makololo. They were forced nearer the Matibele and then killed by Makololo because they had gone nearer. About 20 captives, women and children, were brought and distributed among the people here.[20]

When he returned from the west coast in 1855, Livingstone spent some months at Linyanti with Sekelteu, the new Makololo king, and together they organised Livingstone's journey to the east coast. Apparently, two routes were discussed. One would have followed the route taken by the Zanzibari traders he had met and would have headed towards Zanzibar through Kazembe's kingdom on the Luapula. The alternative was to descend the Zambezi. Here again there were two possibilities:

The Makololo knew all the country eastwards as far as the Kafue, from having lived in former times near the confluence of that river with the Zambesi and they all advised this path in preference to that by the way of Zanzibar ... Some recommended my going to Sesheke, and crossing over in a N.E. direction to the Kafue which is only six days distant ... Others recommended me to go on the south bank of the Zambesi until I had passed the falls, and then get canoes.[21]

However, Livingstone was warned that this route was very difficult terrain. Ultimately, he decided to go by this route but to travel on the north bank, leaving the river between his party and the Ndebele. He was to be accompanied by a guide who knew the route beyond the Falls to the Kafue. Livingstone's party, numbering over a hundred, must have seemed to the Tonga much like a Makololo war party, as he himself admitted.

Accompanied by the Makololo king who had a retinue of 200, Livingstone left on 3 November 1855 and some days later was taken by a guide to the edge of the Victoria Falls, which were, of course, well known not only to the Tonga who lived nearby but also to the Makololo. Reaching the edge of the Falls, Livingstone was able to gaze into the abyss while his Makololo companions amused themselves by throwing stones into the gorge. The next day, he persuaded King Sekeletu to visit the Falls, the king apparently "feeling a little nervous at the probability of being sucked into the gulf before reaching the island".[22] Livingstone reported that "at three spots near these falls ... three Batoka chiefs offered up prayers and sacrifices to the Barimo. They chose their places of prayer within the sound of the roar of the cataract, and in sight of the bright bows in the cloud".

But life for the Batoka people around the Falls was precarious, and Livingstone was told stories of Makololo raiders pursuing their Batoka victims over the edge of the gorge. The Batoka who lived in the region of the Falls were not only periodically subjected to raids by the Makololo but had even come within range of the Mambari traders from Angola, who apparently bought ivory and slaves in return for iron hoes which the Batoka were not able to manufacture for themselves.

This may or may not have been the first journey made by a literate European through the land inhabited by the Tonga, but the diary Livingstone kept, and the book he subsequently wrote, provided the first detailed account of this stretch of the Zambezi and the people who inhabited it. As they travelled north-east-wards, he found much evidence of the effects of the raids to which the Tonga were exposed. Moyara's village, which he came upon 4 days into his journey, he found to be largely depopulated—inhabited only by "four or five" wives—but with a stockade on which were mounted 54 skulls of a Ndebele raiding party that had been successfully ambushed by the Batoka. The country beyond was largely depopulated. "All the surrounding country was formerly densely peopled, though now desolate and still," Livingstone wrote. Two days later, he passed "the remains of a very large town which ... must have been inhabited for a long period".[23]

On 3 December, they reached the furthest place to which Sebituane's Makololo had advanced in their march eastwards. It was littered with the bones of the cattle they had raided and subsequently devoured. Livingstone heard stories of the leader of the first group of raiders to devastate the Batoka country. He was called Pingola and came from the north-east carrying off herds of cattle. Pingola was remembered for shooting arrows that had first been heated in the fire. Livingstone wrote, "After Pingola came Sebituane, and after him the Matabele of Mosilikatse; and these successive inroads have reduced the Batoka to a state in which they naturally rejoice at the prospect of deliverance and peace."[24]

As Livingstone passed through the land of the plateau Tonga, he was principally struck by the lack of population which he attributed to the constant raiding by Ndebele and Makololo. However, he also found some prosperous communities that had somehow survived. Near the Kafue, he saw "a great many little villages among the hills, as if the inhabitants had reason to hide themselves from the observation of their enemies". Although all their cattle had been taken, grain and groundnuts were in plentiful supply, and Livingstone and his large party were generously fed as they crossed the land.

He found little evidence of commerce, though Bisa traders clearly visited the country, and he camped one night sheltering in a hollow baobab which had also been used by the Bisa. Attributing what he saw to the absence of commerce, he commented that some of the population wore no clothes at all, and—perhaps with his Victorian readers in mind—he recalled that he urged them at least to make strategic use of bunches of grass. There were also no guns to be seen. On the other hand, the Tonga did not live in total isolation, and he heard of people who had travelled to the land of the white people. Some of them had not returned, almost, one might say, an early example of the migrations that were to become such a feature of Tonga life in the colonial future. The plateau Tonga, Livingstone thought, were great agriculturalists, but what struck him even more than their industry in growing food was the practice of knocking out their front teeth, which was universally carried out, but for which he could find no explanation.

Livingstone never hesitated to denounce the evil effects of the slave trade, but he thought that the devastation of the Batoka plateau was caused not by the slave trade as such, but by the traditional practice of raiding marginal communities which had always sustained the large central African kingdoms.

In his book, Livingstone also celebrated an unspoiled Africa, innocent as yet of the devastation that he knew would soon follow:

> The plain below us, at the left of the Kafue, had more large game on it than anywhere else I had seen in Africa. Hundreds of buffaloes and zebras grazed on the open spaces, and there stood lordly elephants feeding majestically ... I wished that I had been able to take a photograph of a scene, so seldom beheld, and which is destined, as guns increase, to pass away from earth.[25]

When Livingstone returned to the Middle Zambezi in 1860 with his colleagues from the Zambezi expedition, the plight of the Tonga had become even worse. The right bank of the river was denuded of population "because Moselikatse does not allow anyone to live there who might raise an alarm when he sends out marauders beyond". Again, Livingstone crossed the Batoka plateau and commented as he had in 1855 on the deserted country which had once been well populated. However, although the Batoka were not organised enough to defend themselves and never had "much inclination to fight with men, they are decididly brave hunters of buffaloes and elephants ... The Banyai [*vanhai*], who have long bullied Portuguese traders, were amazed at the daring and bravery of the Batoka in coming at once to close quarters with the elephant".[26]

Always interested to find tendencies which a nineteenth-century Scot would consider progressive, he noted that the Batoka planted fruit trees "in regular rows" and recorded a story he heard of a Batoka traveller bringing back seeds from the Luangwa to plant.

Conditions on the Batoka plateau deteriorated still further after Livingstone's visit, as both the Ndebele and the Lozi led armed forays into the region to carry off cattle and slaves. The Czech explorer, Emil Holub, described how, during Sepopo's reign, the Lozi effectively controlled this region, but after his exile and death in 1876 "the conditions all over the empire became much looser" and "the authority of the Marutse [Lozi] in the eastern provinces had become illusory".[27] In 1882, the Barotse king Lewanika decided to assert his supremacy over the Tonga again and carried out a major raid as far as the Kafue. As a consequence, when Holub tried to travel through the country in 1885, he found the population, unsurprisingly, very hostile, and his experiences were quite different from the friendly reception that Livingstone had received.

The muzungus: Portuguese hunters and slavers penetrate the Middle Zambezi

When Pacheco reoccupied Zumbo in 1862, there were already Portuguese hunters and slavers busy in the area, and their activities soon spread up the valley towards Kariba and beyond. Elephant ivory was the main attraction, but these armed *chicunda* elephant hunters did not hesitate to raid the local population and take slaves. Livingstone himself reported on the activities of a *muzungu* called Sequasha, whose Portuguese name was Sant'anna:

> We passed through a village of twenty large huts, which Sequasha had attacked on his return from the murder of the Chief, Mpangwe. He caught the women and children for slaves, and carried off all the food ... His slaves had broken all the water pots and the mill stones for grinding meal.[28]

In 1877, the famous hunter F.C. Selous travelled through the part of the valley between the Luangwa and Kariba. What he found was recorded in his book, *A Hunter's Wanderings in Africa*. The *muzungus* were not lone individuals like Selous but came with large followings of professional *chicunda* elephant hunters, in reality small armies of men, armed with guns and able to clear whole areas of elephant and other game.[29]

On 13 November, Selous met up with Lorenço Monteiro, "a half-caste Portuguese trader, [who] has established himself, with a large following of Shakundas". From him, Selous obtained guides to take him to the Portuguese trading station at Inhacoe. Before he could leave, fighting broke out between the local Tonga and Monteiro's *chicunda*. Setting out up the river, Selous encountered a large party of 300 Tonga. "If they are to be believed, they have suffered grievous wrongs at the hands of the Shakundas, who, as they assert, have been in the habit of murdering them, ill-using and kidnapping their women and children, burning their corn, stealing their goats etc."

Selous returned to try to negotiate peace with Monteiro. A stand-off ensued, and "during the night the Shakunda on the island beat their war drum and bade defiance to their enemies". Tonga reinforcements arrived, their fighters "with their large feather head-dresses ... and, barring the head-dresses, about half of them were perfectly stark naked". After more negotiations, a peace deal was worked out. Selous suspected this was because another Portuguese trader arrived with a group of *chicunda*, all armed with guns. Selous went across to the island to meet this new arrival, who he described as "a small, sallow, dried-up-looking specimen of humanity, Samoes by name. He had with him several girls, whom he wanted to sell for ivory".

Eventually Selous obtained some Tonga to carry his loads. "The entire clothing worn by four of these men consisted of eight porcupine quills stuck through holes in their ears." As they pursued their journey, they saw on every side burnt-out villages and were told how "their women and children [had been] killed or carried off into slavery by the Shakundas".

Selous and his party skirted the Kariba gorge following a path inland, and on 28 November they reached Inhacoe. This had been a settlement of twenty Portuguese traders who had built substantial houses, but when Selous arrived it had recently been attacked and burnt by Tonga fighters. However, one Portuguese was still operating out of an island in the Zambezi:

> On the highest portion of the island he had his dwelling-place, a square thatched house, with a wide verandah, in front of which, on a flagstaff, flaunted the Portuguese flag. Beside the large house there were several store-rooms and outhouses, and below, occupying half the island, a village of Mendonça's slaves and dependents.

While Selous was there, two more Portuguese arrived. One had "left Portugal at his country's expense"—in other words was a convict—while the other had been a soldier in one of the disastrous Portuguese expeditions against Massangano. Mendonça was a slave hunter and trader and summed up his views on the subject to Selous: "Negro diablo; Africa inferno." Next morning, Selous saw

> ten Batonga women, just captured in the last raid, all chained together. Each had an iron ring round her neck ... While I was here they were

never loosened one from another, but every morning were sent over in a large canoe to the southern shore, to hoe in a corn-field.

Selous then heard that two captured girls had escaped during the night in a canoe. They were brought back, and "my boys informed me that the two girls had been cruelly beaten, and one of the sjamboks, dyed afresh with crimson stains, told its own tale".

Kanyemba

The valley up- and downstream of the Kariba gorge was dominated by Kanyemba, whose Portuguese name was José de Rosario Andrade. Selous described him as a "full-blooded black man". He had had his sons educated at Tete, where they had learnt to speak and write Portuguese, and "upon state occasions he comes out in a sort of Portuguese uniform, with a sword." Kanyemba had some 600 *chicundas*, all armed, 200 or 300 of whom were employed in hunting elephants. Before mounting a slave raid, he always sought permission from Tete to punish the local people for some alleged offence against the Portuguese.

Kanyemba was one of the most powerful and influential of the *muzungus* of the Middle Zambezi, his influence extending from Zumbo to Inhacoe beyond the Kariba gorge, and during his ascendancy this area was ruthlessly subjected to slave raiding and the extermination of region's wildlife. The Tonga of the north bank and the Shona of the south had to endure the depredations of his *chicunda*. He was tolerated by the Portuguese authorities largely because he provided a barrier against the Ndebele, who were also in the business of raiding the valley communities. Kanyemba and the other *muzungu senhores* also always acknowledged a symbolic Portuguese authority and flew Portuguese flags from their stockades. In the 1880s, as the scramble for Africa got underway, this extension of a nominal Portuguese presence would prove invaluable to a hard-pressed country faced by the predatory powers of Britain and Germany.

Kanyemba and his two brothers wielded considerable power over a large part of the Middle Zambezi, particularly on the south of the river which they contested with the Ndebele. When the frontiers were drawn in 1891, most of the area he controlled fell to the British South Africa Company. Kanyemba himself returned to Portuguese territory, but one of his brothers was recognised by the British South Africa Company as chief of the part of the valley now largely populated by *chicunda*. Kanyemba, however, remained the great leader in historical memory, and after his death the medium who conversed with his spirit became a powerful figure in the northern part of Southern Rhodesia/ Zimbabwe, with his medals and Portuguese insignia of office being the sacred objects attached to his shrine. The settlement near the Zambezi opposite Zumbo was even called Kanyemba after him.[30]

The Ndebele kingdom and the wasting of the Zambezi

To the south of the Middle Zambezi, the plateau and the lands beyond the escarpment had seen the establishment of the Karanga kingdoms in the sixteenth and seventeenth centuries. These had been structured like many of the African kingdoms of this region: a ruling elite which received tribute from ethnically diverse and subordinate populations on their borders; alliance with the powerful spirit mediums of the land; and an economy based on cattle ownership and long-distance trade in gold, ivory, copper and other commodities which were exchanged at fairs with the agents of coastal merchants. During the eighteenth century, the plateau had been ruled by the elite Rosvi lineages and their king who bore the title of Changamire. Changamire's influence certainly reached the Portuguese town at Zumbo, which was under his protection, and geography suggests that his influence may have extended over the valley as far as the Victoria Falls.

However, by the early nineteenth century the Rosvi state was weakening, partly as a result of prolonged periods of drought and partly from rivalries within the ruling Rosvi elite. The cohesion of the state was severely damaged in the 1820s and 1830s by the Nguni invasions of Maseko and Zwangendaba, whose armies remained for some years in the country before proceeding north across the Zambezi. The Rosvi state still had not recovered when in 1838–9 a new Nguni army arrived from the south under the leadership of Mzilikatzi. Mzilikatzi had broken away from the rule of the Zulu king Shaka in 1822 and for more than 10 years had built up a state in what was later to become the Transvaal. His original group of not more than 500 Nguni fighters had grown into a sizeable community of tens of thousands through the practice of raiding neighbouring people for captives who were then absorbed into the Nguni society which, like that of the Zulus, was structured round a system of regiments. This new nation became known as the Ndebele.

Defeated by the Boers in 1837, Mzilikatzi led one section of his people north and west and seems to have wanted to settle near Lake Ngami on the edge of the Okavango delta, while another section entered the region still ruled by the Changamire Rosvi. Once the two Ndebele groups were reunited, a permanent Nguni presence in the region around Bulawayo grew gradually into a large kingdom.

Although its military organisation and social structure was clearly derived from its Zulu origins, Mzilikatzi's kingdom adapted to local realities and began to absorb the populations which had previously been ruled by the Rosvi. Alliances were built with local spirit cults, and the population of the kingdom grew through a system of exchanging cattle for a tribute of young men who were then absorbed into the regimental system. The Ndebele also systematically raided the still independent Shona communities in the north and east and the Tonga peoples of the Zambezi valley westwards as far as the Victoria Falls. It seems that the Ndebele aspired to attack and defeat the Makololo and after them the Lozi, whose kingdom occupied the Barotse floodplain.

The Ndebele created a structured society in which the descendants of the original Nguni followers of Mzilikatzi formed an elite known as *zanzi*, who remained exclusive and only married among themselves. Meanwhile, the conquered and assimilated people formed subordinate groups known as *enhla*, and were able to become partially assimilated through the regimental system. As the main structure of the kingdom and its national culture was inseparably linked to the regiments located in regimental towns, it was necessary for there to be a continuous state of warfare so that new generations of Ndebele and young men captured in raids could prove their bravery and fighting spirit and, incidentally, reward themselves with captured cattle and women. From 1860 onwards, Ndebele impis (regiments) annually raided the Shona areas to the north while the remnants of the Rosvi finally disappeared from history.

This was the background to the years of Ndebele raiding in the Zambezi valley. There were clashes with the Makololo near the Victoria Falls where the Ndebele suffered losses, and there were regular forays into the Gwembe valley where the local Tonga population did not have the organisation to provide much resistance. Eventually, large parts of the southern bank of the Zambezi became depopulated as inhabitants fled across the river to find some protection.

However, the Ndebele kingdom never established permanent military control over the valley, as the environment did not allow for cattle rearing and the presence of malaria also discouraged permanent settlement. Moreover, although the Ndebele impis frequently crossed the river, the Zambezi acted as a fairly effective barrier to any permanent expansion of the kingdom to the north.

Ndebele raids could be highly destructive for the valley populations. A raiding party would descend on villages, the huts would be burned, any cattle driven off and some women and children taken as captives. The rest of the population, adult men and the elderly, would be massacred. The economy of the Tonga population of the valley was in effect ruined and established communities were broken up, as their only response was to retreat into inaccessible areas of the escarpment.

Ndebele raids continued until the kingdom was conquered by white settler armies in 1893. The last raid into the north-eastern Shona territories took place in 1892 and the last raid into the Zambezi valley was in 1893. The aftermath of this raid was gruesomely described by the missionary Louis Jalla, who visited the site of one massacre 2 months after it occurred:

> All the prisoners were murdered without exception, and the details given by some eye-witnesses who were left for dead, but revived by the fresh air, make one shudder. Some men were hung by the feet to trees, and left thus with assegais in the body. Others bound to a tree trunk and burnt by slow fire, to judge by their shrivelled and blackened hands. Numbers of little children were strung by the feet to a long perch under which the enemy lighted fires ... When we reached the spot, the camp was just as the enemy had left it. On all sides bones were lying about, scattered by the hyenas or vultures who had been enjoying the carcasses for the last month. Judging by the remains lying among the skeletons, the majority of the prisoners had been women, especially young girls.[31]

It is often maintained that the Ndebele were not slave owners, though the lower ranks of their society had a semi-servile status. Nevertheless, it is clear that they provided a market for the *chicunda* slave hunters from the Lower Zambezi who continued their lucrative profession, selling slaves to the Ndebele, long after the overseas slave trade had dwindled into insignificance.

The establishment of the Ndebele kingdom was more or less contemporary with the Makololo conquest of Barotseland, and it is interesting to compare the two conquest states. In many respects, both fitted the pattern of central African kingship. Both were based on an elite of fighters, only a few hundred in number, coming from the south (the original Karanga dynasties which had formed the Monomotapa and Rosvi kingdoms had also come from the south). Both structured their kingdoms round this ruling elite of southerners and then sought to build alliances with the conquered populations, and both imposed their language as a unifying influence. Both kingdoms had a frontier where frequent raids compelled the population to pay tribute to the centre, often in the form of captives, and both sought to control access to their kingdoms by outsiders. They also sought to regulate key aspects of the economy, for instance, the hunting of elephants.

If there are many superficial similarities, there are also significant differences. In particular, the regimental structures of Ndebele society which enabled them successfully to absorb non-Ndebele into their nation had no real parallel among the Makololo. Moreover, the Makololo never eliminated the old Lozi ruling class and were much less successful in absorbing the pre-existing ruling elites than the Ndebele were with the former Rosvi. In the end, the Makololo were undermined and destroyed by the climate of the Zambezi valley, while the Ndebele continued to thrive in the dry, healthy uplands of the Zimbabwe plateau.

5

THE UPPER ZAMBEZI AND
THE BAROTSE VALLEY

Nineteenth-century travellers describe the Upper Zambezi

The most notable feature of the Upper Zambezi is the floodplain of Barotseland. While many of the rivers that enter the Zambezi also have valleys which flood at the height of the rains, the Barostse floodplain is about 6,000 square kilometres and varies from 30 to 50 kilometres in width. It extends from the junction of the Zambezi with the Kabompo river in the north-west for 230 kilometres downstream to the Ngonye Falls. Beyond the falls, there is a further 150 kilometres to the Victoria Falls, a stretch where the river passes over more than 24 large and small cataracts.

The great Barotse floodplain, through which the Zambezi passes as a wide and peacefully flowing river, is quite different from all other stretches of the river due to its breadth, the extent of the floodplain and the fact that the river is eminently suitable for navigation. Along this stretch of the river are a number of towns of historic importance. Near the mouth of the Chobe river below the Ngonye Falls are the towns of Sesheke and Kazungula on the left bank. Further upstream is Nalolo, the 'second capital' of Barotseland, and then Lealui, which at the end of the nineteenth century had been connected to the Zambezi by a 2-mile-long canal. Limulunga, which lies on high ground at the edge of the Barotse floodplain, is 21 kilometres east of the main channel of the river and was the wet-season residence of the king. Mongu, which became the principal town in the colonial period, was some 15 kilometres from the river. The existence of these towns close to the river can be explained by the fact that, unlike the lower reaches of the Zambezi, the river in Barotseland was always the main highway and principal artery of commerce and communication, connecting all the different parts of the kingdom.

As the river flows eastwards it is partly blocked by the Ngonye Falls at a point where the Kalahari sands meet a large outcrop of sandstone rock. From being up to a mile wide, the Zambezi narrows to 300 feet, the Falls acting as a kind of dam which is largely responsible for the flooding of the valley above it during the wet season. Livingstone believed that the Barotse valley had originally been one great lake before the river carved a passage through the Ngonye Falls, and it is now thought that the whole Upper Zambezi, and the rivers that join it, at one time formed part of the Okavango delta system.

At the Ngonye Falls canoes had to be unloaded and their contents carried for four miles until navigable waters could again be reached. In 1878, the Portuguese traveller Alexandre de Serpa Pinto described how

> the conveyance of the canoes by land was effected by natives of the hamlets of Sioma, people of Calacas or slaves, governed by a Luina chief, who are established there by the Lui [Lozi] government for the express purpose of performing this service, to which they are bound without being entitled to any recompence whatever.[1]

By the end of the nineteenth century, a system of rollers assisted the passage of the canoes. Downstream from the Falls, there is a series of twenty-four rapids before the river reaches the mouth of the Chobe and beyond that the Victoria Falls. Canoes heading upriver from Kazungula and Sesheke were able to negotiate these cataracts at most seasons of the year. In June 1883, the missionary Frederick Arnot described passing the rapids:

> The king sent me away in his largest river boat ... with instructions that I was to be landed while the boat was shooting the rapids ... The boats got through the rapids without serious damage ... I preferred being wetted with the water to getting my legs cut with rocks and reeds and did not leave the boat, but we had a narrow escape at one point.[2]

The junction between the Chobe and the Zambezi became a key strategic point in the history of the region and today is the point where the frontiers of Namibia, Botswana, Zambia and Zimbabwe meet. In the nineteenth century, a ferry operated at the junction of the rivers. The ferryman was answerable to the king, and he controlled what was, in effect, the gateway to the valley upstream. Traders coming from the south with donkeys or mules, as well as those with wagons and spans of oxen, had to wait for permission to cross and then had to swim their beasts across nearly a mile of river. Emil Holub, who crossed the river in 1885, reported that the ferryman, Sinjantu, regularly fed the crocodiles in the river, and as a result they would appear whenever they heard his voice. It was widely believed that the crocodiles respected him, and this gave him huge prestige so that "he was more feared than esteemed and [was] very well known in the whole central Zambezi area".

Arnot described an attempt to use this ferry in August 1882:

> The Zambesi at that point is as broad as the Clyde at Dumbarton, and is very deep from bank to bank; the Chobe is a little narrower. Late in the afternoon the old man started in his canoe, but instead of coming over to us he went a long way up the river and crossed to the island of Inparairie. However, he came down after a time and

landed where we were ... Three trips took us and our bundles across in his cranky canoe. Everything got wet and I had to sit down in water. The edge of the canoe—the trunk of a tree shaped a bit and hollowed out—was scarcely a handbreadth from the water ...[3]

Most traders and hunters arriving from the south brought their wagons as far as the Chobe, but hesitated to advance into regions along the Zambezi believed to be infested by tsetse fly. However, in 1853, Livingstone, with the help of the Makololo in Linyanti, crossed the Chobe with his wagon. "They did it in fine style, swimming and diving among the oxen more like alligators than men and taking the waggons to pieces and carrying them across on a number of canoes lashed together."[4] By the time Emil Holub arrived at the Chobe confluence in 1885, it was quite common for wagons to cross the Zambezi. He gives a graphic description of what was involved in forcing the trek oxen to cross:

The animal was pushed forcibly into the water and had to swim beside the boat. One man rowed in the rear of the boat and a second knelt in the front trying to keep the head of the ox above water by means of a leather strap tied around his horns, or in the case of the donkey by means of his halter. This always caused quite an excitement and was an extremely exhausting job, for only very few animals understand what one wants from them. Usually they kick violently in all directions or they try to jump into the boat with their front legs and thus they endanger the lives of those sitting in the boat. The tribes along the river take for such crossings only their biggest boats in order to keep a certain balance with the stubborn and intractible animals.[5]

As Arnot had found, the canoe operated by the ferryman was impossibly unsafe and inadequate for the task.

On 2 June we began with the crossing of the Zambezi and by 3 June ... we had brought everything across the river. However, because of the strong south-east winds, this would not have been possible even within a week if we had had to rely on those miserable Mashupia canoes cut out of one tree trunk. How inefficient these canoes are can be proved by the fact that these canoes on those two days made only five trips for me and each time could only take the loads of two porters (about fifty kilogrammes) ... The natives cannot use these canoes at all on the broad, choppy river if there is a strong wind blowing, since the canoes can turn over rather easily and the shipwrecked persons are then in great danger for their lives because of the numerous crocodiles.[6]

Above the Ngonye Falls the vast expanse of the river, like a moving lake, became rough and dangerous in high winds. During the rainy season the water could be churned up into waves that frequently swamped the canoes which were the means of river transport. When Livingstone ascended the river in the company of King Sekeletu for the first time in 1853, one of the canoes capsized and a Makololo being carried in it drowned. The river was also full of other hazards, including crocodiles and hippopotamuses. There were communities along the banks who were professional hippopotamus hunters, but most of the traffic on the river was very wary of these animals. Livingstone wrote in his diaries:

He is a dangerous animal by night, but danger is in a measure avoided by winding along the banks by day and taking the middle of the river by night ... A canoe approaching him in his walk appears to him an attack. He strikes it with feet and breaks it to shivers, and generally makes off. A few old gentlemen who have become crusty take to canoe breaking ... When an attack is made on a canoe by an animal bent on destroying the people in it, the Borotse invariably glide down to the bottom. He seeks men on the surface only.[7]

Hippos apart, the lack of major obstructions made the river a highway frequented by the population and provided a corridor linking the various parts of the large kingdom that grew up along the valley. Although in places the riverbanks were thickly wooded, for the most part they were covered with extensive beds of reeds and grass. These were used in the construction and roofing of huts, but in the height of the dry season the reed beds were often swept by fires, which could rage unchecked across the countryside.

Major Gibbons, travelling up the Zambezi in 1898, was particularly struck by the beauty of the river:

> The Zambesi is in fact, one of those scenes which could be more effectively dealt with by the pen of the poet than by the painter's art. A noble expanse of transparent water, studded here and there with treeless islands; a fringe of tall, matted reeds, and about a mile of plain beyond, with a background of tree-clad undulations, make up the view to right and left ... The river is broken up by innumerable tree-clad islands into narrow, rocky channels through which the water rushes and murmurs on its onward course. Above the overhanging branches meet and cast their shade on the watery surface beneath them. Occasional open spaces allow the bright tropical sun to cast his dazzling rays on the dancing torrent.[8]

There were many islands in the river, some of them reed islands rather than islands made of firm ground. Elephants would cross to these islands or sometimes cross the full expanse of the river, particularly when pursued by hunters, and boatmen sometimes camped on the islands to escape the attention of lions, as they did on the lower reaches of the Zambezi. Some of the islands featured in the historical memories of the people, especially the tale of an Ndebele raiding party which was lured onto an island, marooned there and eventually destroyed.

The passage up and down the river bred very skilled boatmen who could hunt from their canoes. Livingstone described how they were

> most expert in the management of their small, thin, light canoes ... the men stand upright in the canoe, though it is not more than fifteen or eighteen inches wide and about fifteen feet long; their paddles, ten feet in length are ... very light, yet as elastic as ash. With these they either punt or paddle, according to the shallowness or depth of the water.[9]

The large canoes reserved for the king and other dignitaries could be more than 30 feet long and had 6 to 8 paddlers who "stand upright and keep the stroke with great precision".[10] Major Gibbons was provided with one of these:

> Three canoes had been lent me; the one in which I travelled was four feet at the beam, and was manned by five paddlers. It was about the largest 'dug-out' canoe I have seen, and though comfortable was very heavy and slow ... the boys called it 'incubu', or hippopotamus, by reason of its ponderous proportions.[11]

In 1911, Arnot returned to the Upper Zambezi region with his wife, and in his diary he described in detail how these canoes, some of which were as much as forty years old, were made:

> We saw a group of canoe carpenters camped around a mahogany log that they had just felled. The first season's work is to trim the outside roughly, and hollow it out while soft and green, leaving the sides of the canoe about six inches thick, covering it over with leaves, branches, and grass. They have to season it for a year, then, returning with supplies of meal and snuff, they camp out for weeks together.

A large party is then held to gather enough people together, and the tree is then dragged a mile or so to the river.

> [The] canoes are then generally sold by the Lunda forest men in this state to Bambowe experts. They allow it another year's soaking in the river before it is pulled up under the shade of a great tree and finished off, the sides varying in thickness from half-an-inch to an inch lower down.[12]

Before the twentieth century, the river provided much of the population with a living. There was plentiful wild game, not yet depleted by firearms and overhunting. Fish also provided a living, and Livingstone recalled that, even in years of drought and famine, fish were always available. Major Gibbons once witnessed a fishing technique that could best be described as a form of trawling:

Close to my tent, and covering some four or five acres of ground, several huge fishing nets were stretched on the ground. These nets are beautifully made out of tan-coloured bark twine, and are at once strong and durable. When in use they are stretched across the river—which at Nalolo is about 250 yards—and dragged forward by men in canoes and on the banks.[13]

Above the Ngonye Falls, the vast plains of the Barotse valley flooded after the winter rains, the flooding beginning in February and generally lasting till May. Here the Zambezi behaved much like the Nile, as Livingstone pointed out. The floods deposited the silt which was brought down and created a rich environment for wildlife, as well as for the rearing of cattle and agriculture. During the floods, the population retreated to small islands of higher ground. Most of these had originated as white ant hills, but Livingstone believed that some of them were artificial and had been raised by human labour, especially during the time of King Santuru, who had immediately preceded the Makololo conquest.

When the floods subsided, the valley was covered with rich grasslands which sustained large herds of cattle. "These thrive wonderfully and give milk copiously to their owners," Livingstone observed. Downstream from the Ngonye Falls the broken country—and especially the escarpment area to the north—was infested with tsetse fly and unsuitable for cattle. It was the Barotse valley above the Falls where conditions existed which allowed cattle breeding, where large populations could make a living and which became the location of the powerful state system that characterised this region.

The founding of the Barotse kingdom

Knowledge about the people who inhabited the Barotse valley and the hundred or so miles of river down to the Victoria Falls is inevitably limited by the lack of any accounts by eyewitnesses prior to the 1850s. However, the peoples of the valley have their own traditions of origin which tell of a substantial movement of people from the north into the upper Zambezi valley in the seventeenth century. The valley was not unpopulated at the time, but the newcomers, who probably belonged to the ruling elite of the Lunda empire, established a hegemony that grew into the Lozi kingdom of historical record. The invaders called themselves A-Luyi and spoke a language known as Siluyi. Traditions recorded that the original leader of the invaders was a woman, Mwamba, and that it was her children who gradually extended their dominance as far down the river as the Kafue, though the limits of the state itself were defined by the Ngonye Falls.

The distinctive institutions of the state evolved during this period, among them the position of the king, or Litunga, and the importance of the royal graves and their keepers; the authority wielded by females of the royal line, the Queen Mother and the royal sisters who controlled sections of the country; the key role of the Ngamela (often referred to as the 'prime minister') and the *kotla* or royal council. However, the A-Luyi, who later were commonly referred to as Rotse or Lozi, were always only a ruling elite, and the population of the valley was made up of around twenty-five ethnically distinct groups, some of whom were assimilated as slaves or clients while the majority continued to live under their own rulers, paying tribute to the A-Luyi kings.

It is tempting to compare the Lozi kingdom with the African kingdoms which established themselves along the lower reaches of the Zambezi: the Karanga and Rosvi kingdoms, the Marave states and the Ndebele. All were founded by invading political and military elites who were able to establish their control over pre-existing communities and who maintained a nominal overlordship over still-larger populations from whom they exacted tribute. However, there were crucial differences, partly explained by the geography of the river valley. The Middle and Lower Zambezi valley has been carved out of the central African plateau and is bordered by rugged escarpment country, often very dry and difficult to cross. Beyond the escarpment are the healthy highlands of the plateaux. It was there that the Karanga, Ndebele and Marave states were based. Although their influence allowed them to demand tribute from the peoples of the valley proper, they themselves never established settlements below the escarpment, and as a consequence never came to depend on the river to travel through their territory. The Zambezi became for them a no-man's land, a frontier and a barrier rather than a highway. The Barotse valley, however, was able to support cattle and was not bounded by unpassable escarpments. Royal towns like Nalolo, Sesheke or Lealui were sited near the river, which was the highway that connected one part of the kingdom with another. This dependence on the Zambezi, and the near proximity of the major settlements to the river, shaped the whole history and culture of the kingdom.

One distinctive feature of the Lozi kingdom resulted from the founding of a second kingdom further down the river, whose ruler was subordinate to the Litunga but in many respects ruled as an independent king. Mutumba Mainga, the distinguished historian of Barotseland and herself a Lozi, describes this unique and complicated arrangement: "Ngombala, the successor of the conqueror Ngalama, sanctioned the founding of a second chieftaincy in the south. This has survived to the present day and is now centred at Nalolo." Complicated traditions surround this division of the kingdom, but

it may represent a considered decision by the Lozi king that a second centre of authority was essential for his enlarged kingdom ... In its present form, the tradition emphasises the seniority of the northern king, who gives the symbols of authority to the founder of the southern kingdom, and the unity of the state since all those concerned are of the same dynasty.[14]

The southern kingdom was called Lwambi and the northern one Namuso, but there was no precise territorial division between them, rather just a separation of jurisdictions.

> Certain sub-districts and villages in the south were directly controlled by the Namuso authority, while certain villages and sub-districts in the north were regarded as belonging directly to the Lwambi authority. The northern ruler was represented by Indunas at the southern Kuta and the southern ruler was similarly represented at the northern court.[15]

As the separate institutions of north and south evolved, it became customary for the ruler of the southern Lwambi to be one of the senior royal women. There was often tension between the northern and southern kingdoms as their political interests conflicted, especially when European traders and travellers began to enter the country and when Mambari slavers from the west brought firearms and began to play a role in Lozi affairs.

During the early nineteenth century, the Barotse kingdom was ruled by a king whose reputation assumed legendary proportions. According to tradition, Mulambwa Santuru became king around 1780 and did not die until shortly before the arrival of the Makololo in 1840. Santuru was a ruler of superior intelligence, a great hunter who delighted in taming the young of wild animals. It was he who planned the building of the mounds on which the settlements stood, and he is also reputed to have planted trees on these mounds to provide shade. Santuru was famous for having a large boat built of planks and sewn together, with an awning of white cloth and twenty paddlers, the original of the Nalikwanda of later times.

The Mambari traders from Angola visited Santuru and offered to buy children, but he gave them large presents of cattle and told them he loved his people too much to think of selling them.

The unwillingness of the Lozi to sell slaves to the Mambari was due to their need to retain the labour of those they themselves had captured in war, but this refusal to take part in the slave trade meant that they did not acquire firearms as early as some other central African peoples. In spite of this, there was a notable immigration of Mbundu (Mambari) settlers from the Angolan highlands during Santuru's reign.

The arrival of the Makololo

In 1824, a group of Sotho speakers led by Sebituane sought to escape from the unsettled conditions in what is now South Africa and headed north into the region that later became Botswana. There they were repeatedly attacked by the Ndebele and robbed of their cattle, and this compelled them to move further westwards into the Kalahari and then north to the banks of the Zambezi. According to Livingstone, who recorded their history, the Zambezi valley and the islands in the river were occupied by Tonga speakers who "feeling perfectly secure in their fastnesses, often allured fugitive and wandering tribes onto uninhabited islets on pretence of ferrying them across, and there left them to perish for the sake of their goods".[16] Sebituane and his followers crossed the Zambezi safely by taking hostage the Tonga ruler who had offered to ferry them over, but he was followed by Ndebele raiding parties. They tried to avoid the raiders by heading eastwards down the river, where they reached the Kafue. Sebituane was then warned, it seems by a spirit medium, not to proceed into Portuguese territory, so instead he turned back up the river towards the great plain occupied by the Lozi. According to Livingstone's account, the medium told him that further up the river there was a "city and a nation of black men—men of the water; their cattle are red; thine own tribe is perishing, and will all be consumed; thou wilt govern the black men".[17]

THE UPPER ZAMBEZI AND THE BAROTSE VALLEY

Around 1840, Sebituane and his followers appeared in the Barotse valley. According to the Plymouth Brother missionary F.S. Arnot, he was invited in by one of Lozi factions in the succession dispute following the death of Santuru. Sebituane overthrew the Lozi government and over a period of about four years gradually established his power throughout the Barotse plain. When the Ndebele also tried to cross the Zambezi, Sebituane is supposed to have used the same trick on them that the river Tonga had employed. The Ndebele were ferried to an island and abandoned there. Fearing further attempts by the Ndebele to cross the Zambezi, the Makololo decided to take full control of the vital river crossings. They also established a royal town at Sesheke only 30 miles upstream from the Chobe confluence, which was the point where invaders from the south tried to cross.

When Livingstone first reached the Zambezi in 1851, the Makololo capital was located at Linyanti south of the river and protected by the Chobe river marshes from Ndebele attacks. This was a long way from the Barotse heartlands up the river where Makololo governors were stationed to control the population. Mutumba Mainga thought the location of the centre of Makololo power in the south was due to the support they had received from the Tonga population.[18]

What emerges from the wars in the region between the Makololo and the Tonga, Lozi and Ndebele was the great importance of the Zambezi river as a highway and as a barrier. Fleets of canoes had to be assembled to bring fighting men to wherever they were needed, and the Makololo, who had previously been pastoralists herding cattle in the dry grasslands of the south, had to take to the water, although they often employed Lozi boatmen. Meanwhile, the Ndebele raiders themselves realised the importance of bringing their own canoes to allow them to cross the rivers, and their last raids had something of the character of naval warfare on the river. This is all in marked contrast to the history of the states of the lower Zambezi. The Karanga and Marave kings never controlled the river or launched fleets of canoes. In fact, there was little serious opposition to the Portuguese when they took control of the highway of the lower river.

Sebituane died in 1851 at the time of Livingstone's first visit to the valley, possibly as a result of a fall from Livingstone's horse which he attempted to ride. When Livingstone returned in 1853, he gave the first detailed account of life in Barotseland under Makololo rule. Livingstone was a privileged visitor and had as a close a relationship with Sekeletu, the son and successor of Sebituane, as he had with the father. It seems likely that Livingstone was both respected and feared because he was believed to be a magician who could deploy powerful medicine. "The people have an unconvincible belief that all we do is by means of medicine ... medicine of the book must be taken or it will never be understood."[19]

The Makololo, Livingstone wrote, were very much an elite as their light skin colour clearly differentiated them from the peoples of the upper Zambezi. The king ruled by placing a number of his Makololo followers in each of the main settlements in the valley. By 1853, however, many of the original followers of Sebituane had died, victims of malaria as well as the passing years, and the birth rate was not high enough to replace the losses. As a result, more and more of the peoples of the valley were being brought into the centres of the Makololo political structures.

Like so many African states established by conquering groups, the Makololo state functioned through the levying of tribute on the conquered peoples. According to Livingstone, the Makololo king received "tribute from a great number of tribes in corn or dura, ground nuts, hoes, spears, honey, canoes, paddles, wooden vessels, tobacco, *mutokuane* (cannabis), various wild fruits (dried), prepared skins, and ivory".[20] This tribute was distributed among his principal followers, according to the distributive practice of African kingship which helped to secure loyalty to the centre. However, little of it reached the rest of the population.

Sebituane was succeeded by his son Sekeletu, though he had originally intended that his daughter should succeed. She had refused the honour but apparently remained an important figure in the kingdom, and may have been a major influence behind the coup attempted by Sekeletu's cousin, Mpepe, in June 1853, in which Livingstone was unwittingly involved. Apparently, Mpepe came to see his cousin and "had made arrangements with his people, who formed about a third of the tribe, to put Sekeletu to death as soon as they met". At the meeting, however, Livingstone was present and was seated between the two cousins. The moment for the planned assassination passed, and the next day Mpepe was killed by his own followers.[21] Sekeletu was still very much in control when Livingstone reached Linyanti, and he travelled with the king in his wagon to Sesheke and on to the capital of the southern part of the kingdom at Nalolo. According to Livingstone's account, on this journey the king was accompanied by about 160 attendants: "we had most of the young men with us and many of the under-chiefs besides … Sekeletu is accompanied by his own Mopato, a number of young men of his own age".[22]

The first appearance of Livingstone in 1851 had coincided with the arrival of a group of Mambari traders from Bié in central Angola. Angolan traders had tried to open up commerce with the Lozi kingdom in the 1830s, but they had found the Lozi unwilling to trade in slaves. The Makololo were less inhibited in this respect, although they tried to keep the trade hidden from Livingstone. The Mambari, who travelled to Linyanti via the Kwando and the Chobe rivers, were now able to buy slaves, chiefly children, in return for European-made goods. Livingstone was particularly annoyed to meet occasional Portuguese traders, whom he usually dismissed as half-castes, as he was intent on maintaining his own claim to be the first 'whiteman' to have travelled in this region. In his private journals, Livingstone describes the Portuguese who accompanied the Mambari as being carried in hammocks (*machillas*), something which Livingstone himself would never have done and which, he claimed, the Africans found effeminate.

The Mambari were already developing the slave trade in the region. "The people who live on the ridges [that border the plain] frequently steal children from adjacent tribes in order to sell them for clothing to the Mambari," but some of these slaves were also retained by the Makololo. In his journals, Livingstone described, "I have seen young girls brought as tribute to Sekeletu twice. They were divided among his people just as other tribute is. They are called children afterwards."[23] The Portuguese trader Silva Porto had already begun to build a settlement and, as a portent of things to come, Livingstone described "a stockade with two houses ... a flagstaff is placed in front for the display of the Portuguese flag, and I suspect for the purpose of proclaiming the sovereignty of Portugal".[24]

The development of trade during the period of Makololo rule, however, was not due solely to the slave trade. Ivory was also in great demand, both in Angola and in southern Africa. Apparently, the rising importance of this trade, which was controlled by the king, was a source of increasing tension among the Makololo. The more conservative believed that the traditional practice of raiding for cattle was preferrable to the ivory trade, which they saw as bringing in more firearms and increasing the power of the king, and it was the Makololo king who enthusiastically supported Livingstone's plan to open up a new route to the west coast.

Livingstone's plan was to travel to the west coast via the Barotse valley and the Upper Zambezi, a different route from that used by the Mambari. Not least among the reasons the Makololo wanted to promote an alternative trade route to the west coast was the poor quality of the goods offered by the Mambari and the low prices they offered for ivory. In his private journals, Livingstone wrote, "one of the Mambari offered me his gun for some beads. They are Portuguese manufacture and so inferior the people in this quarter despise them, and when they are offered for sale not a single tusk is offered."[25] So, twenty-seven men, some of them influential Makololo figures, were detailed to accompany Livingstone on his journey to the coast.

After the departure of Livingstone, Sekeletu's rule became increasingly ineffective as he suffered from leprosy. Livingstone visited the kingdom on his return journey and again in 1860, this time travelling up the river from the east coast. Shortly afterwards, in 1864, Makololo power on the Upper Zambezi finally came to an end when A-Luyi exiles attacked from the north and re-established their ascendancy, killing most of the surviving Makololo men.

The period of Makololo control had ended the isolation of the Barotse valley. Traders from Angola and Zanzibar had opened up trade routes, and Livingstone's arrival and the continuation of his journey to the west coast—and still more the vivid portrayal of the interior in his popular book, which was published in 1856—led to a renewed interest in the route from the Cape northwards to the Zambezi. The Makololo had dominated the valley for twenty-five years, and many members of the elite Lozi families had been educated at the Makololo capital in the retinue of the kings, and thus had acquired some cultural traits from the Makololo. The Makololo were survived by their patrilineal descent system, which they had brought with them. More unexpectedly, their language became the lingua franca of the various peoples of the valley, although the A-Luyi retained their original speech as a court language.

Return of the Lozi

The Lozi who overthrew the Makololo were led by Sipopa, a descendant of the last Litunga to have reigned, who thus restored the ancient ruling Lozi dynasty. It was Sipopa who built his capital at Lealui, near the Zambezi in the upper part of the valley and a long way from Linyanti, which had been the Makololo capital. As this part of the valley flooded in the early months of the year, there was another capital, situated on higher ground, for the wet season. Sipopa was determined to prevent Europeans from entering his kingdom, and for a long time after 1871, when George Westbeech first arrived, he was the only European trader allowed to enter the country. Campaigning downriver, Sipopa renewed the exaction of tribute from the Tonga and, in order to secure trade with Europeans from the south, spent much of his time at Sesheke near the junction of the Zambezi and the Chobe. The Czech explorer, Emil Holub, described him as the "Peter the Great of the Negro rulers".[26]

Norman McLeod, who visited Sipopa in 1875, shortly before he was overthrown, described a royal elephant hunt which gives some idea of the resources the king was able to mobilise: "There were over 200 canoes on the river at once, and about 2000 men. The system of hunting is by fire, beaters etc., to drive the elephants up to the king and his party, about 200, who receive them with a volley." These great royal hunts still continued 20 years later, when Major Gibbons described how

> The great hunts are undertaken in the summer when the river overflows her banks and game ... are concentrated and penned up in large numbers on patches of rising ground which alone remain high and dry above the flood. Every available canoe is manned, and the whole party is landed first on one and then on another of these temporary islands. The game is surrounded and butchered in hundreds with assegais.[27]

Sipopa was determined to arm the Lozi and, according to Emil Holub, during his reign large numbers of firearms of all kinds were imported. Holub estimated that Sipopa acquired 500 flint muskets, 1,500 flintlock muskets, 80 percussion elephant guns, 150 rifles, 30 double-barrel guns, 10 breech loaders and 3 revolvers.[28] As trade with Europeans was a royal prerogative, these firearms were intended to strengthen the power of the king *vis à vis* the other elite families. This arsenal appeared to many contemporaries to epitomise Sipopa's tyranny, and when he was overthrown many of the firearms he had accumulated were thrown into the Zambezi.

In 1876, a rebellion led to the flight of Sipopa and ultimately his death. His nephew briefly succeeded but was ousted by Lewanika (then known as Lobosi), who became king in 1878. As well as establishing control over the huge area of the valley, Lewanika also brought the whole country as far east as the Victoria Falls to accept Lozi overlordship and pay tribute. His conquests included the northern part of the Batoka plateau inhabited by the Mashikalumbwe (later more simply known as the Ila), renowned in the tales told by the early travellers in the region for the way they arranged their hair in strange, tall cones, and for their hostility to European visitors.

The Portuguese traveller, Serpa Pinto, wrote the most detailed description of the Lozi kingdom at the time when Lewanika became king. Serpa Pinto arrived at Lealui in August 1878 with a party who had come from the west coast. He was greeted by the king, which was then only 18 years of age, to whom he gave a present of a Portuguese military uniform. Lewanika

> wore a cashmere mantle over a coloured shirt, and, in lieu of a cravat, had a numerous collection of amulets hanging on his chest. His drawers were of coloured cashmere, displaying Scotch thread stockings, perfectly white, and he had on a pair of low well polished shoes. A large counterpane of smart colours ... and a soft grey hat, adorned with two large and beautiful ostrich-feathers.

Serpa Pinto attended a number of meetings of the *kotla*, or great council.

> It was Lobossi's custom, at sunrise, to leave his quarters, and, at the sound of marimbas and drums, to proceed to the great Square, where he took his seat near a lofty semicircular fence, the centre of which was occupied by the royal chair. Behind him squatted the natives who composed his Court, and on his right were Gambella and the other counsellors, if present. In front of the sovereign, and at about 20 paces distant, stood his musicians in a line, and files of the people were ranged at the sides.[29]

He recorded his impressions of two cases that were tried before the king. One was of a man who had been robbed and, after the thief had been found guilty, was compensated by being given the thief's wife. A second man complained that his wife would not obey him. Twenty others had the same problem, and Serpa Pinto observed that "it seemed to me the women of the Lialui were in a state of complete domestic revolt". The penalty was that the wife "should be bound hand and foot and thrust into the lake, where she was to pass the night with only her head out of water".[30]

At first Serpa Pinto got on well with the king, and on one occasion he recited a Portuguese poem, 'Flores d'Alma' by Thomaz Ribeiro, because Lewanika wanted to hear what the Portuguese language sounded like. However, the Ngambela proved very hostile, as the group around the king wanted to prevent Europeans from entering the kingdom. The political situation in Barotseland was still very precarious. The ex-king Mwanawina, who had been ousted by Lewanika, had escaped and met with some Chikunda elephant hunters on the Kafue who had provided him with protection. Many of Lewanika's council-lors believed that Serpa Pinto was in some way connected with these *muzungus*, and he described in detail how his relations with the Lozi elite deteriorated, though the king had enough authority to oppose the demands that he be killed. Eventually, the king ordered Serpa Pinto to return to Bié, and when he refused, saying that he wanted to travel eastwards towards Zumbo and Tete, a group of armed men attacked his encampment during the night and set it on fire. Serpa Pinto described the event and how the attackers were driven off when one of his men accidentally fired an explosive cartridge at them.

Eventually, Serpa Pinto was provided with three canoes by the king, and he made his way down the river, past the Ngonye Falls to the Chobe confluence and from there to the trading station at Panda ma Tenka. His record of this journey provided the first detail descriptions of the Zambezi cataracts below the Ngonye Falls.

Lewanika also had to respond to the increasing demands of white hunters, traders and missionaries arriving from the south. Among these were a party of Jesuits who asked permission to enter the country. Lewanika refused, but he found it convenient to welcome a select few Europeans, among them the trader George Westbeech who assumed an important role in befriending the king and supplying the Lozi with imported goods. Westbeech had acquired his privileged status because "when the Ma-Mbunda witch-doctors tested chickens with the *moati* poison to see if he should be permitted to advance, none of them died. Hence the Barotsi decided that his presence would be an advantage to the country".[31] The Plymouth Brothers missionary Frederick Arnot also became a friend of the king and spent some time at the capital Lealui, where he ran a school.

The 1884 rebellion

In 1884, a rebellion against Lewanika led by Mataha, the Ngambela, forced the king to flee. A graphic account of this rebellion was written by George Westbeech, which showed clearly the divisions within the Lozi elite:

There had been since Sepopa's days a family of great importance amongst the Barotse called Banosha and who were the prime movers in the insurrections against Sepopa and N'gwanawena and now against Luwanika whom they succeeded in driving away in September 1884 ... they fired several shots into his [Lewanika's] hut but without killing him [He fired back] and thinking he was well armed [they] let him proceed without further opposition, so he went towards the Linyanti River, being joined by his old Prime Minister, Selumbu ... and they after a few days managed to get to the Mashi country. There after some time he was joined by some loyals ...

Mataha, the leader of the rebels, had meanwhile found another member of Sipopa's family, named Akafuna Tatila, to become king:

many were against him and collecting under Samaseku, brother-in-law of Lewanika, and thinking if they won to get back their old king, they fought a battle about 12 miles from Li-a-Liue [Lealui] and were worsted. Samaseku and some hundreds were killed (37 took refuge in some garden huts, were found there, secured inside, the huts were set on fire and they were roasted inside). Those who survived fled to Lewanika ... Now began Mataha to show his nature. Having all the power in his hands ... he began killing off all who were still loyal. Lewanika's mother, brothers and any of his family or children he could get hold of, were butchered ... [Lewanika] sent a good force under Selumbu to enter the valley from the south ... but found ... that Mataha, Tatela, and all who were of their party had fled ... So Selumbu remained master of the valley, augmenting his forces, and sent word to Lewanika to return. Mataha had in the meantime deposed Tatela from the kingship ... In the meantime, Lewanika had advanced and, hearing that Mataha was close by, divided his army into four divisions and awaited his approach outside Li-a-Liue ... the fight began and lasted from 10am to 3pm ... Mataha's army, finding themselves nearly without leaders, threw down their shields and fled. Now began the rout and slaughter, and the flat from Li-a-Liue to Mongu ... is even now covered with skeletons and grinning skulls.[32]

Other accounts suggest that some Mambari traders intervened on behalf of Lewanika and helped secure his victory. Having recounted the massacres and horrors of this war, Westbeech concluded, "one good thing seems to have happened by it, which is that the King has become more manly and appears to have a much more stable character". In a letter to F.S. Arnot, written in 1885, François Coillard, reflecting on the civil war, wrote, "The horizon is dark and the sky very stormy; it seems as if we were witnessing the last days of the Barotse nation." Six months later, he wrote to Arnot, "Liwanika has exterminated his enemies, even those whom he feared might one day become his enemies. I never saw such bloodthirsty people, nor such an unquenchable spirit of revenge. Our hearts bleed for these poor Zambezians."[33]

Firmly back in control by the end of 1885, Lewanika now had to face a wholly unprecedented threat to his kingdom. Until that time, the threat from European traders, hunters and missionaries had been relatively easy to control, but Europeans were now not only seeking ivory and the souls of converts but rights to prospect for minerals. In 1885, the year Lewanika was restored to power, the Berlin Congress had begun the demarcation of spheres of influence for European powers in the Congo–Zambezi region, and in 1886, unbeknownst to Lewanika, the Portuguese had published a map—the so-called Rose Coloured Map—in which they claimed the whole of Lewanika's kingdom for Portugal. The same year, the discovery of the Rand goldfields led to uncontrolled speculation by fortune hunters. In 1888, Charles Rudd obtained a mineral prospecting concession from the Ndebele, which Rhodes persuaded the British government to turn into the concession area of a Charter Company.

Lewanika had used George Westbeech not only as his principal trading partner but also as his adviser in dealing with increasingly importunate Europeans. It was at Westbeech's persuasion that in 1886 Lewanika allowed the French missionary François

Coillard to establish mission stations in the country. Two years later, Westbeech died and Lewanika turned to Coillard to replace him as principal adviser in his dealings with Europeans.

The Barotse king faced huge challenges. As well as his centrally controlled kingdom, the Lozi claimed sovereignty over the peoples along the Zambezi as far as the Victoria Falls—and those on the Batoka plateau as far as the Kafue—and sent raiding parties to force them to pay tribute to Lewanika. Not only was his large kingdom—three times the size of the British Isles—with its control of the Zambezi river, coveted by Britain and Portugal, but also by an increasingly aggressive and expansionist Germany.

6

THE ZAMBEZI WARS

During the eighteenth century, the Lower Zambezi valley had seen a more or less peaceful co-existence between the creole Portuguese community and the neighbouring African kingdoms: the Marave kings, Undi and Lundu, to the north, the remnants of the Monomotapa kingdom on the south bank and the Rosvi state of Changamire dominant on the southern plateau. The relationship of these polities to each other and to the creole Portuguese was cemented by the international trade in gold and ivory, which was increasingly being handled by Indian merchants from the Portuguese towns in western India. Creole society was rooted in the *prazos* where the creole elites extracted tribute from the African *colonos* and organised their followers (now usually known as *chicunda*) into increasingly powerful social units and private armies.

Although many of the creole families either had European origins or had married into European families, the creoles in general were better described as an African ruling elite similar to the elites dominating the large states that had grown up north and south of the river. The creole society had few of the typical characteristics of a European colony—there were no impressive buildings in brick or stone, no plantations run by slaves and no European technology. Trade, agriculture, gold mining, river transport and hunting were all activities performed according to traditional African practices.

In the nineteenth century, however, the world of the Lower Zambezi was to be transformed as the region was hit by a perfect storm of change. This revolutionary transformation was brought about by three developments whose impact was all the more profound because they occurred at the same time, each enhancing the impact of the other two.

These three developments were: first, a prolonged period of climate instability leading to the great drought of the 1820s; second, the invasion of the Zambezi valley by groups of Nguni fighters whose origin lay in the Natal area of South Africa; and third, the rising demand for slaves, primarily to supply the plantations in the French Indian Ocean islands, then to supply markets in Brazil, Cuba and the United States—which could no longer obtain slaves in West Africa—and finally to meet a growing internal market in Africa itself. These three factors each contributed to the other: drought led to a weakening of the African societies of the region, which thus became vulnerable to Nguni attacks, while drought and Nguni raiding in turn fed the slave trade by creating large numbers of the displaced and destitute.

Against these dramas being acted out in the Zambezi valley, the politics in Lisbon were of very little importance, but eventually Portugal's official policy towards its east African colony would add another element contributing to the change that was taking place.

Drought

It seems that southern Africa began to experience a dry phase from the 1790s with increasingly frequent periods of drought.

Drought made ever larger areas of the country uninhabitable and people moved to better-watered regions, often causing severe disruption as groups competed for shrinking areas of good pasture and arable land. Africans had various strategies for dealing with drought, including an increased reliance on wild plants and roots, but the technologies did not exist for digging deeper wells or for mechanised irrigation. As so often happens in African history, the people sought political rather than technological solutions to their problems. As cattle herds dwindled and land became desolate, armed groups moved to seize their neighbours' cattle and to conquer and occupy new land. Societies were forced to abandon settled agriculture and domestic industries like metalworking and weaving. As gold mining, which required water to extract gold from the sand or crushed rocks, became impossible, so warfare, banditry and raiding took over as the default activities of desperate people.

Although the Zambezi was fed by numerous rivers flowing into it from a thousand miles in the interior, the river eventually succumbed to the relentless lack of rainfall. In 1995, and again in 2019, drought reduced the Victoria Falls to a trickle. It is not known if this occurred in the early nineteenth century, but during the great drought that affected the area between 1823 and 1831, the Qua Qua river—which in the wet season took floodwaters from the river to the port of Quelimane—dried up and became blocked with vegetation, cutting off the river settlements from the ocean by that route. The same thing happened to some of the rivers of the delta, and in 1825 the Maindo river was recorded as being completely dry. The creole settlements on the *prazos* along the lower river were either abandoned or reduced to extreme poverty, while armed groups (made up of starving peasants and *chicunda* slaves who deserted the *prazos*), described by the Portuguese as bandits, roamed the valley attacking villages and settled communities.

In 1829, the Portuguese governor of Sena wrote to the governor of the Rivers, "I cannot express to Your Excellency the ruin that these insurgents have caused throughout the district of this town, destroying the *luanes*, some of which are reduced to ashes and causing an immense mortality among the natives." In 1830, another report described how

> last year there was no agriculture of any description because of the lack of population, wiped out by the grim famine from which few have escaped. The chiefs of the kingdom of Barue ... have murdered the *colonos* who had managed to resist the said famine ... They had burnt the *luanes* of the *prazos* so that they were no longer administered.[1]

Starving people tried to reach the Portuguese towns or the seacoast, where many offered themselves to the eager slave traders waiting to fill their ships.

Drought, as so often happens in Africa, was accompanied by the twin scourges of locusts and disease which ravaged the starving population. In 1828, it was reported that the drought had "reduced the *prazos* to complete deserts through famine and the pestiferous smallpox which has reduced the villages of the slaves and *colonos* to mere depositories of corpses". Then, in 1829, another report reached the governor of the Rivers that "day after day the sun was covered by the passage of clouds of these insects [locusts] and they destroyed even the virgin bush, the most extensive fields and the interior for league upon league so that even the herds of wild animals died for lack of food".[2]

The drought not only led to the end of gold mining for a generation but crippled the creole society that had been based on the *prazos*. Many of the *prazo* owners left and retired to India or Brazil, while the town of Sena, at one time the busy capital of the creole community, fell into ruin, becoming almost entirely deserted and reverting to the bush.

Nguni

Meanwhile, the southern plateau country where the Karanga states had flourished for at least 300 years was invaded by a series of armed groups originating from Natal. The first bands arrived in the early 1820s, at the height of the famine when the whole lower Zambezi region had been reduced to chaos by armed marauders. It soon became clear, however, that the invaders were a new phenomenon. An Nguni army led by Nxaba occupied the northern part of the Zimbabwe plateau, seizing cattle, trading slaves with the coast and extorting tribute from any settled community which still managed to survive.

Other groups were led by Zwangendaba and Maseko, who entered the southern Rosvi kingdom, destroying its capital and killing the Changamire. After a few settled years, both these Nguni groups moved northwards, famously crossing the Zambezi during an eclipse of the sun in 1836. Behind them came the Ndebele led by Mzilikatzi, who settled among the surviving Rosvi with his principal town at Bulawayo. Meanwhile, armed bands led by Soshangane also left the Natal region, defeated Nxaba and occupied the whole of the country from the Lower Zambezi south to the Limpopo, establishing the Gaza kingdom, one of the largest tribute-taking monarchies in the history of southern Africa.

The Portuguese settlements along the Zambezi were not permanently occupied by the Gaza king, but they existed on its periphery and annually an impi would arrive to collect tribute from the inhabitants, including the Portuguese creoles. One such tax-gathering event occurred when Livingstone and his companions were present in 1858, and a dramatic print of the event appeared in the account of his expedition that Livingstone subsequently published. Dr John Kirk, a member of the expedition, busy recording events in his diary, described what happened on 14 August 1858:

A party of what the Portuguese call 'Landeens', the natives 'Mabzuite' which are of the Zulu family and under the chief Manakhousi, whose headquarters are somewhere near Inhambane came today ... They all had shields made of cowhide, oval and about 3⅓ feet long ... Their arms are a bundle of assegais and a few hand battle axes. The chief made an oration accompanied with dancing and going through different manoeuvres. The Portuguese are, as far as Shupanga is concerned, tributaries of the Landeens to whom they pay tribute. Thus the poor people of the villages pay to both Landeens and Portuguese.[3]

The old slaver, Vienna, grumbled that he paid 400 dollars to the government and 500 to the Landeens for the privilege of occupying his estate at Shupanga. The 'Landeens', Kirk thought, were "by no means well formed" but were distinguished from the local Tonga "by a split on the ear in which they wear a piece of ivory or a seed with red anillus [a type of beetle]".[4]

Such an event was very similar to the tribute-taking by the Lozi rulers of Barotseland with their periodic visits to outlying communities on the Batoka plateau and into the Lovale and Lunda regions of the upper river.

The slave trade

The slave trade had grown rapidly in the early nineteenth century, with the leading creoles eager participants. However, it received a boost during the drought when destitute people were rounded up to be shipped from the coastal ports. Quelimane briefly became the most important slaving port in eastern Africa, and possibly in the whole of Africa. The other factor, which for a while boosted the slave trade, was the provision in the independence agreement signed between Portugal and Brazil in 1825—on the insistence of the British—that the slave trade to Brazil would end in 1830.

During the first quarter of the century, the slave trade was conducted out of the Portuguese-controlled ports of Mozambique Island and Quelimane with Ibo, Sofala, Inhambane and Lourenço Marques also participating in the trade. The slave trade, as it operated out of Quelimane and the rivers of the Zambezi delta, was vividly described by the British naval officer Frederick Barnard in a book published in 1848. Visiting friends he had made among the Portuguese community in Quelimane in 1843, Barnard reported on the activities of slavers:

> About a week before our arrival, a large bark had embarked from 700 and 800 slaves at Ouilinda, the river to the southward of Quilimane ... the slaves actually went from the town of Quilimane in launches. Three or four days after our last visit, 300 slaves had been burnt alive in a barracoon some distance to the northward, where they had been sent ready for embarkation, one of them slipping his iron collar during the night, and setting fire to the building. Upwards of 2,000 slaves were ready in the neighbourhood of the town for embarkation purchased with merchandise, brought out by American vessels, and slave-vessels were expected from Rio daily ... A brig said to be under Sardinian colours, had attempted to land her captain at Luabo ... but he with three of his boat's crew was drowned in crossing the bar ... The black schooner belonging to Senhor Isidore, which had embarked 400 slaves at Macuze, put back having lost one-half of her human cargo, and relanded the wretched remnant half dead.[5]

However, the nature of the slave trade was changing. In 1834, the victory of the liberals in the Portuguese civil war, and still more the seizure of power in Portugal in 1836 by the Septembrists, threatened the continuation of the Portuguese seaborne slave trade. Pressure from Britain pushed at a door already half-open. In 1836, Portugal formally abolished the slave trade and in 1842 reluctantly accepted the British demand that the trade be declared piracy. A joint Anglo-Portuguese naval force now hunted the slavers up and down the east African coast.

However, the slave trade did not immediately die, as it was supported by many members of the Portuguese community, from the governor downwards. Moreover, there were many minor ports and river mouths where slavers could still lie up unseen before shipping their cargoes. Then, in 1851, Brazil finally stopped the import of slaves, closing one of the last New World markets for east African slaves. The slave trade, however, was to continue to Madagascar and the Gulf and in the form of contracted labour (*engagés*) to the French sugar plantations in Réunion, Nossi Bé and Mayotte. Even so, the Zambezi as a route to the sea for slavers was rapidly closing. Livingstone's companion, John Kirk, recorded meeting a retired slave trader in August 1858:

> Sr Vienna is an old slave trader, but seems to have reformed, finding it rather unprofitable. He had shipped 4,000 slaves, some from Angola some from Quillimane. Out of 12 ships, he has men in, he has had five taken as prizes. He is very indignant at one of the prizes which he considers as having been taken unjustly. The others, he says, were fair prizes. He ran the risk and lost them in a contraband trade. He says that when well supplied with food and water, they lose almost none [of the slaves], except from skin disease, but when water runs short, the mortality becomes enormous.[6]

The creole slavers now had to find internal markets, and the slave trade became largely an African affair as the tribute-taking states—the Barotse, the Ndebele and the other Nguni and Yao polities that established themselves in the area north of the river—continued to recruit a slave labour force, slave wives and slave soldiers into their armies.

Changing Portuguese attitudes towards east Africa

Revolutionary change in Portugal had a long period of gestation. Beginning with Pombal's economic and educational radicalism in the 1770s, Portugal received an injection of French ideas from the Napoleonic occupation of the Iberian Peninsula of 1808–14. The country underwent a growing sense of crisis as the royal government remained rooted in Brazil and Portuguese affairs and were managed by a Council of Regency at perpetual loggerheads with Lord Beresford, the army's autocratic commander. In 1821, there was a liberal uprising which promised a new dawn, but its work was largely undone when the king's younger son, Dom Miguel, seized the throne in 1827. By 1832, tension in Portugal had reached the point of civil war, and the armed struggle for power continued until 1834 when the liberal party triumphed and installed Dona Maria II on a very shaky throne.

The victory of the liberals was the victory of new ideas about the ordering of society and the conduct of the economy. Radical measures were adopted, which included the dissolution of the monastic orders and the confiscation of their property, the ending of all residual rights of the Crown in land and the abolition of the privileges of the noble class. Although the liberals soon split between a radical element—the Septembrists—and the more conservative constitutional monarchists, the promotion of the principles of economic liberalism, free trade, private ownership of land and removal of restraints on capital were shared by all. The same principles were to be applied in the colonies and were coupled with the abolition of the slave trade and eventually slavery itself. As early as 1832, the measures with regard to property were nominally applied in Africa, and further measures announced in 1838 and 1854 spelt out the formal abolition of the *prazos*, which were replaced by a system whereby land would be rented. Meanwhile, the overseas slave trade was abolished in 1836, and co-operation with the British in its suppression initiated. In 1854, it was announced that slavery itself would cease in the colonies in 20 years' time.

None of these measures were easily enforced in eastern Africa, where the Portuguese authorities had few administrative resources at their disposal which could bring about any immediate change to the creole world of the Zambezi valley. However, these measures prepared the ground for a series of armed conflicts that would be played out between 1845 and the end of the century, which are collectively known as the Zambezi Wars.

The beginning of the Zambezi Wars

The liberals in Portugal not only wanted to end the slave trade but also to develop a plantation economy in the areas of Africa where the Portuguese were the dominant influence. They were also wary of the increasing presence of the British on the coast, first in the form of the Admiralty's hydrographic survey, then in the form of the anti-slave trade squadrons and the presence of British consuls in Zanzibar and the Comoros Islands. It was in this context of changing attitudes towards the slave trade, as well as a changing relationship between Zambezia and the world beyond the river delta, that the wars of the mid-century must be understood. Above all else, the Portuguese wanted to wrest control of the river from the creole warlords who controlled it. However, with very little military capacity to deploy in pursuit of their aims, the Portuguese found they had to depend on the highly undependable forces of 'loyal' creoles.

By the 1840s, the Zambezi valley had recovered from the drought years of the first two decades of the century. As the climate resumed its normal pattern of seasonal rains followed by flooding of the river, the communities of the valley gradually rebuilt themselves. But there were fundamental changes: the old creole families which had controlled the *prazos*, trading in gold and ivory with the Indian merchants of Mozambique Island and the other coastal ports, had mostly gone. The *prazos*, abandoned during the drought and the Nguni raids, had been taken over by a new breed of creole warlord. The Lower Zambezi was now dominated by six families, all but one of them of East Asian origin. These families established their control over sections of the Zambezi valley, acquiring titles to the abandoned *prazos* from the Portuguese government and basing their rule on large, fortified strongholds called *aringas*, the largest of which were like fortified towns where the heads of the families lived surrounded by their *chicunda* clients and soldiers.

These warlords controlled traffic on the river and traded in slaves rustled by their armed followers from the populations north and south of the river. Their activities widened the reach of creole control. They usurped the authority of the formerly powerful Marave chiefs Undi and Lundu, establishing their own polities in their place. On the north bank near the Luangwa confluence, the Caetano Pereiras conquered their 'kingdom' of Macanga, while on the Shire river another Indian family, the Vas dos Anjos, ruled a state called Massingire with their stronghold at Shamo (*Enshamu*), dominating the river like robber barons of medieval times.

South of the river an Indian ivory trader, Manuel António de Sousa, gradually established a state which challenged the authority of the Gaza kingdom after its founder, Soshangane, died and the kingdom was plunged into civil war. Most notorious of all was the da Cruz family, of Thai origin, whose *aringa* lay close to the Zambezi on the right bank below the Ruenya confluence, threateningly close to Tete.

These powerful creole families controlled the river settlements and rejoiced in their Portuguese names and military ranks, which provided a fig leaf of legitimacy to their depredations as they raided surrounding communities and sent their captives downriver to the waiting slavers.

The first phase of the Zambezi Wars

The earliest phases of the Zambezi Wars broke out in the 1840s, when the Pereiras of Macanga, under their formidable chieftain

Chissaca, came in conflict with the da Cruz family, who controlled the river below Tete from their riverside stronghold of Massangano. The da Cruz family emerged from these conflicts with their power considerably enhanced. The Portuguese tried to deal with the power of the da Cruz family by raising forces from among the other warlords and advancing on the da Cruz *aringa* at Massangano in 1845. Confusion and rout followed, with African carriers and auxiliaries fleeing once the da Cruz warriors made an appearance.

The failure of these expeditions was partly offset by a successful attack on the *aringa* of the Vas dos Anjos on the Shire river. Livingstone and his colleagues were witnesses to this 'victory' by government forces, which was apparently achieved without a shot being fired, except for Portuguese guns firing at so-called rebel groups from across the river. In his diary, John Kirk described not only the powerful fortress of a creole warlord but also the Portuguese method of waging war. In September 1858, he paid a visit to the governor in command of the Portuguese forces and observed that "the Portuguese army burn before them, in order to prevent attacks and also to keep the rebels from falling on them in the bush in the rear". The Portuguese force had taken the Vas dos Anjos stronghold of Shamo:

> This was the chief place of the rebels, the town of Mariano [Paul Mariano Vas dos Anjos] which for four years he had been strengthening and which had now fallen into the hands of the army, as we learned afterwards, without a shot ... The house of Mariano was of stone, with large verandah, tiled roof. It stood on the side of a large circle which had a Baobab tree in the centre. Most of the other houses were of reeds, very nicely made and remarkably well thatched ... Near Mariano's house stood his dining hall, a large oblong with thatch roof on wooden poles, the floor of mud with mud sides about three feet high. The central square was separated from the others by a stockade in part and by thick bush. It had a number of gates, from

which you passed by crooked paths among the bush to other open spaces where were the houses of the common people, also well made.[7]

The town was protected on one side by the Shire river and surrounded by a stockade, which was being replaced by a brick wall "about five feet thick and at the Shire was pierced for artillery. The guns were found in position". Large quantities of plunder were taken and shipped off in canoes, accompanied by Kirk who wanted to commandeer the canoes to go down to the coast.

In the wake of this success, an attack was made on the independent Islamic state of Angoche halfway up the coast between Quelimane and Mozambique Island, which fell to a force raised by the Zambezi warlord Alves da Silva. The following year, 1862, the official expedition led by Albino Manuel Pacheco re-established a Portuguese presence at Zumbo at the confluence of the Luangwa with the Zambezi.

Livingstone's Zambezi expedition and Lower Zambezi society

The Lower Zambezi basin and its extension north along the Shire river as far as Lake Malawi had, meanwhile, been thoroughly explored and mapped. There had been sketch maps of the Zambezi region produced in the seventeenth century whose details appeared on printed maps in the eighteenth century. Then, in the early nineteenth century, the British Admiralty sent Commodore Owen to carry out a hydrographic survey of the East African coast between 1821 and 1826. However, his survey did little more than chart the rivers of the delta, and it was a German naturalist, Wilhelm Peters, who first studied the Zambezi river system and the valley's flora and fauna during a 6-year period between 1842 and 1848. Livingstone then mapped the upper reaches of the Zambezi during his travels there in 1853–6. In 1858, he returned with a team that included a geologist and a naturalist to survey the lower river, the Shire and Lake

Malawi in detail. This prompted the Portuguese to produce their own map of the river as far as the Kafue confluence in 1867.

Livingstone and his team remained working in the Lower Zambezi region until 1864, and the account of this expedition, written by himself and his brother Charles, supplemented by his diaries and the diaries of the geologist Richard Thornton and naturalist John Kirk (all of which were published in the twentieth century), give an extraordinarily detailed picture of life on the river, which can be supplemented by Pacheco's written account of his mission to re-establish the fair at Zumbo in 1861–2.

Livingstone had brought with him the first steamer to attempt the navigation of the Zambezi. Making use of this vessel, the *MaRobert*, the expedition soon discovered that there was no reliable point of entry into the delta from the sea. Livingstone used the so-called Kongone mouth, but this was only navigable when the river was in flood, and Kirk described at length the bewildering tangle of creeks, inlets and waterways, many of which disappeared into the marshes of the delta. Once the main stream of the river was reached, at the point the Portuguese called the Boca do Rio, the main channel of the river meandered through a maze of sandy shallows and islands on which the steamer constantly ran aground. Nevertheless, difficult as this navigation was, Livingstone did manage to take his steamer beyond Tete and also up the Shire river, only to find his progress up both rivers barred by impassable cataracts.

During the 6 years that the British expedition was active in the Zambezi region, the indefatigable Livingstone travelled up and down the river, making an expedition up to Barotseland to return some of the companions who had accompanied him down the river in 1855. During this period, the people who inhabited the river valley were met and described in some detail. What is immediately striking is how little had changed on the lower river since João dos Santos and António Gomes described it in the early seventeenth century. In the outside world, the scientific and industrial revolutions had transformed human understanding of the world and with it the global economy, but little of this had influenced the peoples of the Zambezi.

River traffic, with the attendant hazards of crocodiles and hippopotamuses, had altered little. John Kirk, tirelessly interested in every aspect of river life, was fascinated by the giant canoes which carried the commerce of the river. While staying at Shupanga, he observed the first stages of the construction of one of these vessels:

> They are cut in the forest, in the interior and there roughly cut out, then dragged down, over the branches of trees to the Zambezi. They are of enormous size and cost about £100. The transport occupies often three months. The hawsers are made sometimes of the leaf of the Palm, called Musheo, sometimes of the stems of a twiner, with side ropes and cross bits of wood to haul by ... After being cut and roughly formed and hollowed out in the forest, they are brought down here to be finished when the helm is fixed and the whole smoothed, frequently the centre part cracks and comes out, leaving a large hole in the end. This is fastened in again with iron and caulked with bast ... The large canoes which are made here ... continue good for from 15–20 years ... I saw a canoe which they had begun to hollow out. This was done by lighting a fire of wood along the upper side of the trunk as it lay. I suppose when they have done as much as safely may be done in this way they commence with their small axes and Adzes to cut it out.[8]

Richard Thornton, who also saw the canoe, added that

> it was 34 feet long, 3 feet wide at the top & 2 from the stern. About 80 natives were hauling away at ropes of creepers, one rope in front & 2 from the stern. They laid a road of long poles about 4 feet apart for her to pass over, then hauled all together to a kind of song, till they reached the water.

He also adds the interesting information that the men working on the canoe were using "English adzes, planing tools, chisels, saws etc.".[9]

Some of the canoes could carry up to one ton of cargo:

> The canoes have six paddles three on a side and two pilots, one fore
> and one aft, the fore one with a long pole, the after one steering.
> The crew sit on three or four cross boughs right in the stern and dig
> away with clumsy paddles at the water.[10]

This is not exactly the picture of the skilful paddlers of the
Upper Zambezi standing in their canoes and tirelessly propelling
their craft hour after hour.

The African canoe makers had perfected their craft and found
no reason to change a tradition which had developed to meet the
peculiar characteristics of Zambezi navigation. Watching the
labours of Livingstone's steamer, which staggered from sandbank
to sandbank, ran out of fuel and could barely get up enough
steam pressure, they saw no advantages in—and no reason to
adopt—the obviously inadequate technology of the Europeans.

The town of Sena had recovered somewhat from the disasters
of the great drought, but Kirk found that the course of the
Zambezi had altered and left the town stranded some distance
away from the river.

> The town of Senna is built on the right bank of the river or was in
> former times when the main stream took the opposite side to what
> it does now but at present the water communication is a narrow
> canal between sand banks which will only allow a canoe to pass ...
> The town is situate[d] on a plain with a gentle rise of the ground
> behind and a double hill about a mile off of basalt and about 400
> feet high. The houses of Senna are at present in a better state than
> they have been for long. The principal is that of Senhor Ferrao
> which is a substantial and large house with a fine verandah in front.
> There are only a few other houses of stone and lime. Many are of
> reeds plastered over with mud while the generality are of reeds
> entirely and they are very comfortable places now. How they may
> be in the rainy season, I don't know. There is a chapel and three
> bells in front, two of them cracked, the third was one of trophy

from the stockade of Shamoa. The fort is an oblong building of no strength. The walls are cracked at one place from the discharge of artillery on the arrival of the Governor from the war and then one of the pieces came down on the ground. The whole town is enclosed in a stockade of wooden poles stuck in the ground and fastened by a bundle of branches ... between the different houses there are deep pits from which clay has been dug. These become full of water in the wet season and the vegetable matter and filth of all sorts begin to putrify which will in great measure account for the ill health of the residents.[11]

Kirk made a point of studying the crafts and technologies of the inhabitants of the valley. In Sena, he was taken on a tour of the local workshops by none other than Albino Manuel Pacheco, who 2 years later led the expedition to Zumbo and wrote his own account of Zambezia.

He took me to see the manufactures of Senna, first to the goldsmith. Here under a reed shed he had two or three men busy making gold ornaments. He shewed me a ring of the finest filigree work and made of the finest unalloyed gold. The platting of the wire was very fine. It seemed very superior to any filigree work ... The gold we saw in rods about four inches long and from an eighth to a quarter thick square and hammered. This is then thinned off at one end and drawn through a plate of iron. Passing it successively through smaller holes, it is drawn. By means of pliers. His tools were in part European as he possessed a half round file. The next trade we saw was that of blacksmith. Then we went to the shoemakers and saw some of the specimens of their work, very well done and seemed substantial. They work sometimes in native leather, which is cow hide tanned in mimosa bark.[12]

Later, he described in rather confused detail a lathe used by an African carver, a rare example of a machine in use in pre-colonial Africa. Livingstone was less tolerant of the technological backwardness, as he saw it, of the creole community.

It is astonishing to anyone who has seen the works for irrigation in other countries, as at the Cape and in Egypt, that no attempt has ever been made to lead out the water either of the Zambesi or any of its tributaries; no machinery has ever been used to raise it even from the stream, but droughts and starvation are endured, as if they were inevitable dispensations of Providence, incapable of being mitigated.[13]

The second phase of the Zambezi Wars

The fighting, which had ended with the capture of Shamo and the expedition to Angoche in 1861, had proved relatively successful for the Portuguese government. However, the next phase of the Zambezi Wars was a series of disasters of unprecedented dimensions. Between 1867 and 1869, no less than four military expeditions were sent against the da Cruz stronghold of Massangano. Four armies were destroyed, and the Portuguese were forced to come to terms with their da Cruz opponents. After this, there would be no renewal of the conflict until the 1880s, when circumstances on the Zambezi were very different. In the meantime, the creole *senhores* practised their depredations with impunity.

The Portuguese were well aware that Livingstone had revealed to the world some aspects of life on the Zambezi which would not do Portugal's reputation any good in the liberal circles of Europe: in particular, the existence of slavery and evidence that the slave trade was as active as ever, even though it was now largely directed towards internal markets. The departure of Livingstone's expedition therefore prompted the government in Lisbon to try once again to assert its authority throughout the valley. The problem, as always, was the presence of the da Cruz stronghold of Massangano at the junction of the Ruenya river which commanded the passage up the Zambezi between Sena and Tete. However, dealing with the da Cruz family was no easy matter, as the Portuguese depended on the support of other Zambezi warlords to wage its wars.

The head of the da Cruz clan since 1855 was António da Cruz, known by his African sobriquet of Bonga. He and members of his family had been leasing *prazos* on both sides of the river, and they were behaving in an increasingly violent way towards traffic on the river. Six of Livingstone's African companions had been murdered when they rashly visited Massangano.

In July 1867, the governor of Tete, Miguel Gouveia, mounted a punitive expedition against Massangano. His forces were ambushed and large numbers of them killed. The Portuguese government determined to avenge this outrage, but they were unable to assemble an armed force powerful enough to defeat the fighters of the da Cruz family on their home ground. However, they pressed ahead and unnecessarily suffered further humiliating defeats. In November 1867, a force of 400 Portuguese soldiers arrived, to be joined by auxiliaries raised on the Sena *prazos* and fighters commanded by Manuel António de Sousa, who had already established himself as the principal rival of the da Cruz family south of the river. This army advanced through the rainy season up the Zambezi valley and actually laid siege to Massangano. However, their small field guns were unable to breach the living walls of the *aringa*, and the commander himself came down with malaria. In December, the army withdrew towards Quelimane, having achieved nothing except to enhance Bonga's reputation.

Sound advice for the Portuguese would have been to leave well alone and work behind the scenes to undermine Bonga's authority. Instead, another army, with a regiment of European troops, was sent under Guilherme de Portugal e Vasconcellos. This time the army advanced during the dry season and reached Massangano in July 1868. The army once again laid siege to the *aringa* and was able to fire into it from the high ground behind the town. It seems that Bonga, facing imminent defeat, tried to escape from this trap with his followers. Breaking suddenly out of the stockade, he caught the Portuguese unprepared and massacred a large part of their army. Two hundred and sixty Portuguese soldiers were killed in the fighting, and soon rows of the heads of those who had been captured were decorating the walls.

Finally, Lisbon tried to organise a serious military expedition, assembling nearly a thousand troops from Portugal and Goa. It was commanded by a former governor of Tete, António Tavares de Almeida, and was equipped with a battery of mountain guns. The army was slow to assemble and did not have proper forward bases from which to operate. It did not reach Massangano until November 1869, by which time large numbers of the soldiers were suffering with fever. Only one month after reaching Massangano, Tavares de Almeida decided he would have to withdraw his forces. As he tried to organise a retreat, his men were attacked from the *aringa* and the army disintegrated and fled. Once again, the da Cruz forces reaped a plentiful harvest of heads, while the Portuguese army disappeared down the river.

In this final campaign, the da Cruz family had been helped by the rulers of the kingdom of Barue, still independent but fearful that, if the Portuguese succeeded in capturing Massangano, Barue might well become the next target.

There was an epilogue to Tavares de Almeida's defeat. Some of the Indian soldiers who had managed to escape stayed in Zambezia and began to trade on their own account, playing a significant role in the commercial revolution that was soon underway in the coastal area.

The da Cruz family remained in control of their stronghold and continued to take tolls on the river. Eventually, in June 1875, they made their peace with the Portuguese in Tete. Bonga agreed to return some of the government property and allow the remains of the dead Portuguese soldiers to be buried. He died on 8 September 1879 and was buried with full military honours, a requiem mass subsequently being said for him by a Jesuit priest.

After Bonga's death, there was no immediate revival of hostilities. In 1880, Manuel António de Sousa invaded Barue with his *chicunda* army and took control of the kingdom, establishing himself as the most powerful of the creole *senhores* on the lower river, and it was his private army that was summoned by the Portuguese to deal with the next major outbreak of hostilities in 1884. This time, the centre of disturbances was not the da Cruz in Massangano, but the old Vas dos Anjos *prazo* of Massingire.

The feudal regime on the Zambezi

Those familiar with the struggle between Europe's feudal regimes and the modern state, for example in France, will find much that is familiar in the story of the Zambezi Wars. Feudalism, in its later phases, was an organisation of society in which people's identity was not defined by being born a citizen of a state but by being born to depend on and serve an overlord whose position rested primarily on the ownership of land. Since the seventeenth century, those who lived along the stretches of the Zambezi that were controlled by the Portuguese creoles had owed tribute and service to the *senhores* and *senhoras* who leased the *prazos*. Although many *colonos* still lived in traditional lineage-based villages, increasing numbers had become *chicunda*, directly dependent on their *senhor*. By the nineteenth century, the relationship of dependency between the *senhor*, the *chicunda* and the peasantry had become very deeply rooted, and much of it carried over into the twentieth century when the *prazo senhores* were replaced by plantation companies.

The seigneurial regime on the *prazos* acquired a culture that was highly distinctive, not least because of the important role played by women in the upper echelons of Zambezi society. In the nineteenth century, these were usually referred to as *Donas*—ladies. The families which ruled the *prazos* often had few if any direct links to Portugal. Many of them had their origins in Goa, but as a result of marriage with local women, after a generation or two the members of these families were physically indistinguishable from their African neighbours. Nevertheless, they maintained a separate identity from the African population and were often simply referred to as *muzungus* (a term which Africans used generally to describe white men). The *muzungus*, however black their skin may have been, were honorary whites.

Seigneurial society was either based on a *luane*—a country property—or on an *aringa*. At the centre of a *luane* was a large house built in the traditional Zambezian style—low and square, with a roof that was usually thatched and deep verandahs that ran round all four sides of the building. Around the central house would be a village of huts which housed the *chicunda* who provided personal service for the *senhores*, performing all the necessary tasks on the estate. The *aringa* was rather different. Like the feudal castle of the later European Middle Ages, *aringas*—which housed the *prazo senhor*—could be the size of large villages or towns with the *senhor's* house in the centre. The walls, which could be a mile or more round, were made of green stakes which rooted and formed a wall of living trees, impossible for an attacker to breach except with heavy artillery. The *aringa* would house the private army of the *senhor* or *dona*.

A distinctive feature of *muzungu* culture was the *machilla*, the hammock in which the *muzungu senhor* or *dona* reclined, and which was carried by two or sometimes four carriers. The *machilla* might be highly decorated with gold or, ivory or leopard skins. It was already a recognised status symbol when, in the seventeenth century, António Gomes recorded the wife of a recent convert to Christianity being carried to church in a *machilla* draped with Persian carpets. When sallying out abroad or attending church, the *dona* would be accompanied by numerous servants, and often dozens of the women of her household.

The *prazo senhores* notoriously lived partly in the European and partly in the African worlds. *Muzungus* were all known by African as well as Portuguese names. In their houses they often had European furnishings and luxuries, but many of them were unable to write or even speak Portuguese. The men would seek rank in the Portuguese militia or titles, in particular the title of *capitão-mor* or *sargento-mor*, which enabled them to obtain firearms and other supplies to carry out their alleged administrative duties. *Donas* would try to make matches with Portuguese soldiers or officials, their children undoubtedly gaining in status from being light-skinned. Both Lacerda and Gamitto, the Portuguese explorers who visited Kazembe and wrote about their journeys, married local *Donas*. *Muzungu* men seldom bothered with legal marriages and took wives according to African custom. In many cases, it was important African women who sought these liaisons and took the initiative in finding a Portuguese man who would oblige them. António da Cruz's father, known as Nhaude, boasted of being a grandson of the Monomotapa.

However, the epithet that was once used with regard to law enforcers in the American Wild West—"Sheriffs don't have wives, they have widows"—certainly applied to the husbands of the Zambezi *Donas*, and many of these formidable ladies managed to get through a number of husbands over the course of their lifetime. However, as José Capela points out, although marriages may have been marked by their informality, the *muzungu* men were often very anxious to have their children baptised. Capela cites Manuel António de Sousa, who brought his 'wife' and their child to the priest so that both could be baptised at the same time.

Gamitto, on his way to the court of Kazembe in 1831, described one of the Zambezi *senhores*, João Pedro Xavier de Silva Botelho, being received in some style in his *luane*:

Over a hundred blacks were waiting here for [him]. When they saw him they broke into loud shouting and singing, and travelled on beside him, surrounding the palanquin in which he was being carried. The closer we got to the habitation, the greater their numbers became so that when Botelho arrived at the Luane ... there were more than six hundred people singing and dancing with drums around him ... Botelho was received with 21 rounds fired from two one-pound pieces he has there, and with the hoisting of the Portuguese flag.

And he goes on:

the life of a senhor ... consists in eating, smoking and sleeping, being surrounded by young black women and giving himself up to continual sensuality. When he sits at table he is surrounded by slaves, their arms folded, awaiting orders, or busying themselves changing dishes—but not changing knives and forks because he eats by hand in the normal fashion of the natives ...

The *senhor* then washes his hands, lights his pipe and smokes:

A slave holds the pipe while two or three slaves pummel him, giving light blows with both hands or fists on his calves, thighs and buttocks until he falls asleep. This operation continues during sleep ... and the same happens at night, the slaves complying being of both sexes but always young.[14]

The private lives of the *muzungus* of Zambezia suggest a world where European custom was transformed by the African environment and flourished in the absence of those formal restraints that operated, to some extent at least, in nineteenth-century Europe.

In January 1860, John Kirk met the African wife of the old slave trader Vienna.

She gave us a curious history of the manners of the Portuguese. Irema is no half-caste. He bought her and her sister when she was young, perhaps 9 or 10 years old. He used her as he now does two of similar age. Now, as she says, she then knew nothing, still he slept with her every night. When she got a little older he promised to keep to her alone and she has made a first rate house-keeper to him and he, being blind, has put all in her care. Now she has had three children and he is tired of her. She may be about 18 years old. Now, he has two young girls whom he uses and neglects her ... The argument ended in the conclusion that she was now to do as he did and take whom she pleased.[15]

Muzungu men, and sometimes the women as well, often acquired reputations for extreme cruelty. As there was no real check of any kind on their conduct, and as they were surrounded by crowds of servile followers, many of them allowed their darker instincts free rein. Chanetta, one of the last rulers of Macanga, is said to have thrown five of his wives, whom he suspected of adultery, to the crocodiles in the Revubwe river where his capital was located. Carl Wiese described a *muzungu* disembowelling an old man so that the famous *rabo da guerra*, the buffalo tail that was brandished by a magician in the vanguard of an army, could be dipped in his blood.

In 1885, Kankuni, the current ruler of Macanga, invited the Jesuit priest Victor Courtois to visit him to baptise his children. Kankuni met him dressed in the uniform of a *capitão-mor*, wearing a plumed hat and a belt decorated with the symbols of freemasonry. Courtois claimed that Kankuni had 300 wives. The priest visited the burial place of the earlier Caetano Pereiras, which had originally been a Catholic chapel but now consisted of three huts in which were various items of Catholic ritual and the weapons of the dead kings. It was in the charge of a *chicunda*, whose job was to remember the histories of the previous Pereiras. When revisited 1891, it was found that a regular Zambezian spirit medium was in charge of consulting the spirits of the dead kings. The story of the Pereira mausoleum shows perfectly how the *muzungu senhores* lived astride two worlds, and how they derived their authority from their position as African kings and at the same time as representatives of a remote and shadowy, but increasingly important, Portuguese government.

Some of the women acquired reputations as lurid as their men folk. José Capela in his fascinating book *Donas, Senhores e Escravos* quotes the description of Dona Luisa da Cruz by Augusto de Castilho, the commander famous for the eventual conquest of Massangano in 1888: "Her justice was summary: behind her *aringa* of Guengue there was a small lake infested with enormous crocodiles. [Into this] she ordered her victims, accused of robbery, adultery, witchcraft etc, to be thrown, bound hand and foot."

He claimed she was guilty of eighty such murders. The French traveller Paul Guyot, who published a French translation of Pacheco's *Viagem de Tete a Zumbo*, recorded meeting *Dona* Paula da Cruz, one of Bonga's daughters. She was 18 years old and did not speak a word of Portuguese. She had been married at fifteen and had a son. After an argument with her husband, she had had him seized by her men, bound in a *fumba* (a sort of sleeping bag used by Africans) and sent to the "next world via the Zambezi and the teeth of the crocodiles". Guyot had dinner with her, which she ate with her hand, after which they retired to sit on her veranda and drank *pombe*.[16]

European travellers took pleasure in pinning similar stories of atrocities to the names of other rulers and warlords of the Zambezi region—for instance, some of the Barotse royals or the Ndebele king Mzilikatzi—and this cannot but remind the historian of the monsters of European feudal legend, for example, Gilles de Rais or Elizabeth Bathory. Were these tales of atrocity real or were they part of the persona that rulers or feudal lords needed to cultivate in order to maintain control over their subjects and followers? Or were they largely the invention of Europeans who had a vested interest in portraying the savagery of an Africa they wanted to take over and 'civilise'?

7

THE 'SCRAMBLE FOR AFRICA'
AND THE ZAMBEZI

Anglo-Portuguese agreements over the navigation of the Zambezi

Before Livingstone turned the spotlight of his famous *Missionary Travels* on the Zambezi river and its people, there had been little international interest in the river, which was barely even known to the outside world. In the 1840s, a German scientist Wilhelm Peters had spent 6 years in the Zambezi valley examining and describing its flora and fauna. However, he only began the publication of his seven volumes in 1852. The Portuguese had not published any work of note, Gamitto's *Muata Cazembe* (*King Kazembe*) only appearing in 1854. For some reason, the exploration of the Zambezi never aroused the interest of nineteenth-century scientists in the same way as discovering the source of the Nile or the course of the Niger.

Livingstone believed the Zambezi could provide a highway into the interior and open Africa for commerce and missionary work. However, this optimism unravelled as his government-supported expedition, which arrived by steamer in 1858, learned the hard way the problems of trying to navigate the shallows and sandbanks of the river, before confronting the brutal realities of the Cahora Bassa rocks that filled the bed of the gorge. The Zambezi was very much not the highway into the interior Livingstone had hope for.

However, if the Zambezi could be entered from the sea only with difficulty, there was another point of access which Livingstone had vividly described in his writing. He had originally reached the Upper Zambezi travelling north through what is modern Botswana. He had reached the upper river at its junction with the Chobe and had travelled west through the Barotse floodplain. There, he had become aware that Mambari traders from Angola had also reached the upper river travelling along the Cuando river, as had some Swahili traders from Zanzibar. Livingstone's subsequent visit to the Victoria Falls and his vivid description of them in his best-selling *Missionary Travels* meant that many hunters and travellers would follow his path northwards to visit what was soon recognised as one of the natural wonders of the world. In the following decades, the Victoria Falls became, in effect, Africa's first major tourist attraction.

However, none of this concerned international statesmen or bothered the chancelleries of Europe, and Portugal remained the only European country concerned with affairs on the great river.

What brought the Zambezi more into the public eye was the decision in 1875 by the two principal Scottish churches to establish missions in the Shire Highlands, on what was then called Lake Nyasa (now Lake Malawi). These missions were conceived as memorials to Livingstone, who had died in 1873 in central Africa, and intended to further his campaign against the slave trade. However, unlike the ill-conceived and disastrous UMCA mission which had briefly established itself on the Shire in 1861–2, these missions were to be linked to a commercial enterprise, the African Lakes Company, which was established in

1878. This enterprise, it was hoped, would realise Livingstone's ambition to develop commerce in the region as well as provide support for the missions.

The Scottish missions were located far beyond any region that the Portuguese could realistically lay claim to, but their only route to the outside world lay up the Zambezi and Shire rivers through territory that was claimed, and after a fashion controlled, by Portugal. Freedom of access for missionaries and traders now became a regular point of discussion between the Portuguese and British governments. The problem was partly solved in 1877 when the Portuguese agreed to a new, much lower, tariff for goods entering the Zambezi. Still, there remained much scope for further disagreement. For example, the Portuguese granted a short-lived concession to a private company to operate steamers on the Zambezi, thus, apparently, preventing any British-owned steamer from operating there. Moreover, although the Scottish missions were convinced they lay outside Portuguese jurisdiction, it was not clear exactly where the inland frontier of Portuguese jurisdiction was located.

Meanwhile, Portugal and Britain had been drawn into negotiations over the control of Delagoa Bay, a deep-water harbour from which there was relatively close access to the developing mines of the Transvaal. In 1875, arbitration by the president of France, Marshal Macmahon, had awarded sovereignty over the bay to Portugal. When in 1877 Britain annexed the Transvaal and began to plan a railway to the coast, relations with Portugal rose to the top of the international agenda.

The deal that emerged, largely negotiated by Robert Morier, Britain's minister in Lisbon, made provision for a British-financed railway to be built to the port of Lourenço Marques in Delagoa Bay and for a low tariff on all goods imported by Britain through the port itself, while the low tariffs already agreed for the Zambezi were confirmed and embodied in the treaty. When this treaty failed to pass the two houses of the Portuguese Cortes, the future of freedom of navigation was revisited in the so-called Congo Treaty. The Congo Treaty was, in effect, an attempt by Britain and Portugal to settle on a bilateral basis the future of commerce on—and by implication access to—the Zambezi and the Congo/Zaire rivers. Had this treaty been accepted, it would have conformed with Britain's long-standing policy of promoting free trade. Objectively, it should have met the interests of both parties without overly interfering with the interests of the African kingdoms of central Africa, but it snagged on the hidden rocks of British objections to Portuguese slaving, protectionism and Catholic religious identity.

The treaty ran into difficulties as it progressed downstream through diplomatic to political channels. In Britain, the strong liberal, anti-slave trade lobby saw it as confirming the position of the Portuguese, who were considered to be inveterate slavers, in both east and west Africa. In Portugal, it was seen as opening up their colonies to British trade, British influence and ultimately British control.

While the treaty struggled with its progress in both countries, the international situation had begun to change. King Leopold of the Belgians had created his International African Association, which had its focus on central Africa, while in the south of Africa, Britain handed back independence to the Boers of the Transvaal in 1881. This latter development meant that Portugal and the Transvaal could, in theory, proceed with plans for a railway without requiring Britain's collaboration. However, it was Bismarck's decision to involve Germany in African affairs, and in 1884 to summon the Berlin Conference, which finally put an end to the Anglo-Portuguese treaties.

Meanwhile, a growing interest in the affairs of central Africa, demonstrated by Scottish missionaries on the lower Zambezi as well as travellers, hunters and ivory traders heading up from the south to hunt elephants and visit the Victoria Falls, had led to the founding of the Lisbon Geographical Society in November 1875. The publicly stated object of this society was to "promote and assist the study and progress of geography and related sciences in the country", but this society was not a mere scientific organisation. The intention was to link its scientific activities to an openly avowed 'forward' policy in Africa. Exploration was to pave the way for increased Portuguese trade with Africa, the expansion of Portuguese settlements and the assertion of Portuguese sovereignty in the interior.

Sponsored by the Society, a Portuguese expedition headed for the upper Zambezi in 1877. After delays and disagreements that led to the members of the expedition going in different directions, Major Serpa Pinto reached the Barotse capital at Lealui in 1878 and proceeded south and eastwards to complete a formal Portuguese 'crossing of Africa'. Serpa Pinto did little of scientific importance, but his arrival at Lealui heralded a clear Portuguese intention to claim this region of the Upper Zambezi as an area of Portuguese influence.

In the same year, on the Lower Zambezi, a Portuguese diplomat, Joaquim Paiva de Andrade, had convinced the Portuguese government to grant him a timber and mining concession which extended over much of the south bank of the river. However, this clearly overlapped with regions which the Gaza king claimed as part of his kingdom, while also threatening to impinge on areas which were regularly raided by the Ndebele. The major African states of the region were in this way being drawn into a rivalry with the Portuguese.

None of these activities meant that the international community saw the Zambezi river itself as central to its concerns. Indeed, the fact that the river system was effectively split into three rather separate parts by the Victoria Falls and the Cahora Bassa gorge meant that the river was not viewed as a continuous system that could be exploited commercially. In the same vein, the fact that those who travelled along the river into the interior were usually stricken with malaria meant that no one saw it as an area for potential colonisation either.

The Rose-Coloured Map

The Berlin Conference was for the most part concerned with the future of the Niger and the Congo/Zaire rivers. However, it also outlined an agreement that the Zambezi basin together with the basin of the Congo/Zaire would be a free-trade area, even though the full extent of the drainage basins of the two rivers was as yet unknown. The Conference also recognised the existence of Leopold's Congo Free State, but, as no firm inland frontiers were established, it was inevitable that there would be a scramble to see who could occupy which areas of central Africa first. The Conference agreed what criteria were to be employed before any country could claim territory in Africa. The main criterion was to be 'effective occupation' rather than 'prior discovery', as the Portuguese had claimed. If the original idea of insisting on 'effective occupation' had been to limit the extent of claims, the effect was exactly the opposite, as this clause was responsible more than anything else for promoting the scramble for African territory.

These decisions for the moment existed only on paper, but they did not bode well for the future of African kingdoms. The Lozi and the Ndebele, their immediate neighbours down the river, would have to confront the threat posed by industrialised nations, with huge technological superiority, determined to wrest their land and natural resources from them. These African kingdoms had neither the military strength nor the skills which literacy and a wider understanding of the world would have given them, and thus they were not well equipped to deal with these threats.

In this 'scramble' for central African territory, the Portuguese led the way, partly because they already had a commercial presence in much of central Africa, even if this did not really amount to effective occupation. The Portuguese had published the first detailed map of the lower reaches of the Zambezi in 1867, and in 1883 they set up a cartographic commission to map in detail the country between Angola and Mozambique.

In 1884, in pursuit of this aim, two Portuguese officers, Hermenegildo de Brito Capello and Roberto Ivens, set out on an avowedly scientific mission which was to take them across the continent, arriving back in Portugal in 1886. The two explorers departed from the west coast, reached the upper Zambezi and travelled up the river to the confluence with the Kabompo, before heading inland to Msiri's kingdom of Garenganze. Their crossing of Africa established a route connecting Angola with the Lower Zambezi and did a lot to explore the watershed between the Zambezi and Zaire river basins. Their journey had at last made a reality out of the idea of the *contracosta*, a route connecting Mozambique and Angola, which had been a subject of speculation since the sixteenth century, although the path they had followed had wandered far to the north of Barotseland. In 1886, the Portuguese published their famous Rose-Coloured Map (*Mapa Cor-de-Rosa*), which they attached to agreements that were being negotiated with France and Germany to fix the frontiers of possessions that were contiguous with those of Portugal.

The Rose-Coloured Map (Map 5) clearly showed a broad band of territory stretching across Africa over which Portugal claimed sovereignty. This included all of the main stream of the Zambezi and most of the Zambezi drainage basin that was known at the time. However, what was excluded is revealing. The map excluded the well-trodden route northwards from the Cape to the Zambezi and the whole of the region south of the Cunene and Cubango/Chobe rivers, which were now clearly acknowledged to be in the German sphere of interest. In this map, the Zambezi was for the first time treated as a single river system that was destined to fall under Portuguese control.[1]

With Germany and France now acquiescing, Portugal had to establish its claim to the effective occupation of this territory. It seemed as if its ambitions might be substantially realised. Although there had been no formal acceptance of the claims made in the Rose-Coloured Map, neither the French nor the Germans had protested against its being attached to the frontier agreements which they had negotiated with Portugal. In 1888, Britain had even offered to recognise Portugal's claim to the area north of the Zambezi in return for Portugal recognising the area south of the river to be a British sphere of influence.

The competition for influence south of the Zambezi

So far, the concessions that had been granted to Paiva de Andrade in 1878 had not resulted in significant investment or economic activity of any kind. This was partly because the Lower Zambezi region remained very disturbed. In 1880, Manuel António de Sousa had used his private army to seize control of the hitherto independent African kingdom of Barue. Then, in 1884, there had been a war on the lower Shire as fighters from the old Vas dos Anjos lands of Massingire took control of the lower reaches of the river and endangered the operations of the African Lakes Company and the Opium Company, the embryo of Portuguese plantation capitalism. More serious was the continued da Cruz presence at Massangano, which periodically led to the closure of the Zambezi downstream from Tete. The Portuguese knew that, in the increasingly competitive climate of the 1880s, they had to establish full control of the lower river, a feat which had eluded them in the 1860s.

Government armed forces captured Massangano in 1887 only to find that the *aringa* had been abandoned. However, the following year the da Cruz returned to reoccupy the site and a final campaign had to be mounted in 1888 to end their occupation of Massangano. A government fort was now built and a garrison installed. Meanwhile, Paiva de Andrade formed an alliance with Manuel António de Sousa, and together they invaded the high veldt of what was later to be Mashonaland. There they met resistance and were forced to retreat.

Meanwhile, the Portuguese were organising other expeditions with the intention of occupying the country around the outpost at Zumbo and establishing Portuguese occupation of the Shire valley. There, of course, they threatened directly the communications of the Scottish missions and the independence of the so-called Makololo, descendants of Livingstone's former companions who were allies of the missions and had established their control over land on the lower reaches of the river.

While the focus of Lisbon's attention had largely shifted to eastern Africa, expeditions were also sent from Angola into the areas of the old Lunda empire, which the Portuguese found to be an empty shell of what had once been the powerful state, ruled over by the Mwant Yaav (Mwata Yamvo), which in the early nineteenth century had controlled so much of West Central Africa.

Cecil Rhodes

In spite of all efforts by the Portuguese, the future of Central Africa would not be determined by Portugal but by Cecil Rhodes, the millionaire owner of the Kimberley diamond mines.

In 1881, Britain had been obliged to abandon its attempt to form a federation of South African states and now sought to maintain its position in southern Africa through the surrogacy of Cape Colony. This gave considerable leverage to the Cape politicians, many of whom were Afrikaners. In 1885, the fear that the Transvaalers would link up with the Germans who had declared a protectorate on the coast of South West Africa, led to Britain declaring a protectorate over Bechuanaland. This had the effect of extending British influence as far as the Zambezi and placing a wedge of British territory between Transvaal and the Germans. Already the road north from Cape Colony to the Zambezi—a road which since Livingstone's day had seen a continuous stream of hunters, travellers and missionaries, and which had become known as the Missionary Road—had acquired a certain strategic importance as it passed through the narrow strip of fertile land between the Transvaal border and the Kalahari desert.

In 1886, the discovery of the Witwatersrand gold fields had raised the possibility that the Transvaal Boers would now use their newly acquired resources to expand their republic to the north and eastwards to the sea. Rhodes and his backers, who included the powerful Rothschild bankers, were convinced that similar gold-bearing reef existed further to the north, where it was known there had been extensive gold mining by the African population for hundreds of years. Rhodes was determined to control the mineral resources of this region south of the Zambezi that was known to be gold bearing, and in a series of dramatic moves his agents secured mineral concessions from the Ndebele king, and from the British government a Charter which enabled his British South Africa Company (BSAC), which had been established in October 1888, to turn the concessions they had obtained into a colony. The Charter took effect from December 1889.

Rhodes also cast his eye north of the Zambezi into lands between the Upper Zambezi and Lake Malawi. Here nothing much was known beyond the fact that copper existed in large quantities. Was there also gold or other valuable minerals? This was wildly speculative, but the terms of the Charter which he had obtained from the British government left open the possibility of expansion north of the Zambezi. The Charter conferred on the company full financial and administrative responsibility for the countries "lying immediately to the north of British Bechuanaland ... to the north and west of the South African Republic and to the west of Portuguese dominions". Where exactly Portuguese dominions ended was not clear, and there was no northern limit to the concession. This vagueness Rhodes interpreted as an open invitation to obtain as much of central Africa as he could.

These ambitions were decked out in clever language which imagined the possibility of a British-owned Cape-to-Cairo rail-way—an idea which had been passed around in imperialist circles for at least 10 years and was eagerly espoused by Harry Johnston, who became the first Commissioner (i.e., administrator) of the Nyasaland Protectorate. An essential part of the package that Rhodes had negotiated was his undertaking to finance the build-ing of a railway north from Cape Colony towards the Zambezi. Rhodes was an accomplished propagandist, and his 'Cape to Cairo' proposal would prove one of the most successful of all populist slogans, creating a wave of enthusiasm and speculation that more sober politicians in London would be unable to resist. The idea of a Cape-to-Cairo railway was an economic absurdity, but it conjured up images of imperial might that won the day.

Rhodes's ambitions cut right through the lands tinted pink on the Rose-Coloured Map and threatened open conflict between British interests and those of Portugal. In 1889, much of the advantage on the ground lay with Portugal, whose expeditions were establishing administrative and military posts throughout Zambezia and the Shire river valley, and even in parts of Mashonaland. However, what gave Rhodes virtually a free hand was the British government intervention in January 1890, pre-senting Portugal with an ultimatum the essence of which was the demand that the Portuguese call a halt to all the expeditions they had sent out to establish their effective occupation of central

Africa. An ultimatum, backed with the threat of war, was a drastic step to take, particularly towards an old ally with whom the peaceful resolution of problems had so recently been given a high priority. Its declaration seems to have been influenced by the vigorous protests of the Scottish missions on Lake Malawi and in the Shire highlands at the advance of an armed Portuguese expedition on the Shire. Worried about public opinion in Scotland and, for the moment, ill in bed with flu, Lord Salisbury agreed to send the ultimatum.

Portuguese public opinion was outraged, and republicans pinned much of the blame on the monarchy. However, Portugal had no option but to agree to halt its expeditions. There was no similar commitment on the British side, and Rhodes now had a free hand to exploit the situation. His pioneer column advanced into what was to become Southern Rhodesia, and an armed unit confronted the Portuguese in Manica, taking Manuel António de Sousa and Paiva de Andrade prisoner. Agents were also sent to the Zambezi to make treaties with African rulers. Alfred Sharpe went north and Frank Lochner headed west to meet the king of Barotseland. Meanwhile, Rhodes agreed to pay the expenses of a British protectorate over the area where the Scottish missions were established.

In a short and decisive war in 1893, Rhodes's forces destroyed the Ndebele kingdom. Rhodes, however, did not have it all his own way. His agents failed to gain control of the copper-rich region ruled over by Msiri that later became known as Katanga. This area was secured by Leopold for his Congo Free State in 1891. The same year, Rhodes's men attempted but failed to gain a concession from the Gaza king, which would have extended his territory to the Indian Ocean through what later became southern Mozambique. Moreover, the British government, alarmed at the irresponsible buccaneering of Rhodes and his men, refused to recognise an eastward extension of the British South Africa

Company concession after a column of Rhodes's men, in an anticipation of the disastrous Jameson Raid, headed down from Manica to seize control of the port of Beira.

However, unexpectedly, it was Germany that placed the most effective limit on Rhodes's expansion.

The Caprivi Strip

Since Bismarck first decided to take an active interest in Africa in 1884, the Germans had been carving out colonies for themselves in South West Africa, Cameroon, Togo and the territories of the Sultan of Zanzibar. The extreme colonial party envisaged an unbroken band of German colonies linking South West Africa with German East Africa, a German version of Portugal's Rose-Coloured Map. Meanwhile, Emin Pasha in Equatoria threatened a German presence near the headwaters of the Nile. Very much alive, also, was the fear that Germany would find a way of establishing an alliance with the Transvaal and challenge Britain's dominance in South Africa.

In fact, even before the fall of Bismarck in 1890 and his replacement by Leo von Caprivi, Germany had begun to lose interest in extending its African empire, and Salisbury, the British prime minister, was pushing at an open door in proposing a comprehensive settlement of outstanding African questions. This was negotiated during the early months of 1890, while Rhodes was pushing his agents and mercenaries deep into the centre of Africa.

The agreement with Germany tidied up many issues. The Germans were allowed to take over all the territories of the Sultan of Zanzibar except the island itself, the border being drawn in such a way that Mount Kilimanjaro (known at the time as Kaiser Wilhelm Spitze) fell within the frontiers of the German colony. Germany abandoned any claims to expand into Equatoria and the Nile valley as well as the ambition to link its East African with its South West African territories. Moreover, the ambitions of some British imperial enthusiasts to secure territory between German East Africa and the Congo Free State, in the form of a strip of land along which the futuristic Cape-to-Cairo railway would run, was also abandoned. These concessions were sweetened by Britain agreeing to cede to Germany Heligoland, a strategically placed island in the North Sea.

Surprisingly, however, Germany did obtain another concession. Germany demanded that, if it abandoned its ambitions to link its colonies together, it must at the very least have access to the Zambezi river. So it was agreed that a 280-mile strip of territory would be added to German South West Africa, linking the colony to the strategic point where the Chobe river entered the Zambezi and which was the head of the road northwards from South Africa. This area of land, which included the Linyanti region which had been the location of the Makololo capital, was a recognised part of the Barotse kingdom and was not Britain's to give away. It became known as the Caprivizipfel (or Caprivi Strip) after the German chancellor Leo von Caprivi, who had succeeded Bismarck.

In all the frenetic politicking of the 1888–90 period, the Zambezi river itself had not really been an objective. The British and Portuguese were well aware that the river did not constitute a highway that could be easily navigated, let alone used to access the interior, and the British were more concerned with securing a route for a railway from the south than securing the river itself. In fact, the Zambezi mostly came into play in the negotiations because the regions immediately to the south and the north of the river came to be referred to as 'Zambezia'.

The negotiations between Britain and Germany had brought the Caprivi Strip into existence. There seemed to be no conceivable reason for this extraordinary geographical anomaly, as navigation of the Zambezi was blocked downstream from the Chobe confluence by the Victoria Falls and upstream by the Ngonye Falls. Although it seems highly improbable, a myth has grown up that no one in the German foreign office knew about the Victoria Falls or the other impediments to Zambezi navigation, and they thought the Caprivi Strip would give Germany a route to the Indian Ocean. This myth is still repeated in respectable publications.[2]

In fact, Germany had shown an interest in having access to the Zambezi as early as 1886, and, during the negotiations with Portugal over the border between Angola and South West Africa, an inland frontier for Germany's South West African colony had been agreed which would follow the right bank of the Cubango and Chobe rivers as far as the Katima rapids on the Zambezi and downstream to the Chobe confluence with the Zambezi. This agreement was eventually confirmed in July 1887 and was reflected in the version of the Rose-Coloured Map that was attached to the treaty. Any idea that Germany might have had of extending the whole of South West Africa as far as the Zambezi was abandoned when Britain established the western boundary of the Bechuanaland Protectorate, leaving the Caprivi Strip as vestige of what had been a grander but now abandoned project. Germany's insistence that it must have access to the Zambezi, even if the frontiers of its colony fell a long way short of that point, was largely an assertion of power and potentially allowed it to be considered as one of the riverain states to be consulted in any international negotiations over the future of the river. This is, indeed, what happened, and the Caprivi Strip was to give Germany and later South Africa and independent Namibia a say in all international negotiations that might concern the river. A rather similar arrangement extended the German colony of Cameroon inland to the shores of Lake Chad.

After 1890, the Germans made no attempt to establish any kind of presence near the Zambezi, and the region continued to be ruled by the Lozi until 1908. In that year, the Germans refused a British offer to exchange the Caprivi Strip for an equivalent strip of Bechuanaland and at last decided to occupy their small section of the Zambezi's southern shore. The Lozi all left the region taking with them not only their own but everyone else's cattle, while a small town, called Schuckmannsburg after the governor of the German colony, was built 2 miles from the banks of the river on part of the floodplain. This town, never much bigger than a military post, had a very short life. In September 1914, forces sent by the British occupied the town and received the German surrender. Apparently, it had been thought that the Germans might try to mount an invasion of British Central Africa from that remote location on the river.

After the German surrender, Schuckmannsburg was abandoned and the town of Katina Mulilo opposite Sesheke grew as the principal town of the Caprivi Strip. No part of the region was ever returned to Barotseland, although it had been confidently expected by Lewanika and his successor that this would be one of the adjustments to colonial boundaries following the First World War.

The Anglo–Portuguese agreements

Following the ultimatum of January 1890, Britain and Portugal began negotiations to resolve the conflict of interests that had arisen. Portugal refused at first to abandon the Rose-Coloured Map, and the preliminary agreement that was negotiated made provision for a communications corridor that would link Portugal's east African and west African territories. This corridor would run roughly along the Zambezi river, which was thus accorded the role it could never actually play, that of providing a transport corridor. This compromise was inherently impractical, worse even than the Caprivi Strip as a solution to European rivalries, and was rejected by the Portuguese government.

Negotiations continued into 1891, and finally a deal was struck which outlined the boundaries of Mozambique with British Central Africa. The corridor was abandoned, and in return Mozambique was given an extensive chunk of territory north of Tete. Along the eastern border, the frontier ran along the tops of the Manica mountains, dividing that region between Britain and Portugal but ending any hope that Rhodes's central African empire would acquire a corridor to the sea. British and Portuguese spheres on the Shire were fixed at the point where the Ruo river entered the Shire, which had been the frontier that had effectively been frozen when the ultimatum was issued.

The Zambezi divided

Looking at how events progressed from the sobering distance of 130 years, it is difficult to make sense of the European powers' obsessive scramble for African territory. Much of the land contested had never been visited by any of the claimants and could not easily be found on any map. Any glance at the political map of Africa shows how, ignorant of the geography and ethnography of the continent, the officials in the European chancelleries simply fell back on ruling lines across empty maps, slicing carelessly through river valleys and traditional African communities. In the twenty-first century, the posturing of empire builders—the 'men on the spot'—appears as little short of absurd. We still see their visages: Leopold and Salisbury with their patriarchal beards hiding who knows what psychological insecurities, and Harry Johnston and Brito Capello with their truly magnificent moustaches. It would not be inappropriate if their heads could have been mounted on the wall alongside the wild animals they and their contemporaries so heedlessly slaughtered.

And once these men had coloured the map of Africa with their national colours, it was not clear what they intended to do with these vast and, in reality, unwanted tracts. On one thing, however, they all agreed: the African inhabitants would be made to pay for the privilege of being civilised.

The Zambezi river, divided into its three sections by impassable cataracts, was now also divided by politics: the Upper Zambezi partitioned with Angola but otherwise providing the spinal cord of the Barotseland protectorate, the Middle Zambezi the frontier between Northern and Southern Rhodesia and the Lower Zambezi continuing to be what it had been since the sixteenth century, the backbone of a Portuguese creole-dominated state.

THE FALLS FROM THE WESTERN END OF THE CHASM .

(From the Leaping Water and Three Hill Cliff, to Garden Island)

1. Victoria Falls by Thomas Baines, 1865

2. Cahora Bassa dam and gorge

3. Postcard of Chinde during floods

THE COURT HOUSE. FLOOD TIME.

[To face p. 324.

4. The Courthouse Lealui during the annual floods

5. The Dona Ana Bridge, spanning the Lower Zambezi

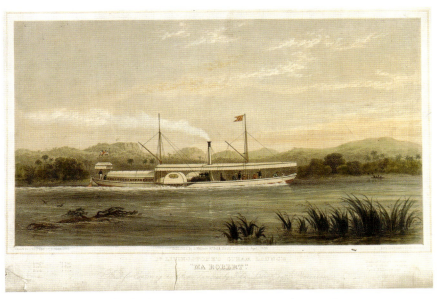

6. Ma Robert, D. Livingstone's steamboat, 1858

7. Nalikuanda, ceremonial barge of the Litunga of Barotseland

8. Portuguese gunboat on the Zambezi, 1913

Fig. 8. Empire of Monomotapa by João Teixeira Albernaz II. *Atlas de 1665* Archives Nationales, Paris.

9. Map of the Lower Zambezi

10. Canoe on the Lower Zambezi at Bandar, 1964

11. Site of the *aringa* of Massangano. Site of repeated battles between Portuguese and the da Cruz, 1964

12. Photo taken by the author when crossing the Zambezi by bridge, behind a steam locomotive, 1964

13. A traditional Lower Zambezi house at Tete, 1964

14. District Commissioner Balovale departing by boat, 1935

15. Barotseland boatmen, 1935

16. A river boat on the Upper Zambezi, 1935

8

BAROTSELAND IN THE TWENTIETH CENTURY

Barotseland becomes a protectorate

In the 1880s and 1890s, as the European chancelleries haggled over their respective spheres of influence in central Africa, the major African states were excluded from any but the most nominal role in deciding the region's future. The Ndebele king, Lobengula, had been lured into making mineral concessions which had opened the way to a European takeover of Mashonaland. He could only watch anxiously as white settlers, gold prospectors and gunmen poured north into regions that up to that time had paid tribute to him. Higher up the Zambezi, the Barotse king also felt the near approach of European adventurers and empire builders.

The civil conflict that had torn the whole Barotse kingdom apart in 1884 was only resolved with the return of Lewanika in 1885. Even then, the purging continued, with the supporters of the rebels being rounded up and murdered along with any members of their families not able to flee in time. The purges continued throughout 1886, and the Lozi were indeed fortunate that, as events unfolded, they did not have to pay the price for their internal dissensions.

The Lozi ruling elite were split over the course of action that should be taken in the face of threats from Europeans, and many wanted their king to refuse to deal with any of them. In 1888, Lewanika's principal European adviser, George Westbeech, had died. The king had allowed François Coillard and his companions to establish a mission in the country in 1886, but it seems that he wanted to find a replacement to fill the vital economic role Westbeech had played in the kingdom. In June 1889, Lewanika was approached by a trader and hunter, Henry Ware, who brought a large number of gifts, including modern rifles, and claimed to be a representative of the British government.

Apparently on François Coillard's advice, Lewanika granted a mineral concession to Ware covering the Batoka country north of the Falls as far as the Kafue, a region that had paid tribute to the Lozi king but had never been formally incorporated into his kingdom. The concession also included extensive rights over water, timber and railway track. The king was to be paid £2000 a year and was to be given 4 per cent on all minerals extracted. Lewanika was strongly opposed by many of the indunas in his kingdom, who said that he was selling his whole kingdom. The agreement with Ware seemed to promise advantages that would secure Lewanika's protection against threats from both internal and external enemies and help the king to consolidate his position in the country. However, Ware was not a representative of the British government, as soon became apparent when he sold his concession to Cecil Rhodes.

As early as 1886, Lewanika had considered seeking British protection, and the idea of a protectorate was still very much in his mind when Rhodes's agent Frank Lochner reached Barotseland in April 1890. Lochner arrived amid political tensions he did not entirely understand. Lewanika was not secure on his throne and faced a rival focus of authority in the town of Sesheke. Here opposition to the idea of a protectorate came from a group of senior Lozi, often referred to as the 'Sesheke chiefs', who ruled the area around Sesheke and the Chobe confluence and who were linked with the Mulena Mukwae, the queen mother. Each party saw something to gain from an agreement with Britain, but likewise each feared the other party gaining an advantage.

Lewanika was greatly influenced by François Coillard, who was well aware of the dangers that would result from a refusal to negotiate with the European powers. It was Coillard who urged Lewanika to seek British protection with an agreement similar to that of the British protectorate over Bechuanaland, which had guaranteed the position of Khama and prevented his kingdom from being attacked and broken up by the Transvaal Boers and the Ndebele. Coillard persuaded Lewanika that he needed British protection not only against a possible German or Portuguese take-over but also as an insurance against a free-for-all invasion by a horde of elephant hunters, gold prospectors and concession seekers. It was this advice, supported by messages from Khama himself, that persuaded Lewanika to listen to Lochner and agree to a British protectorate. In June 1890, after consultation with a large number of his supporters in Lealui, Lewanika eventually signed the document that became known as the Lochner Concession.

This Concession, which effectively excluded the Portuguese, the Germans and King Leopold, served the immediate purposes of the British government, and those of Cecil Rhodes, but it was to be some time before the Barotse kingdom was safely reeled in as a protectorate. The trouble was that Lochner had not been an emissary of the British government but an agent of Rhodes's British South Africa Company, a point soon seized upon by Lewanika's opponents. After Lochner left, Lewanika came to believe that he had been deceived and maintained that he had only signed in the belief that he had agreed to the protection of the British Crown not that of Rhodes's company. In 1892, he even tried to renounce the treaty signed with Lochner.

The British meanwhile made an agreement with the Portuguese in 1891 and, after a year of great internal agitation in Barotseland, the British government confirmed that the protection offered to Lewanika was indeed that of the British government. In 1894, an agreement was signed with King Leopold which drew the frontier between the chartered territory and that of the Congo Free State along the Zambezi–Zaire watershed, as far as this was known at the time.

However, no British officials arrived in Barotseland, and Lewanika was aware that the boundaries of his kingdom had not been agreed. The Linyanti area between the Zambezi and the Chobe had already been lost to Germany in the Anglo–German agreement of July 1890, and Lewanika's claims to rule as far down the river as the Victoria Falls and over the Batoka plateau country between the Zambezi and the Kafue were now being challenged, as was his control of the upper reaches of the Zambezi beyond the confluence with the Lungwebungo river. According to Major Gibbons, in 1892 Lewanika sent an armed expedition into the Batoka plateau to try assert his authority, and that "many Mashukalumbwe chiefs have acknowledged Liwanika as their paramount chief, and send a tusk, a leopard skin, or foodstuffs annually as a tribute and acknowledgment of suzerainty. In this way they escape being raided, and are practically as independent as ever they were".[1]

The same year, Lewanika answered a plea from some of the hard-pressed Lunda and sent an expedition up the Zambezi in an attempt to impose his authority in the region inhabited by the Lunda and Lovale people. However, the wisdom of seeking some form of protection for his own kingdom was made only too clear when Lewanika heard of a fresh Ndebele raid across the Zambezi, and news of the murder of his neighbour Msiri by Leopold's henchman Stairs in December 1891. Subsequently, in 1893, a powerful Ndebele impi crossed the Zambezi and devastated the country of the Tonga, who were nominally Lewanika's subjects.

In any event, it was not until 1895 that any British presence manifested itself in the Barotseland. Even then, confusingly, it was officials of the British South Africa Company, as Britain had handed the administration of the protectorate over to Rhodes's Company after all.

Had Lewanika not signed the Lochner Concession, he would have faced the prospect of his kingdom being taken over by the Portuguese, who had already staked their claim in the Rose-Coloured Map, or possibly by Leopold's Congo Free State, or even conceivably by the Germans who had already secured the Linyanti triangle between the Zambezi and the Chobe, which had always been considered part of the Barotse kingdom. The possible fate that awaited Barotseland was made vividly clear when in 1893 Rhodes's company picked a fight with the Ndebele, annihilated Lobengula's army and annexed his kingdom.

The Lozi kingdom of Barotseland was the only kingdom in Central Africa to survive the establishment of colonial rule. This was largely due to the fact that, unlike the kingdom of the Ndebele, Barotseland did not have mineral wealth that could be exploited, and it was too remote and unhealthy to be attractive to European colonists. Significantly, the Lochner Concession had made no mention of any right to make land grants to white settlers. Meanwhile, the Jameson Raid of January 1896, followed by the Mashona/Matabele rebellion in Southern Rhodesia, so discredited the British South Africa Company that plans that had been drawn up to extend to Barotseland the terms of the Matabele Order in Council were dropped. The decision was then taken to bring the Barotseland Protectorate under the direct control of the High Commissioner in South Africa, leaving the British South Africa Company, which owned the mineral concessions, to pay for any resident in Lealui. The first resident, R.T. Coryndon, established himself at the Barotse capital in 1897.

However, these factors alone would not have ensured the kingdom's survival but for the skill shown by the king over a number of years in negotiating the relations with the colonial authorities and balancing the politics of his own kingdom.

Lewanika

Many of those who visited Barotseland recorded their impressions of Lewanika, the man who dominated the kingdom's affairs from 1878 until his death in 1916. The king had been known as Lobosi, but he assumed the name Lewanika (meaning 'conqueror') after his victory over the rebels in 1885. The French missionary François Coillard met Lewanika shortly after his restoration to the throne in 1886. The relationship that grew up between the two men was close, but the historical record seems often to privilege unnecessarily the paternal advice of the missionary. An example of this can be seen in C.W. Mackintosh's biography of Coillard, which was published in 1907:

> though he [Lewanika] had returned to his own, [he] was poor and destitute; all his property had been destroyed except his carved armchair or throne, he had no garments to wear, though the Barotsi for many years past had adopted the practice of clothing from the West Coast traders; of his flourishing town hardly a single hut remained. "Tell me how to govern my kingdom?" he entreated. The reply was:

> "Take the secret spear from under your cloak and throw it away; renounce vengeance once for all; attach your people to yourself by making their welfare your first object; put a stop to theft; give them justice, quiet sleep, and food to eat".

"What are the riches of a kingdom?" asked Lewanika. "The wealth of mine is ivory, and soon there will be none left. What shall we do then?"[2]

In a letter written in April 1886, Coillard wrote of Lewanika, "he is intelligent, somewhat childlike in intimate discourse, and none the worse for that".[3] According to Major Gibbons, Lewanika was

> a tall, very black man ... He wore a light coat, a patterned waistcoat and a pair of tweed trousers. A low, broad-brimmed, white felt hat protected his head, and a well fitting pair of boots his feet. The upper lip and cheeks were shaven, and a pointed beard, curly and crisp, covered the chin.[4]

When writing about Lewanika and the Mokwae, many European travellers gave the British reader the descriptions of sexual promiscuity and bloodthirsty cruelty that they expected of African potentates, but some of the narrative was more counter-intuitive. According to Gibbons, Lewanika devoted much of his spare time to woodwork, at which he proved exceptionally skilled. This is echoed by Coillard:

> The Barotsi royal family posseses this gift of craftsmanship in the highest degree. King Lewanika can construct anything from a house to an ivory carved hairpin, and is an adept in basket work ... His sister, Queen Mokwae, among other accomplishments, has proved herself an adept in what we should call 'poker-painting'.[5]

In his diary, Coillard described this more fully:

> Queen Mokwae, pointing with her finger to the doorpost, "Do you see him there?" she said. "It is Mathaha! [the chief of the revolution who had just been put to death]." And, indeed, I saw, burnt with red-hot irons in the wood, in quite the Egyptian style, the portrait of a human being holding his chin in his right hand, which, it appears, was a favourite habit of Mathahal's. "Look at him well!" she shrieked imitating his attitude.

And he continues with this recitation of royal artistic talent:

> Mokwae's daughter, Akanagisoa, inherits her mother's talent of portraiture, and once painted a series of likenesses in coloured earths on

the walls of her hut, just like the Egyptian paintings in the National Gallery. It cannot be said, however, that the pursuit of Art has in any way softened her manners or made them less ferocious.[6]

In 1910, Arnot visited Lewanika and his sister, 30 years after they had first made each other's acquaintance. The Mokwae was now a woman of substantial size.

her majesty had on a straw hat, with pink ribbon and aigrette plumes stuck all round ... [she] invited us to sit down to lunch, and this time her majesty's chair consisted of a settee sufficient for two people ... She spread herself out with a contented smile between the wooden arms, like her own Zambesi river flowing comfortably between her banks.[7]

When Gibbons was granted an audience, he recalled that he was offered "a rickety Portuguese chair" to sit in. Lewanika told him, "you must sit quietly in that chair, or else it will probably collapse". He recalled that Lewanika spoke "in a quick, somewhat nervous manner, at times almost stammering in his hurry to get out his sentence". He told Gibbons that "Lobengula used to talk of Khama and of me as if we were his cattle". Although by that time the protectorate agreement with Britain had been secured, Lewanika was deeply suspicious of the situation that faced him.

He has an idea that part of his country might be taken from him on the plea that there is little or no outward and visible sign of his authority in some of his more distant possessions. For this reason he has recently been distributing Marotse chiefs among the Matoka as rulers of districts and headmen of villages.

In this, of course, he was right, and although the British confirmed Lewanika's sovereignty over the Lunda and Lovale on the upper river, the Batoka plateau was eventually detached from Barotseland.[8]

Lewanika's summer capital was Lealui.

In the middle of the town of Lialui a strong circular palisade about ten feet high encloses the private premises of Liwanika. In the centre stands an oblong hut about forty-five feet by twenty, substantially built and well thatched with coarse grass. Here the king himself lives. Opposite is a smaller oblong building open in front; native made mats cover the floor and decorate the back and side walls. In this shelter the king usually receives and gossips with his chiefs on matters trivial and important. Immediately inside the palisade is a circle of huts of the usual round native pattern. Each of these is occupied by a royal wife of whom there are fourteen, though not very long ago the ladies of the harem numbered twenty. Liwanika is a regular attendant at church, but has not become a professed Christian on account of the wife difficulty.[9]

In fact, Lewanika had been told by his chief supporters that he would lose his throne if he became a Christian.

The Lozi king has his wings clipped

Even before the definitive ruling that established Barotseland as a British protectorate, Lewanika had been involved in a series of negotiations with the British South Africa Company and other British authorities to determine exactly what colonial rule involved. This relationship continued to be modified up to the end of British rule in 1964. It was a relationship, therefore, that continually evolved through negotiation and was never one where the colonial authorities simply imposed themselves by force. There was always give and take, as in any negotiated relationship, and this continued even after the independence of Zambia in 1964, erasing any clear separation between the colonial and postcolonial periods.

In the 1899 Order in Council, it was made clear that Barotseland was now part of Queen Victoria's dominions. Lewanika's jurisdiction was formally limited, and his kingdom became not unlike that of the Indian princes who ruled under the watchful eye of a Resident appointed by the Raj. As Eric Stokes wrote, the grants to be made by him would only be operative so far as they were ratified by Her Majesty, and were not inconsistent with the Order in Council. "The Order marked the loss of sovereignty. Henceforth Lewanika's authority rested, formally speaking, on sufferance and not autochthonous right."[10]

However, Lewanika had made some shrewd bargains. In the negotiations which preceded the Order in Council, he had agreed to a reduction of the annual payment from the British South Africa Company to £850 in return for formal recognition that his sovereignty extended over virtually all North Western Rhodesia. The British South Africa Company was willing to go along with what was, in effect, a rewriting of history, because according to the Lochner Concession it acquired the mineral rights in any area that came under Barotse control. This arrangement recognised that the Barotse kingdom extended up the river to include the Lovale and Lunda peoples, whose previous links with the Lozi had been confined to the occasional raid, which they usually beat off. On the other hand, Lewanika had agreed to allow the British South Africa Company to grant land to white settlers, not in the Barotse valley itself but in the Batoka and Ila highlands through which the railway to the north would run, and which the Lozi had claimed only by right of regularly raiding the people and taking tribute from them.

Subsequently, Lewanika's position as an independent ruler was chipped away, first by new regulations over the collection of hut tax. In 1905, joint collection of the tax was agreed upon, with 10 per cent being paid into a fund for use by the Lozi. In 1906, slavery was formally abolished, and the king relinquished his right to try cases outside the central Barotse area. Lewanika accepted that even in the heart of his kingdom his jurisdiction would not cover murder or witchcraft. Finally, he relinquished his right to appoint indunas to reside in the Batoka and Ila districts. In 1909, he gave up all control over land outside the reserved area of the Barotse valley in return for its extension to include the western regions of the Zambezi. According to Eric Stokes, "the 1909 Concession marked the full acceptance of the logic of partition [as] Lewanika ... abandoned all his claims and interests outside Barotseland proper".[11] In 1924, after Lewanika's death, his successor gave up his right as king to require 12 days' labour from all Lozi.

When Lewanika died in 1916 and was succeeded by his son Yeta III, the educated Lozi who advised the new king continued to press his claims to a wider jurisdiction for Barotseland, but these claims finally weakened when Yeta's income was bolstered by an additional grant from the government. In 1941, after years of increasingly embittered dispute, the Luena/Lovale and Lunda peoples of the Balovale district were separated from Barotseland in another major excision from the Barotse kingdom. Their claim that historically they had never been subjects of the Lozi king was accepted by the government. The Barotseland that still enjoyed protectorate status was now pared down to the floodplain and the surrounding marginal areas, less than half the area that Lewanika claimed to have ruled at the beginning of his reign, or even at the time of the Lochner Concession.

By the original protectorate agreement, the king could rule his people, but his laws had to be compatible with the laws of England. This provision wore away the king's freedom of action, and the colonial authorities gradually imposed new laws and new practices that brought about fundamental change. As Max Gluckman put it, "the British government has developed a considerable number of activities—public works, schools, hospitals and dispensaries, transport services, veterinary treatment", though he emphasised that much of this was done with the active collaboration of the king and his officials.

However, as the years went by the sphere in which the king was the active ruler shrank, and his power became increasingly the soft power exercised by tradition, influence, prestige and the extent to which he continued to represent the opinions and sentiments of the people of the floodplain.

The institutions of Barotseland

What was it that made Barotseland so unique and set it apart from other areas of central Africa that came under colonial rule? To understand this, one has to look back to the kingdom that emerged in 1864 from 25 years of Makololo rule.

Barotseland was a hierarchically organised kingdom rather than a culturally homogenous nation-state. The ruling Lozi elite controlled the land, the fishing resources, most of the cattle and the game rights. The relationship of the king to these elite families was carefully regulated. The king had to consult in the *kotla* assembly and shared a great deal of his authority with the Ngamela, a sort of prime minister or chief adviser. In the nineteenth century, the king commanded huge resources as land rights, fishing rights, hunting and external trade, the import of guns, the product of raids on neighbouring peoples and the tribute paid by his subjects had all been royal monopolies, as was the tribute paid by subject people on the margins of the kingdom. In addition, all subjects owed the king labour service.

Mutumba Mainga emphasises the importance of the tribute paid to the king. She quotes A. Bertrand, writing in 1898, "certain tribes must annually send the king a fixed impost of canoes, building wood, cattle, grain, milk, wild honey, fish, game, skins, iron spear heads etc.", while Coillard described the "long strings of people" bringing "honey, pelts, wild fruits, fishing tackle, mats etc.—the produce of the fields, of the chase, and of industry".[12] These lists recall the tribute paid to the *senhora* of the *prazo* of Gorongosa listed in chapter three.

This tribute vastly increased the wealth at the king's disposal, but in practice royal authority was closely tied to the way this wealth was distributed. As Max Gluckman wrote:

> The people emphasize most in chiefs the quality of generosity ... and even today, constantly recount the distribution of goods and food by the king among his people. The subject people were drawn into this distribution. After European trade-goods entered the country this continued; and missionaries have described how King Lewanika, after the arrival of a trade-caravan, shared out the cloth among all the people present until every man flaunted a half-yard of cloth.[13]

All members of the royal family had potential to be recognised as king, and rebellions that occurred, as when Lewanika was forced into exile in 1884, opened the way for another member of the family to take the throne.

Of special significance was the way that the kingship was shared between the Litunga (king) in Lealui and the Mokwai, the senior Lozi royal woman, who ruled with her own *kotla* in Nalolo, 25 miles distant. The existence of two capitals reflected a historical tradition that the Lozi state had originally been formed by the union of two kingdoms, while the size of the Lozi kingdom made it impossible, in practice, for the whole to be controlled from a single capital located in the north. The tradition grew up of having two capitals, each ruled by a senior royal with their own *kotla*, although the northern kingdom was always considered paramount. Mutumba Mainga claimed that "its main function was to maintain the unity of the Lozi state and to safeguard the supremacy of the central kingship in the north".[14]

Major Gibbons described the position of the Mokwai Matauka.

> Nalolo is the second town in importance in the Marotse empire, and is presided over by the queen of the country. An interesting and unique custom places this lady—known as the Mokwai—in the position she holds. By the unwritten constitution of Marotseland the

eldest sister of the ruling king shares both his prerogatives and his rights. He is not at liberty to take any important step in the government of his country without his sister's sanction and advice, though of course he stands in the position of a senior partner, and I imagine has his own way when he wants it. Within her district the Mokwai enjoys absolute sway over her subjects. She is at liberty to take unto herself a husband or depose him at will.[15]

He added that the Mokwai he met was on husband number seven, having murdered number six herself, and he went on to describe a meeting with her.

The following morning, having previously sent my greetings to the 'Mokwai' or ruling princess of the Sesheke district, I paid her a visit ... A neat palisade of reeds bound together and some ten feet high surrounds a courtyard, in the centre of which stands an oblong hut about thirty feet long and half that width. It is neatly thatched with coarse river grass, while the walls are constructed of cement made of ant-heap earth and cow-dung mixed, and supported internally by upright stakes. We found this young lady lounging on a mat beneath a reed-built shade. She is about twenty-three years of age, very black, decidedly presentable in appearance and refined in feature. Round each eye is a circular blue scar-tattoo mark. The two front teeth of a pearly white row are so filed as to form a reversed V. The wool, allowed to grow fairly long, is well combed out, thick and fuzzy, and in one side of it an ivory-carved dagger is thrust. A coloured robe passing over the left and under the right shoulder covers her person. To this young person, who is niece to Liwanika, the ruling of the Masubia and a section of the Matutela is entrusted, though her cousin Latia has powers of direction in the more important matters of government. A tall, good-looking young Masubia sat next to her. He bears the title 'Mokwetunga' or 'son-in-law of the king', and is at once her husband and her slave.[16]

In the twentieth century, the custom of placing senior royals in different parts of the country was extended. D.W. Stirke, whose book, published in 1922, described how this had developed shortly before Lewanika's death in 1916:

> A younger sister, Mbwanjikana, is Mokwai of Libonda, and Lewanika's eldest son Litia ... is stationed at Sesheke ... The two sisters and [Litia] are subordinate to Lewanika but all three have their Kotlas (Parliaments) and Prime Minister. There is a right of appeal from any of these subordinate Kotlas to the Lialui Kotla.[17]

Outside the immediate circle of the royal family, a key figure in the Lozi hierarchy was the Natamoyo whose function in the state was described by Stirke.

> Natamoyo means the 'father of life' ... Should any man—Chief, induna, or private person—be pursuing anyone with the desire or intention of killing him, the hunted person was safe directly he could reach the Natamoyo or his palisade ... Natamoyo also had the power to veto an execution when discussed in the Kotla, but his chief value lay in his being a haven of refuge.[18]

The Natamoyo could also be appealed to by anyone who alleged that he had been unjustly treated by a chief.

This office had had particular importance in the days before Lewanika gathered enough authority to put an end to trials by ordeal and witchcraft executions, trials which were subsequently forbidden by the colonial authorities. All early writers about Barotseland in the nineteenth century commented on the frequency of witchcraft trials and the subsequent executions by burning. Major Gibbons described what was involved;

> The prevailing treatment meted out to the person condemned of exerting evil charms was, until Liwanika discountenanced the practice, cruel in the extreme. In the case of anyone accused of witchcraft or suspected of any other crime, the 'ordeal of hot water' was resorted to, by which the accused was compelled to submerge his hands in boiling water. If, subsequently, the skin peeled off, he was guilty, and condemned, if accused of witchcraft, to the flames. The

unfortunate victim was hung by the feet from the branch of a tree, under him a large fire made, and roasted to death. The people stood round silently watching the effect of the fire until the heat caused the bursting of the entrails. At this point the evil spirit was supposed to have been burned out.[19]

Mutumba Mainga placed the prevalence of witchcraft trials in the context of the conflict between two religious cults, or more properly the exponents of two religious ideas. On the one hand was the importance of the royal graves and their guardians, who had great influence and whose consultations with the ancestors find many parallels in the history of other Central African monarchies, the kingdom of the Monomotapa being the clearest example. The rival religious influence was wielded by the witch finders which, Mainga claimed, were particularly associated with Mbunda immigrants from Angola.[20] The Mbunda had become increasingly involved in Lozi politics, and when, in December 1892, Lewanika finally moved against their dominance it was because the Mbunda witchfinders had actually laid accusations against the king himself, and Lewanika felt strong enough finally to assert himself.

Coillard gave a vivid description of this showdown in his diary:

In the large, rectangular shed of the lekhothla ... six or seven old Ma-Mbunda, squatting on some skins, were convulsively shaking baskets filled with every conceivable object, bits of human skeletons, bones of strange animals, spines and scales of fish, rare shells, curious seeds, the hairs of wild beasts etc. ... The people, packed like herrings, looked on with craning necks staring eyes, and mouths agape. And all this ... under the very eyes of the king, whom they thus accused of the nation's misfortunes. Shortly afterwards, the king's messenger had assembled the crowd, given his message, and finished by crying "Seize them". Everyone threw themselves on the wretched Ma-Mbunda, and fought for the pleasure of throttling them, when a second messenger arrived, who ordered the release of the miserable men, and warned them to have more respect for the Throne in future. The Ma-Mbundas had already profited by the moment's confusion to escape.[21]

In fact, the decline in the influence of the Mbunda witch finders was more drawn out, and divination for witchcraft only came to an end in 1897 when, according to Alphonse Jalla, Lewanika ruled that "where witchcraft was concerned it was the accuser not the accused who was to be punished".[22]

The king always ruled with the consent of the *kotla*, where the people were represented in a complicated system of precedence and hereditary right. The power of the king was often dependent on the skill, or lack of skill, with which he could influence or manipulate the three 'houses' of the *kotla*.

The Zambezi flood

As in ancient Egypt, the annual flooding of the river is the single most important event in national life and the most important influence in the culture of the peoples of the Barotse plain. In normal years, the Zambezi begins to rise in December, and from January through to May much of the floodplain is under water, with February and March being the peak months. Max Gluckman described in 1952 how the people of the Zambezi were accustomed to deal with the flooding. People who live in villages in the plain had to relocate either to small islands or further to the edges of the flooded area. Many of the mounds had been formed around white ant hills and had been built up by human labour over a number of years, but few could support large numbers of people and their cattle. For the most part, cattle were driven to the margins of the plain, where the population also worked small seasonal gardens.

Among the most important traditions of the monarchy were the rituals surrounding the annual floods. According to tradition, no one could move from the villages in the floodplain until the king himself began his own move. Gluckman vividly described this annual ceremony, which was known as Kuomboka and was every bit as significant as the rituals that surrounded the flooding of the Nile in Ancient Egypt:

> The Lozi calendar is largely defined by the state of the flood. The two great national events of the year are the moves of the king between his plain and his margin capitals. In theory no one should move out before he does. When the flood is rising his people may be living in discomfort as the water creeps up to their huts, and rodents, snakes, and warrior ants invade their homes. The royal drummers sing songs beseeching him to save the people and move. At last, after new moon, sacrifices are made at all the royal graves. The national drums are beaten at night. The king begins the drumming, followed by his chief councillor (the NGAMBELA) and then by other councillors in order of rank. After that, young men struggle for the honour of sounding the drums. These thunder over the Plain and men ... come hurrying to escort the king on his voyage.

Central to the ritual was the king's ceremonial barge, known as the Nalikwanda. The legendary king, Santuru, was supposed to have been the first to build such a boat.

> [The king] travels in a barge with forty paddlers, all princes and counsellors, dressed in bright cloths and caps, and wearing headdresses with long black plumes. Behind his white shelter his personal bands play. The national drums travel in a separate barge, for they represent the people ... A whole fleet of other barges (the queen's, the chief councillor's, the king's baggage barge, the councillors baggage barge) and of dugouts escort the king.[23]

D.W. Stirke described the event in the last years of Lewanika's reign and published photographs to illustrate his account.

> The boat is called 'Nalikwanda' and is always spoken of as a man and when being prepared for the excursion has a 'beard' made of plaited

reeds hung onto the bow and stem. Over the shelter ('lutanka') erected in the middle of the boats, is a big figure representing an elephant—the crest of the chief. The Mokwai of Nalolo and Litia [the heir to the throne] also perform this ceremony and have a bull and an eland respectively as their crests.[24]

In 1902, Lewanika had attended the coronation of Edward VII in London and had acquired the uniform of a British admiral. This became part of the regalia worn by Litungas on their annual voyage.

Changes to a traditional way of life

Barotseland's population had been divided between freemen, who might be ethnically Lozi or belong to one of the other twenty or so separate ethnic groups in the country, and *bazike* (slaves). Although the Lozi constituted a social elite which monopolised political power, they were not as exclusive as might be imagined. They married freely with other ethnic groups and in the past had often integrated into their families children acquired as war captives or presented in lieu of tribute. Until slavery was officially abolished in 1906, slaves made up at least half the total population and, although they possessed some rights as subjects of the king, like slaves in other societies they performed all the unskilled labour, could be bought and sold, and could be punished by their owners. During Lewanika's time, slaves were used to maintain royal and aristocratic gardens and to dig canals. Slavery was above all a question of status, and slave families would long remain a largely despised and excluded underclass in Lozi society, their numbers continually replenished by raids on neighbouring people.

The political turbulence of the nineteenth century had resulted in important changes to national institutions, which had had to adapt to changing circumstances, but there were economic changes as well. Firearms had been introduced and had spread widely in society, leading, among other things, to the virtual disappearance of elephants from the valley and its immediate environs. Agriculture was the occupation of virtually the whole population, and the hoe and axe were the most important implements of agricultural production. Hoes came from the Mbunda settled in the eastern part of the floodplain. Wooden spades had been used for digging the canals, but, towards the end of the nineteenth century, iron spades began to be produced. Maize, also introduced in the nineteenth century, led to the draining of new fields and the irrigation of crops.

The Paris mission had, in a limited way, been an agent for many of these changes, and Lewanika had wanted to encourage the introduction of schools. The mission schools had created an appetite for education, and in 1906 the Barotseland National School was founded with government funding. The younger generation of elite families, including members of the royal family, attended and became literate. Many of them, including Lewanika's heir, Litia, adopted Christianity.

After the establishment of the protectorate, many Lozi began to take employment in the modern sector of the colonial economy as it started to take shape. However, Barotseland itself remained insulated from many of the changes that were taking place elsewhere. There were no mines, industries or commercial farms in the kingdom, and no railway was built into the valley. At the end of the colonial period, there was only a single paved road leading to the administrative capital at Mongu. Protected by its treaties and agreements with the British, the Lozi of the Barotse valley had relatively little change forced upon them, while their traditional institutions, with their endless round of consultations, undoubtedly fostered a conservative outlook. Barotseland basked in its surviving way of life and was maintained by Britain as a kind of "museum of traditional rule".[25]

With the coming of colonial rule and the building of the railway northwards from the Victoria Falls towards the Copper Belt, migration of people both into and out of Barotseland became increasingly common. People went in search of paid employment or moved nearer to the railway where there were flourishing markets. And there were other causes for migration. The kingdom bordered on Angola, and in the 1930s the forced-labour practices of the Portuguese in that country led to large numbers of migrants crossing into Barotseland. By and large, these newcomers were absorbed into the population with little tension, as the long-established relationship between the king and the people, with reciprocal rights and duties, enabled outsiders to become subjects of the king with little fuss.

Moreover, with the exception of the near relatives of the king, there were no problems about intermarriage between different ethnic groups. The Lozi state had always been made up of a multiplicity of peoples speaking different dialects and recognising separate identities. All these different groups could be integrated into the wider nation, as long as they acknowledged their loyalty to the king. Loyalty meant paying tribute and recognising that they owed labour services to the king, but in return they expected that he give them land or other resources by which to live, a kind of social contract which in most cases proved fairly successful. In the same way, children and slaves taken in raids could also be integrated into the wider nation.

Barotseland and Caprivi after independence

In 1964, Northern Rhodesia became independent as the Republic of Zambia. The Barotseland Agreement of that year established Barotseland as a self-governing region, effectively continuing the previous relations with the colonial government. However, the ruling party in Zambia, under Kenneth Kaunda, was determined to end Barotseland's separate status, and by a constitutional amendment abrogated the 1964 Agreement and renamed Barotseland as the Western Province. Since then, the Lozi have maintained that abrogating the 1964 Agreement had the effect of abrogating the agreement by which Barotseland became part of Zambia, ergo it was now an independent entity.

This has been the basis for a growing independence movement. There have been cases in the International Court and submissions to various African arbitration bodies, none of which have made much progress. Between 2010 and 2014, there were protest riots in Mongu associated with the formation of the Barotse Freedom Movement (BFM) and the Movement for the Restoration of Barotseland. This has led to the formation of the Barotseland National Freedom Alliance, which has joined the Unrepresented Nations and Peoples Organization (UNPO) in order to enlist support from a worldwide audience. However, in spite of this activity, the separatist movements have never gained mass support.

After the expulsion of the Germans, the Caprivi Strip remained part of South West Africa, administratively separated from Barotseland, though there was continuous contact for the people with those across the Zambezi. A Caprivi independence movement, CANU (Caprivi African National Union), was founded in 1964 when colonial liberation movements were in full flood. But in the 1970s, as the security situation in South West Africa and South Africa deteriorated, the South Africans built military installations to secure the frontier from those seeking to enter from newly independent Zambia. They also built infrastructure and sought to gain the support of the population of Caprivi by building schools and other facilities. The population of the Caprivi Strip, although in origin part of the multi-ethnic Barotse kingdom, had begun to acquire its own identity, and this was accentuated by South African policies. After the independence of Namibia in 1990, there were growing tensions as the new SWAPO government began to impose its presence, which led to large numbers of Caprivians migrating to Botswana in 1998 and 1999. However, there does not seem to have been much contact between separatists in Caprivi and Barotseland, and the historical unity of the two areas is not an issue in twenty-first century politics.

9

THE LOWER ZAMBEZI IN THE 20th CENTURY

By the end of the nineteenth century, the creole society of the Lower Zambezi was under constant scrutiny from the increasing number of travellers navigating the lower river on their way to the Scottish missions in the Shire Highlands and on Lake Nyasa/Malawi. Other travellers were reaching the Zambezi overland from the south, and reports of the disturbed political state of the region were appearing in the world's press.

The regime of the *prazos* had created a feudal society where creole *senhores* with their *chicunda* followers (in effect private armies) dominated and extracted tribute and labour services from a peasant population living in fragmented lineage-based villages. In Portugal, the liberal victory in the civil war in 1834 had initiated a period of change in which political leaders like Mouzinho da Silveira, Sá da Bandeira and Costa Cabral sought to dismantle the control of the Crown, the Church and the aristocracy over the kingdom's resources, to replace it with a system of landownership which favoured the capitalist exploitation of the land and a capitalist system of economic and social relations. It was hoped that a similar transformation could be brought about in Africa and that, on the Lower Zambezi, the feudal domains of the creole warlords could be transformed into prosperous plantations.

This was the thrust of a series of laws which sought to change the three-life tenure of the *prazos* into leasehold property and replace slavery with a system of free-wage labour. As with similar ambitious attempts to transform society—for example, in Russia—it proved easier to pass legislation than to achieve real change on the ground, and throughout most of the nineteenth century the creole *senhores* remained firmly in control of their feudal domains.

In the delta region and around Quelimane, where the government was able to exert some control, there was a tentative experiment of replacing the rule of the *prazo senhores* with direct state control, which for the peasantry involved the replacement of tribute and services to a *senhor* with taxes paid directly to the government. Such reforms proved very unsettling, and the *colonos* actively resisted government attempts to take a census of the population. The armed resistance of the African peasants was complicated by the activities of the creole *senhores* and their *chicunda* followers, who saw themselves as being marginalised by the new commercial developments and who tried to profit from the situation by either fuelling peasant discontent or lending their support to the government in suppressing it.

The disturbances in 1878 known as the Matuka rebellion were put down, but a fresh war broke out in 1884, originating in the Massingire area, which had been the domain of the Vas dos Anjos, and spreading along the north bank of the Zambezi towards Quelimane. Again, the government turned to one of the warlords, Manuel António de Sousa, to suppress the rebellion.

These wars had shown just how ineffective the government's control really was. As for introducing change of this kind higher upriver, around Tete, the realities were spelt out to Lisbon by the governor–general in 1881:

Will the renters of the *prazos* who today are real feudal *senhores*—and more than feudal *senhores* for they virtually never render homage and fealty to the sovereign power—will these men who are absolute and dominant ... be willing to allow themselves to become simple proprietors of small estates subordinated to the common law in an area where all the Africans recognise them as *senhor*.[1]

Such was the situation when Portugal was forced to confront the threat of Cecil Rhodes and the aggressive expansionist policies emanating from South Africa.

Once again, the government was forced to confront the realities of the feudal society of Zambezia. While fresh, and this time successful, attempts were made to subdue Massangano, a commission was appointed in November 1888 to examine the problem of the *prazos*. Early in 1889, it produced a series of recommendations which were designed to place the system on a new basis more in tune with the capitalist age. The *prazos* were not abolished but would instead be reconfigured to achieve regional economic development. Those that were deemed to have been pacified would be leased by the state for a fixed rent for a period of 30 years, and in return the lessee would assume administrative and police responsibilities. The lessee would have the duty to collect the traditional head tax—the *mussoco*—half of which was to be paid in the form of labour, a system which had already been tried by the Opium Company to provide labour for its plantations at Mopeia. In this way, it was hoped that whoever leased the *prazos* could obtain both capital from the *mussoco*, as well as labour to undertake the agricultural development, which was a condition of the lease. The recommendations of the Commission, which were implemented in 1892, included detailed obligations laid on those who leased the *prazos* as well as measures to protect the African peasant from exploitation, thereby avoiding, it was hoped, the repeated peasant jacqueries that had plagued the *prazos* of the lower river during the previous decade.

A second category of *prazo* was identified. It included those that were not yet pacified. In effect, all the *prazos* beyond the Lupata gorge fell into this category. Here the tenant had the sole obligation of pacifying them and only then would they have to assume the obligations attached to the first category.

The Lower Zambezi divided

The division of the *prazos* into two categories merely established in law a reality that had already been taking place on the ground. Ever since the formal abolition of slavery and the reduction in tariffs in the 1870s, there had been a boom in agricultural production in the delta and the region around Quelimane that had easy access to the coast. African farmers produced increasing amounts of sesame, groundnuts and copra which were sold to the Indian agents of international trading companies. Some Portuguese entrepreneurs also began to establish businesses in the hope of cashing in on this expanding commodity trade, but also in the hope of finally, after centuries of unfulfilled ambitions, establishing a plantation economy. Among these was the company founded by Ignacio de Paiva Raposo, which planned to produce opium for the Chinese market. However, opium production faltered when the poppy fields were destroyed during the Massingire rising of 1884.

It is not entirely clear what the intention of this new *prazo* legislation really was. It seems that António Ennes, the governor–general who devised the detailed regulations for the new system, envisaged the Zambezi becoming a new São Tomé, with Portuguese entrepreneurs establishing plantations similar to the cocoa *roças* of the Guinea Islands. However, in the 1880s the system in São Tomé was already changing as banks and commercial companies were taking over the *roças* from the original cocoa entrepreneurs. Portugal did not have a large class of entrepreneurs with capital to invest, and putting all the *prazos* up for auction provided a perfect opportunity for international investors to acquire prime land concessions. The large mining and timber concession that had already been made to Paiva de Andrada covered many of the *prazos* on the right bank of the river. These were now consolidated into the Moçambique Company, which received a charter in 1892 and assumed the task of administering the whole region between the Zambezi and the Sabi rivers. It was similar in concept to the charter companies that Britain was using to rule its vast acquisitions in East and Central Africa. Although this company assumed control of all the *prazos* on the right bank of the river, it never made any attempt to implement the *prazo* legislation and instead contented itself with subleasing to other companies and collecting the *mussoco* from the African inhabitants.[2]

The *prazos* further up the river did not offer good prospects for plantation companies, partly because the geography was unfavourable with the dry conditions and the relatively narrow valley floor between the escarpments, but also because the region was so unsettled ('unpacified', in the parlance of the time). As a result, the *prazos* that were deemed to be unpacified were leased en bloc by the Zambesia Company, which was established in 1892 under the direction of a British entrepreneur, Albert Ochs, who also obtained a controlling interest in the Moçambique Company. The Zambesia Company did not have any capacity either to pacify or develop the region and contented itself with subletting its *prazos*, thereby handing them back to the class of creole *senhor* which continued traditional forms of tribute collection and the exacting of labour services to which they now added the lucrative business of recruiting labour for the South African mines.

The Zambesia Company also bid for some of the *prazos* on the lower part of the river. The other *prazos* in the delta region and in the hinterland of Quelimane, with a few exceptions, were taken up by internationally financed concession companies.

Among these were the Luabo Company and the Boror Company, both partly French owned. These companies sought to impose trading monopolies in their *prazos* and collect the head taxes for which they recruited company police, the so-called *cypaes*. Gradually, however, they turned to growing crops. The Boror Company in particular became a major producer of copra, using their rights under the new *prazo* legislation to obtain labour from the peasants on their lands.

Among the other concessionaires, the most important was the Mozambique Sugar Company, an enterprise started by a British entrepreneur, John Peter Hornung, who was married to the daughter of Paiva Raposo (of Opium Company fame) and who took advantage of the patriotic sentiment in Portugal that followed the British ultimatum of January 1890 to raise finance for his enterprise. This company was soon to morph into Sena Sugar, and would become one of the largest enterprises operating not only in the Lower Zambezi region but in the whole of Mozambique.

The economic and social relations on the Lower Zambezi were now passing from feudalism to a capitalist phase. The creole warlords and their associates were being superseded by faceless commercial companies eager to exploit the resources of the region. To put a seal on the process, a new universal labour law was introduced in 1899 which imposed a labour obligation on all the inhabitants of the colony. Meanwhile, price controls and changes to tariffs and marketing regulations finally spelt the end of the relatively free market conditions that had operated since the 1870s and which had allowed African farmers and Indian commercial agents to take full advantage.

Chinde

All these developments were only possible because, for the first time since the early 1800s, the annual floods of the Zambezi had once again opened up a viable river route to the sea. The rivers of the delta had, from time to time, been used by ships to gain access to the Zambezi, and in the seventeenth century there had been plans to build a fort to defend the route via the Luabo river. In the mid-nineteenth century, Livingstone had successfully used the Kongone mouth for 3 or 4 years before it too closed due to local erosion. It is always assumed that Livingstone's hopes of turning the Zambezi into a commercial highway into the interior were dashed by the discovery of the Cahora Bassa rapids, but the failure to find a viable port of entry through the delta into the river was probably equally significant. The shifting sands of the delta had meant that no reliable river channel could be identified and no permanent port of entry could be built. The delta rivers remained an uncharted maze of waterways used by smugglers and those carrying on the illegal slave trade.

However, by 1889, the so-called Chinde mouth was proving accessible to steamers. For some years this enabled the Zambezi to have its own seaport, with the result that commercial shipping, including boats bound for the Scottish missions on the Shire, no longer had to rely on the tortuous route up the Qua Qua from Quelimane with overland porterage during the dry season. In 1891, the British negotiated a concession at Chinde and a town grew up around the port. In 1893, it was visited by the British Consul, R.C.F. Maugham, and in 1909 he gave a vivid description of it in his book *Zambesia*:

> the British Concession, securely fenced in, and fulfilling the func-
> tions of a gigantic bonded warehouse, contained the tidily built
> offices of the transport companies and shipping agents who con-
> trolled the river traffic, and the tastefully laid out gardens and
> cement tennis court of the British Central Africa Protectorate Agent
> and Vice-Consul. Along one side of this ran the river, at whose
> tendency to eat away the sandy bank householders were already
> beginning to look with disquietude. Gradually the disappearance of

the bank increased until it attained to alarming proportions, and buildings had to be hurriedly taken down at great expense, and reerected in positions promising greater safety.

The Zambezi floods had begun to take away what they had generously provided in 1889. Land at Chinde washed away, and the town had to be relocated further back from the river. Arriving at the port, Maugham described

> several stern wheel river steamers in ingeniously constructed dry docks, either 'resting' as they say in the theatrical profession, or undergoing repairs, their appearance suggesting that of so many gigantic and indignant hens sitting on an equal number of enormous nests ... every sort of craft is huddled in one confused pell mell, from the smartly painted, five-oared agent's gig, to the large, unwieldy iron lighter.

After three centuries of discussion and inaction, the British had now moved in to build a modern town of sorts at one of the Zambezi's mouths. Maugham describes the crowd in the town:

> Almost naked Zambezi boys, or 'lower river boys' as one speedily learns to call them. A couple of Scottish engineers, coatless, shirt sleeves rolled up, double terai hat faded and shapeless well back on the head, pipe inevitable, evidently in difficulties with their razors ... They stroll along, jostling one or two tidy-looking Mohammedans in red fezes, evidently from the cultured native atmosphere of Zanzibar. A leisurely khaki-clad Customs guard ... discusses some important point of local customs tariff with a group of dressy Indian merchants, with gold embroidered caps and spangled waistoats A little further along you see a handsome brass-mounted machila spread with a showy leopard skin rug and carried by four muscular A-Mahindo with wild-looking cock's feathers perkily stuck in their small, jaunty scarlet fezes.[3]

In 1910, the residents built a tennis court, apparently so that they could relax in temperatures that often exceeded 100 degrees (one thinks inevitably of Noel Coward's song, 'Mad Dogs and Englishmen'). According to Michael Main, to reduce the glare from its cement surface, the Senior Naval Officer had coated it with olive-green paint [and] the Assistant Agent had ventured his considerable artistic talents in a riotous display of beautifully painted flowers, neatly arranged in and occupying most of the four corners of the court. It is reported that many players, dancing lightly from buttercup to marigold, sunflower to rose, violet to iris, found the experience unnerving.[4]

In contrast to Maugham, the mining engineer Owen Letcher, who travelled widely in central Africa between 1902 and 1912, gave a melancholic, almost apocalyptic, description of Chinde. Upon descending the Shire river and entering the Zambezi, "hot, sandy Chinde was soon reached. The place is rapidly being washed away by the sea, and ... I should not care very much if the Indian Ocean devoured the place in one bound". If the traveller enjoyed good health,

> the variegated roofs of the township, the mangrove patches, and the tender hues of the bush all blending with river, sea, and sky, and giving to it the torpid touch of the tropics, the master-brush of creation's artist. How different does it all appear when disease has fretted away fancy, and malady has steeped one's very bones in a vindictive flight of thought against all Nature! ... For this is the Golgotha of the East Coast.

Letcher pursued his theme of death—the dying town, eaten away by the sea, and the dying inhabitants wracked with fever and the diseases of Africa:

> There are two burial-grounds in Chinde, the new cemetery and an old graveyard. It is in the latter place of skulls that the remains of Stairs, who dared the darkness of the Congo forests with Stanley were laid to rest ... Great Britain has her tenement of commerce here, just as God has His acres for the worn-out bodies of those who made that commerce possible. A small strip of land bounded by a palisade stretches down to the river front. This is the British Concession where all goods for and from British Central Africa are landed and

> stored free of duty ... so it is that Chinde, where the lazy Portuguese
> police sleep in the sandy streets, and the British trader watches with
> anxiety the irresistable advance of ocean tide and river wavelet, plumes
> itself with the mock feathers of a meagre commerce ... God has set
> His seal of doom on this place. Each little wavelet has its appointed
> task to do, and the day is not far distant when Chinde will lie below
> golden sands and muddy ooze, as deep as Pompeii and Herculaneum
> were buried by the lava of Vesuvius. For Chinde has defied the inexo-
> rable laws, and a house built on the sands cannot stand.[5]

The river continued to undermine the foreshore, and the town
was devastated by a cyclone in 1919 and again in 1922.
Meanwhile, a seaport was being developed further south at Beira,
near the old port of Sofala which had also been washed away in
the swirling tides and sand of the coastal waters. When a railway
was built from Beira to the Zambezi at Sena, the British sur-
rendered their concession in 1923 and Chinde sank further into
insignificance, surviving only as the port that served the Sena
Sugar Company. However, it never quite disappeared, and the
small town somehow survived offering anchorage for any shallow-draft boat that wanted to land there.

Pacification

It was not until 1902, 10 years after the new *prazo* legislation had
come into effect, that relative peace descended on the whole of
the Lower Zambezi. The Portuguese authorities had lacked the
resources either to police the region or to establish any effective
civil government, and the attempt to transfer government
responsibilities to the lessees of the *prazos* meant that throughout the region there was confusion and lack of co-ordination.
The new *prazo* owners tried to recruit *cypaes* to assert their control and found they had to turn to the creole *senhores* with their
chicunda followers. These old social formations were not willing

to surrender the authority they exerted over the population, and many of them still ruled semi-independent domains.

In 1891, the whole process of 'pacification' was already in disarray when the government's principal supporter, Manuel António de Sousa, was captured by the British South Africa Company police in Manica, with the result that the whole of the area he had controlled on the south side of the Zambezi, which included the kingdom of Barue, was thrown into chaos. The exiled Barue ruling dynasty returned, and in Sousa's *prazos* authority fell into the hands of his *chicunda* captains.

A further element of instability was the threat of attacks from Gaza. The Moçambique Company, whose charter nominally covered the whole region as far south as the Sabi, had to negotiate an agreement with the Gaza kings which allowed Gaza impis to continue to collect tribute from the population. With the defeat and disintegration of the Gaza kingdom in 1895, large numbers of former Gaza soldiers were recruited as mercenaries and brought to Zambezia, adding to the violence and disorder. Mercenaries were also recruited from the independent *chicunda* 'republic' of Maganja da Costa along the coast north of Quelimane.

Throughout the middle of the decade, armies—partly under Portuguese command but made up of *chicunda*, Gaza and Maganja mercenaries—were employed to 'pacify' the *prazos* both north and south of the Zambezi. Although the Portuguese themselves had only very limited military capacity, they never failed to find willing collaborators among the African populations, for whom raiding their neighbours for cattle or captives was an established tradition. These campaigns were in reality little more than raids with widespread killings, looting of villages and kidnapping of women, while famine conditions throughout Zambezia brought back memories of the worst days of the 1820s.

By 1902, however, mercenary forces under Portuguese command had once again taken control of Barue and the old Sousa *prazos* on the south bank. The Pereira domain of Macanga had been occupied, and the *chicunda* 'republic' of Maganja da Costa had also been brought to submission. The world which had been dominated by the creole *senhores* was now virtually dead, and Zambezia was about to experience 50 years of rule by plantation companies and labour recruitment agencies. Although feudalism had now been replaced once and for all by a capitalist regime, it was a capitalism which was to inherit many of the characteristics of the old feudal system, employing a similar *modus operandi* and many of the same personnel.

One result of a decade of civil disturbance and warfare was that the ordinary African population became highly mobile, moving to escape the violence and the ravages of the military campaigns. Once the fighting died down, retaining a high level of mobility was a means of avoiding labour obligations and tax payments. Migration—temporary, seasonal or permanent—was to become part of the life experience of the Lower Zambezi peoples for the next half-century.

Maugham's vision of a natural paradise

Consul Maugham travelled from Chinde up the river to Tete in a Portuguese river steamer sometime around 1908, making a slight diversion up the Shire river on the way. He observed the Zambezi from aboard the steamer and described a kind of natural paradise which contrasted vividly with the desolation of the wars that had devastated the interior during the decade of the 'pacification'.

Steaming up the Chinde river, Maugham commented unfavourably on the mangroves that lined the river in the delta:

> Within the mangrove forests ... there is always a darkness and gloom ... the foliage shuts out the day. In the semi-twilight thus produced you see, in your mournful, squelching progress through this moist muddy land of disordered dreams, the ghostly night-jar rise noise-

lessly from beneath your feet; a horned owl glares suspicious disapproval; a scuttling brood of land crabs disappear down their yawning, muddy holes.

Emerging from the Chinde river, he reached the Zambezi, 800–900 yards wide with sandy banks 15 feet high: "literally honeycombed for long distances by swifts and sand martins, and their parent birds wheel and circle round their tiny strongholds". The boat passed floating islands of vegetation, crocodiles in the water and a "vast congregation of Zambesi water fowl. Giant grey herons stand sentry-like watching the water ... snowy egrets shoot out their long, yellow beaks, with a snaky motion of the neck, at the small fish and other tiny forms of river life". Maugham goes on to describe the richness of bird life: ducks, geese, sandpipers, plovers, curlews, weaver birds, kites and fish eagles.

Maugham passed the Franciscan mission at Chupanga, where Livingstone's wife was buried, and described the

> increased luxuriance of the tropical vegetation. The high river-banks are covered with an exuberant growth of low bushes. Palms of various kinds become very numerous; immense baobabs, clumps of stiff euphorbias and groves of feathery albizzias mingle with acacias of several kinds ... Climbing plants quite cover the bushes and lower trees in places and hang down lovely transparent green trailers gemmed with deep mauve, white centred convolvulus blooms to gaze Narcissus-like, in placid admiration of their beauties in the calmly flowing water beneath.[6]

This rich and romantic account of the natural world of the river echoes the impressions of the first missionaries who wrote in the seventeenth century describing the trees, flowers and rich birdlife of the river. Maugham also reflected that twenty steamers were now plying the river. One can see in this a sinister warning of how the twentieth century would soon impact on this natural wonderland: these steamers would consume thousands of tons of timber, bringing insatiable, trigger-happy hunters who would soon carry out a barely controlled slaughter of the wildlife, while twentieth century civilisation would bring about the flooding of large extents of the river valley with man-made lakes.

Indians

Merchants from India had always been prominent in Indian Ocean trade, and many had taken part in the Portuguese settlement of the Zambezi valley. The Jesuit, António Gomes, had been an enthusiastic supporter of a policy that would encourage Indians to settle in Zambezia:

> The people from India are industrious and they will make salt pans by the sea, wheat fields, palm-tree plantations, fisheries etc. In this way they will all make a good living because the land is good for everything and in the end they can all be farmers and develop other industries that can benefit everyone ... There are so many poor people in India and they would not suffer so much poverty if they came to these lands. As they are people who aspire to have their own house and whatever goes with it, they would strive to do many of the things that are not done [here] for lack of industry ... In India there are so many poor orphan girls, both the daughters of Portuguese and of native people, that at small expense a lot could be done for the service of our Lord and the public good.[7]

In the eighteenth and early nineteenth centuries, men with backgrounds in India had established influential *prazo* dynasties while Indian capital had dominated the trade in ivory and slaves. In the nineteenth century, a number of Indians also arrived with the military contingent sent from Goa in 1869. Some of these stayed behind after disaster overtook the expedition and established themselves in the ivory trade. The growth of trade in agricultural produce in the 1870s encouraged a further influx of Indians, primarily from British India, who were always known as Banyans. They acted as trading agents in the interior and, when the *prazo* companies gradually put a squeeze on their activities, many of them turned to being employed agents of the companies.

When the British Consul, Maugham, wrote his description of Zambezia in 1909, the Banyans were a well-established element in the Zambezi population. Maugham's description of them is in language typical of the period, but it is clear that he considered them an important influence in transforming Zambezian society:

> Not only is he [the typical Banyan] wonderfully impervious to the effects of climate but he possesses that inestimable faculty of easily acquiring a fluent knowledge of the native tongue ... He has successfully monopolised the whole of this class of commerce ... His manner of life, domestic in the extreme, is nevertheless so thrifty, so frugal, and his wants, bounded by a little curry and rice, are so inexpensive, that few there are who cannot remit a few rupees to India.[8]

Although discouraged officially by the Portuguese authorities, the presence of Indian traders, especially those who established stores in the interior where Africans could sell the crops they produced, contributed to creating a commercial infrastructure to support colonial rule.

Company rule

With the passing of the labour regulations of 1899 and the final pacification of Barue and Macanga in 1902, the Lower Zambezi was to experience 30 years when the *prazos* were under company rule. All but a handful of the *prazos* were now let to one of six major plantation companies, which exercised almost total control over the populations who lived on the land.

Gradually the companies moved from simply living off the tax they collected, to establishing a more or less profitable agricultural economy. Experiments were made in growing, coffee, tea, sisal, copra and, of course, sugar. Of these, copra, sugar and later tea were the most profitable. A regular labour supply was essential for plantation agriculture, and most of the companies leased a number of *prazos* which they used only for the labour to be obtained from their populations. Although the terms of the *prazo* leases allowed the companies to collect part of the African tax in the form of labour, this only amounted to a few weeks in the year, and the rapid turnover of this labour force meant it was hugely inefficient.

Among the plantation companies, the real success story was that of Hornung's Mozambique Sugar Company, which in the early years of the twentieth century moved aggressively to sublease, take over and otherwise acquire control of rival sugar producers and a number of *prazos*. Ultimately, as its first historian put it, Hornung "administered, policed, levied taxes, monopolized trade, and controlled labour from some 14,000 square miles of Mozambique", including the concession port of Chinde.[9]

Although plantations along the Zambezi employed large amounts of unskilled labour, workers were also recruited for unpaid work on roads, and men were conscripted into the *cypaes* and other branches of the armed forces, often to be sent abroad. Penal labour could also be imposed for crimes, and this might involve exile to the cocoa plantations of São Tomé from which there was seldom any return. Nevertheless, much of this labour was seasonal and depended on the labourers being able to support themselves and their families with traditional village agriculture, and the more efficient of the plantation companies ameliorated the oppression of the labour regime and jealously protected their labour supplies for their own operations.

The African population adopted varied strategies to avoid the payment of *mussoco* and the labour obligations. The most successful was migration. Migration from the Zambezi valley to British Africa—either the Rhodesias or the Nyasaland Protectorate—was relatively easy, and there migrants were often welcomed as they swelled the populations of those colonies. There were also possibilities for internal migration. The various *prazos*, being under the control of different companies, had different labour practices and different levels of efficiency. Some paid better wages and were less strict in exacting payment of tax. There were thus huge advantages in moving from one *prazo* to another, or in crossing the Zambezi to the territory of the Moçambique Company, or to Barue and the Tete district, which were still under direct government administration.

The best opportunities were presented to migrants heading to South Africa or to work on Rhodesian farms. The Rand recruitment organisation, WNLA, operated in some *prazos*, and Rhodesian farmers and mine owners were also allowed to recruit by a formal agreement made with the Mozambique government. In many parts of the valley, the attempts by company police to extract tax or recruit labourers became a sort of cat-and-mouse game, and the fact that company police used violent methods, often tantamount to kidnapping, was evidence that in normal circumstances evasion of labour obligations by the African population was only too frequent. However, those mice who were caught often experienced brutal treatment and semi-starvation in the plantation compounds, where the death rate among workers was high and health facilities few.[10]

Company control of the *prazos* meant that the whole Zambezi valley was fragmented into a crazy mosaic of different jurisdictions and practices. There was no consistent administration and absolutely no systematic attempt to create the skeleton infrastructure of a modern state.

If, in some respects, the companies with their managers and African *capitães* continued many of the practices of the old feudal *senhores*, in others they represented the arrival of the modern world. For the first time, some of the *prazos*, particularly those on the lower river, saw serious investment in fixed capital.

Hornung's sugar enterprises had imported steam-driven ploughs ahead of the curve, laid rail tracks throughout their plantations and had paddle steamers and barges operating on the Zambezi. According to Paul Lapperre's recent study of Sena Sugar, "At the onset of the Great War, the combined Fowler plough fleet in Mopeia, Caia and Marromeu consisted of 15 sets of compound steam engines with some 30 ploughs. The fleet is probably the largest in the world owned by a single owner."[11]

By 1914, Sena Sugar was producing nearly 30,000 tons of sugar a year, and by 1921 this had risen to just short of 40,000 tons. Offices and accommodation for European staff led to the building of company towns, very different from the old traditional Zambezi *luanes* with their deep verandas and compounds housing servants and livestock.

The First World War and the Zambezi rebellion

By 1914, Mozambique did not exist as a single entity. The vast colony that Portugal had acquired in the negotiations of 1890–91 was fragmented, two-thirds of it under the rule of companies, almost all of which were owned by foreign capital. It was interspersed with pockets of territory under direct government control and ruled from scattered *postos militares* from which attempts were made, often in vain, to extract tax from a local population determined to resist in any way it could.

This was the situation when, in 1916, the Lisbon government made the fateful decision to enter the First World War on the side of the Allies. The republican regime, recently installed in 1910, hoped that by joining the Allies it would gain British protection for its African territories, as well as support for the regime's insecure position within Portugal itself. However, there was a German army on the loose in the territory immediately to the north of Mozambique. Portuguese forces were sent to northern Mozambique, and to support military operations tens of thousands of carriers were forcibly recruited, many of them from the population of the Zambezi valley. By the time the war ended, it was thought that nearly 100,000 carriers had been recruited to support the war effort.

In March 1917, revolt broke out in Barue in opposition to the forced labour levies. The revolt spread up the river along both banks, and the Portuguese had to retreat into their towns and abandon the countryside. The revolt was in many ways the last flare-up of the Zambezi Wars of the previous century. Although its leadership came from Barue's ruling family—who had been in exile since 1902—and from the Kaguru spirit medium, the revolt was joined by former *chicunda* and descendants of the old *prazo senhores* who had been effectively dispossessed. The revolt was, as much as anything else, the result of the chaotic state of colonial control on the upper reaches of the river, as it did not spread into the region downstream of Sena and the Shire confluence, where the plantation companies were better organised.

The British on the Mozambique border looked on nervously. The hunter Wilfrid Robertson was visiting the frontier post at Feira across the Luangwa from Zumbo when the revolt reached that point:

> The rebellion was widespread through northern Mozambique; and the spark that had set alight the long-standing disaffection was the old, old trouble—the *corvé* of the gentle Portuguese. But the rebels had not the slightest intention of having the British on their hands also ... and there was no sign of unrest even among the tribes whose blood-brothers a few miles away were up in arms.

Three Portuguese hastily paddled across from Zumbo together with a West African who had been encamped nearby.

> Not much was to be got out of the white refugees, but the negro had kept his wits about him. To the astonished Englishmen he announced

that the Portuguese had bolted in such haste that they had left a big stock of military rifles and ammunition in the fort—a windfall for the rebels.

One of the English in Feira volunteered to go to bring them back.

The fort was reached, the door broken open, and the rifles and ammunition found. Their removal necessitated two journeys over the half-mile between Zumbo and the river ... hardly was he safely out of the water than the pursuers reached the bank, shaking their spears and muskets in baffled rage.[12]

Inevitably, this tale recalls the incident of the Portuguese royal family fleeing for Brazil, crossing the Lisbon bar just as Napoleon's army entered the city and fired a few cannonballs after the fast-disappearing warships.

While the revolt was still unfolding along the river, the Germans invaded Mozambique from the north. An initial raid was followed by a large-scale invasion by General Paul von Lettow Vorbek in November 1917. The general divided his forces into four columns and advanced, almost without resistance, towards the Zambezi, capturing Portuguese military posts, plundering settlements and rousing the local population to resist the government. Vorbeck's men almost reached the Zambezi itself in June 1918, before retreating northward again.

With the end of the war in November 1918, the Portuguese were able to concentrate on ending the Zambezi revolt and to do so reverted to the measures of nineteenth-century warfare. African irregular forces were raised on the *prazos*, and Nguni, possibly as many as 30,000, from the northern Angonia region were mobilised and turned loose on the rebel-held areas. The revolt was over by 1919, though outbreaks of guerrilla activity continued into 1920 as many of the rebels fled into the largely inaccessible escarpment area of Southern Rhodesia.

THE LOWER ZAMBEZI IN THE 20TH CENTURY

The Zambezi revolt and the German invasion formed part of a pattern that was deeply etched into Mozambique's history where armed bands, living off plunder and capturing women and children to swell their numbers, established themselves in the heart of states that were too decentralised and fundamentally weak to resist. The Portuguese colonial state in the second decade of the century was as weak and decentralised as the old Marave kingdoms and Shona states south of the river that had not been able to resist the Zambezi warlords and organised Nguni war bands of the nineteenth century.

Nor were these to be the last episodes of depredations on the civilian population by militarised war bands, as the catastrophic civil war of the 1980s would reveal.

The Trans-Zambezia railway and the Lower Zambezi bridge

The nineteenth century had been an age of railway building, and Mozambique had not escaped the speculation and political manoeuvring associated with railway investment. Two railways had eventually been built, one to connect the Rand with the port of Lourenço Marques and one from the newly established colony of Southern Rhodesia to the port of Beira in the territory of the Moçambique Company. Neither of these railways had served the Zambezi valley, although the construction of a line along the south bank would have presented few engineering problems, and a line on the north bank would have overcome the age-old difficulty of using Quelimane as the port of entry to Zambezia.

Plans for a Zambezi railway ran into diplomatic difficulties before the First World War, as the Anglo-German agreements over the future of eastern Africa had allocated northern Mozambique as a German sphere of interest while southern Mozambique was in the British sphere. There were unresolved issues over who would build and own any railway that was constructed and who would principally benefit from it. Moreover, the plantation companies were only interested in local railways that would connect their plantations with the coast. The shortest route for a railway from Nyasaland would have headed directly to Quelimane, but political considerations continued to intervene. The only line that was eventually built was a short one linking the port to some of the *prazos* immediately inland.

In a report to the Foreign Office dated January 1914, vice-consul Rule reported that a railway from Quelimane to Tete had received formal government approval, "but its construction is hardly likely to be rapid". Any extension to Beira, he wrote, would require a 1.5-mile bridge across the Zambezi. Clearly, this idea was being given at least some consideration.

So no railway along the Zambezi was built, and the broad expanse of the river continued to divide Mozambique in two, while the British Nyasaland Protectorate was effectively land-locked with no easy access to the wider world. The steamers operating out of Chinde mostly provided a transport service for the sugar plantations of Sena Sugar, while an irregular paddle steamer made the 7-day journey upriver to Tete when conditions in the river allowed. Vice-consul Rule described how "groundings were frequent, and it was no uncommon experience to spend half a day on a sand bank ... while the sand around the steamer [is] cleared away with spades and the boat eventually pushed off by the combined muscular efforts of the captain, passengers and crew".[13] To cross the river from one side to the other, the traveller had to depend on local craft, which often meant traditional Zambezi canoes.

However, a new scheme was advanced after the war which was designed to make Beira, not Quelimane, the main port for the Zambezi region. Behind this vision was Libert Oury, who was planning to link his business empire, based on control of the Moçambique Company, with Sena Sugar and the coal fields known to exist on the north bank of the Zambezi opposite Tete. Oury built a coalition of interests and won support from the British government for the idea that a railway from Beira could provide access to the outside world for Nyasaland. With British government guarantees, the railway went ahead in 1920 and reached the southern bank of the Zambezi in 1922, where it was connected to the transport networks of Sena Sugar. Notoriously, the debt incurred by the construction and operation of this loss-making railway was to be serviced by the taxes paid by Africans in the Nyasaland Protectorate.

All the railway achieved was to bring goods from Beira to the southern bank of the Zambezi. A broad stretch of the river lay between its terminus and the north bank, where another railway had been built into the Shire Highlands. This solution to Nyasaland's isolation was far from satisfactory.

> At certain points ... the track was subject to inundation when the Zambezi was in high flood, with consequent damage to the permanent way and disorganisation of traffic, while the ferry traffic across the river ... was carried on under very severe conditions and with great difficulty. The vagaries of the river Zambezi during the low river season ... rendered it impossible to establish wharves and permanent cranes, and merchandise had to be handled by hand ... Sandbanks form in a night, and it frequently happened that ferry steamers had to be assisted across shallow places by big gangs of natives pushing and polling them.[14]

Once again the silt, sands and floods of the Zambezi were putting apparently insuperable obstacles in the way of human ambitions. So a campaign began for a bridge.

In 1905, the first bridge had been built across the Zambezi, spanning the gorge below the Victoria Falls and designed to carry Cecil Rhodes's railway north to the Copper Belt. The bridge had been built in Britain and transferred along the Bechuanaland railway in sections. Even before this bridge was completed, a steam locomotive had been winched across the gorge on a cable. Ten years earlier, life along the Zambezi had been lived according to rhythms that had not altered greatly for centuries, and the peoples had lived by technologies little more complicated than those employed by village craftsmen. Now the industrial world of the twentieth century had arrived in dramatic fashion.

The Victoria Falls bridge was only 300 metres long. Bridging the river on the Lower Zambezi would require a bridge more than ten times that length. Again, the politics moved far more slowly than the engineering. The final pieces were only in place by 1931, when building the bridge was justified on the grounds that it would be a major stimulus for the depression-hit British steel industry.

Once again, the bridge was designed in Britain, shipped out to the Indian Ocean and carried in sections along the railway from Beira. The crossing would be 2¼ miles long and would have to stand 27 feet above the highest flood level in order to permit the passage of river steamers.

A large industrial town was built to house all the machinery and workshops, and to provide accommodation for the workers. A hundred and sixty non-African personnel were employed, drawn from India and East and South Africa, who all had to be trained in bridge-building technology but "no Indian labour was at any time employed on the works, and such work as pneumatic riveting, locomotive and stationary engine driving, rough fitting and carpentry was all done by African natives".[15] This is interesting and prompts certain thoughts. The great Lower Zambezi Bridge was an example of the modern industrial world being introduced into Africa as a prefabricated, preordained and established fact, rather like the Rand gold mines. Africans adapted quickly in order to participate in this new world, but it had little long-term effect on their lives. A modern industrial town grew up overnight, but when the bridge was completed it disappeared, leaving little trace, and the industrially trained workforce returned to their traditional villages.

The contractors claimed that they had installed modern water-purifying and sanitation facilities and had solved the problem of malaria, with only four cases occurring during the construction, "although previously the district had had a deservedly bad reputation for malaria".[16] A European compound was built, comfortably furnished with "ice-making and cold storage plant, electric light, fans etc. and later ... recreation facilities were added in the form of a club room and billiard table, tennis court, squash court and a 9-hole golf course". For the African workers, "large carefully sited compounds consisting of well built reed thatched huts of the general pattern to which they were accustomed but better built". Rations consisted of 2¼ lbs of mealie meal, 6 oz of groundnuts and ¾ oz salt a day, 1 lb of fresh beef twice a week and ¾ lb of dry fish or beans four times a week. A hospital was built and "a small force of native police were employed".[17]

Such carefully chosen official words no doubt hide a different reality, and it is by no means clear from the report that all the African labour were volunteers.

The bridge took 4 years to complete. At 12,064 feet, it was larger than any railway bridge in the world except for the San Francisco–Oakland Bay bridge, though this had an island in the middle which made it, in effect, two bridges. The bridge used 17,000 tons of steel and 73,202 cubic metres of concrete. It had a walkway and a single-rail track, but no roadway. When it was completed—one of the great engineering feats of the day, as it had to be built in unstable sandy conditions—it proved next to useless. Only a few trains per week crossed the river, though if someone wanted to bring their car or lorry across, it was possible to hire a locomotive, drive the car onto a goods truck and be steamed across, as the author of this book did in 1963. The opening of coalfields on the north bank opposite Tete, which was supposed to give the bridge a steady income from bunkering coal heading to Beira, was indefinitely delayed.

The bridge was in fact a great dinosaur of the age of steam, built just as motor traffic was beginning to cross the Zambezi on the ferry at Tete, opening up a modern highway to the north. There continued to be no direct transport links joining the north of Mozambique with the south until 1973 when, in the last year of colonial rule, a road bridge was at last constructed at Tete.

The Moatize coal fields

Richard Thornton, the geologist who had accompanied Livingstone on his Zambezi expedition in 1858, had been provided with a list of ninety-nine coal outcrops by the Portuguese and explored those on the Moatize river, a tributary of the Revubwe river, that entered the Zambezi opposite Tete. In subsequent years, these had been further explored but it was not until after the First World War that the Société Minière et Géologique du Zambèze was formed to exploit the coalfields. Charles Spence, who was later to write a well-received book on the economy of Mozambique, while travelling through northern Mozambique in 1943, visited the Moatize coalfields which lay some 10 miles from the Zambezi.[18]

> As a coal mine it was not a very imposing sight; there was certainly plenty of evidence of coal to be seen, black dust and small coal pebbles on the entrance road, the small trucks of the minute narrow-gauge railway filled with coal bricks, and the tip-trucks coming up from the level of the river with the same load. All this implied a coal mine, but there was no dump and no shaft elevator with two wheels above such as one usually sees on such mines.

The operation of the mine was severely limited because the coal had to be transported by barge on the Zambezi, 10 miles away.

Since the river was only navigable six months in the year, their operations were naturally confined to this period, but even so they could only supply the Sena Sugar Estates at Mopeia further down the river and the Trans-Zambesia railway at Sena ... There was one other interesting point about this mine and that was that they could not work the boilers at all during the dry season as the river stopped flowing until the next rains came. This would not have mattered under normal circumstances as there was always water below the sandy river bed, but for some reason or another, probably due to some salt deposits further up, all water pumped from below during the dry season was salty and consequently damaging to the boilers.

The seam that Spence was shown was 65 feet thick and 400 yards wide, and he was told that another similar seam had been recently discovered nearby: "We followed the Decauville track he had laid, rather cunningly I thought, with wooden rails instead of the usual iron ones owing to the lack of material." As the mine could not be worked for half the year, the manager had taken to growing groundnuts to help pay for the mine's operation. It was while clearing ground for the planting that the new seam had been discovered.

A railway linking the coal mines to the Trans-Zambezia railway was only completed in 1949. Even so, the serious exploitation of the coalfields would only begin in the twenty-first century, after independence and after the civil war that followed independence was over.

The end of the prazos

In 1930, while engineers were pondering the problems of bridging the Zambezi, the old regime of the *prazos* was reaching the end of its life. That year, the leases of many of the *prazos* finally expired. The government in Lisbon, in the middle of its own revolution, decided that the system was outdated and beyond reform, and in August 1930 a law summarily brought the regime to an end. The holders of the *prazos* which still had time on their leases were pressured to surrender them to the government. There remained two *prazos* not owned by companies and still in private hands—a last remnant of a feudal system stretching back to the beginning of the seventeenth century.

It is true that some successful plantations had grown up on the lower reaches of the Zambezi, notably those of Sena Sugar, whose properties extended from the original *prazo* of Maganja aquem Shire—where the Opium Company had once tried to create a narcotics empire—through the delta to include Luabo and the extensive lands on the right bank, which were rented from the Moçambique Company. However, most of the *prazos* had seen no economic development and had been used simply as labour reserves. Above all, the *prazos* had become a byword for all kinds of abuses practised against their inhabitants, abuses that had led to the serious revolt of 1917.

Now a new strain of capitalism was to replace the paternal, quasi-feudalism of the old system. The administration of the *prazos* was to be replaced by a civil administration, staffed by a professional colonial service. The new district officers, like their counterparts in British Africa, were to be responsible for seeing that the inhabitants paid their taxes, that they fulfilled their labour obligations and that a basic infrastructure of health, transport and education was put in place in their districts. The plantation companies now had to recruit their labour in an open market, although in practice most of them depended on the district officers to put pressure on the Africans, who were sup-posed to be free to find their own employment, to work for the plantation companies.

Then, as the decade advanced, the government put into opera-tion a scheme to compel African villagers to grow cotton, a scheme originally developed in the Belgian Congo and tried with some success by the Moçambique Company.

The scheme would be administered by cotton concession companies, which would be responsible for providing seed and supervising the growing of the crop. Eventually, the companies would also purchase what the Africans produced at fixed prices.

By 1938, the Junta de Exportação de Algodão Colonial had been set up, cotton concession areas had been mapped out and a system of fixed prices for every stage of cotton production and export had been introduced. The system involved the African peasants within each concession area being required to grow cotton on their land. Theoretically, one hectare had to be planted for every adult male and half a hectare for every female. However, the policy was not always well thought out or soundly administered. In much of the area that was leased to concessionaires, cotton could not be grown profitably, and the returns to both the peasant farmers and the concession companies were low. Moreover, the system produced poor-quality cotton, as many growers were careless or inexperienced, and some of them sabotaged the scheme by damaging plants or boiling the seed to make it sterile.

A rice concession scheme was begun in 1941 with the setting up of the Divisão do Fomento Orizícola. Output rose from an initial figure of 100 tons to 12,000 tons by 1946. Charles Spence described the system in his travel diary in 1943:

> The system in this country is for the natives to do the growing, whilst hulling and cleaning the rice is in the hands of concessionaires who buy from the native the unhulled rice, hull it, clean it and polish it and then sell it to the traders. Concessions are divided into districts each concession holder having a monopoly in his own district, the natives not being permitted to sell to anyone else. Prices to the natives for unhulled rice, to the traders for ready milled rice and again retail to the natives by the traders are all controlled by the Portuguese government through the price controller.[19]

He adds, "at present controlled prices are high, in fact over three times the cost of pre-war imported rice from Burma".

This system was soon extended throughout the Lower Zambezi and the delta region, engaging the African population in forced crop growing. To some extent, it limited the extent to which men and women had to be compelled to leave their homes to work on plantations and changed the work obligation so that they were forced to till their own fields to meet cotton or rice quotas. Sena Sugar was an early cotton concessionaire, and it manipulated the scheme so that local labour and locally grown food was still available for its sugar plantations which, by then, employed 30,000 labourers.

In 1942, the demands for labour during the wartime boom in tropical products led to a reimposition of the old regulations of 1899. But after the war there was a return to a more market-oriented attitude towards labour and crop growing, though the continuation of the plantation economy in the Lower Zambezi continued to shape social relations as it had for two or three generations, reflecting something of the feudal paternalism of the old *prazo* system with its traditional relations of patron and client.

10

THE MIDDLE ZAMBEZI

THE COLONIAL EXPERIENCE

The Victoria Falls and the passage of the Middle Zambezi

David Livingstone first made the Victoria Falls known to the world when he published his *Missionary Travels* in 1856. The Falls are one of the most spectacular sights in the world: the cloud of spray that can be seen from up to 10 miles away, the rainbow that spans the gorge and the way the great river cascades into a crack in the surface of the earth 300 feet below and then swirls away through 20 miles of a winding gorge.

The Falls were, of course, well known to the local Tonga inhabitants who called them Seonga or Chongwe (Shongwe, according to Livingstone), and to the Makololo, who knew them as Mosi-oa-Tunya ('the smoke that sounds') and occasionally visited the region to extract tribute. As Livingstone admitted, "Of these [waters] we had often heard since we came into the country." Indeed, one of the questions asked by Sebituane during his first visit was, "have you smoke that sounds in your country?"

Livingstone was taken to the Falls in the company of the Makololo king Sekeletu and a large royal party. As the river was at its lowest in November, he was able to go in a small canoe to the very edge of the Falls and look into the gorge. Although in his book Livingstone famously wrote that "scenes so lovely must have been gazed upon by angels in their flight", this poetic extravagance is not typical of his writing; according to his biographer, Tim Jeal, it was added at the suggestion of his publisher. Most of the rest of Livingstone's description concerns his unsuccessful attempt to measure the width of the Falls and his various advice and warnings for future travellers.

From the moment Livingstone's description appeared in print, the Falls became southern Africa's first major tourist attraction. Hunters, traders and self-appointed explorers turned aside from killing wild animals and posturing as dauntless heroes taming savage Africa to visit the Falls.

However, Livingstone was less daring pioneer explorer and more lucky adventurer who happened to be at the head of what soon became a procession. Livingstone's companion, William Cotton Oswald, had already marked the position of the Falls on a hand-drawn map after his return from the Zambezi in 1851, and the hunter James Chapman claimed he had already been within a few miles of the Falls, near enough to see the plumes of spray rising from the gorge.

On his first visit, Livingstone tried to measure the width and depth of the Falls, even reaching over the edge and letting a line down into the gorge. He returned again with his brother Charles and John Kirk in June 1860, when he was able to make more accurate measurements and drawings of the Falls. Already by this time the drama of the Falls was attracting other visitors, as they lay within a few days of relatively easy travel from the mouth of the Chobe river, which was fast becoming the head of the wagon trail leading north through Tswana country. When Livingstone reached the Falls for the second time in 1860, he and his party met William Baldwin, who had made his way to the Falls apparently using only a pocket compass.

Thomas Baines and James Chapman visited the Falls in July 1862. Baines, like Livingstone, went to the very edge of the falls and looked into the gorge, something which terrified Chapman. Baines was a talented artist, and his drawings and paintings of the Falls became famous. Sir Richard Glyn, grandson of a Lord Mayor of London, together with his brother Robert and four companions, reached the Falls in July 1863, and in July 1869 Thomas Leask travelled through Ndebele country, opening another route to the Falls. The route was now becoming somewhat congested. When the German Edward Mohr reached the Falls in 1870, again in the company of Thomas Baines, he mentioned meeting three Englishmen and two Norwegians. The following year, the trader George Westbeech visited the Falls for the first time. The outside world had suddenly broken upon the Upper Zambezi after centuries of it being effectively isolated from the non-African world.

By the middle of the nineteenth century, it was known that the Cahora Bassa rapids could not be passed by boats, but it was still thought that the middle sections of the river, up to the Victoria Falls, might prove navigable. In 1860, Thomas Baines and James Chapman decided to bring a specially designed copper boat overland from Walvis Bay, launch it on the Zambezi below the Falls and take it down the river to the sea. Although their boat eventually reached the Zambezi, having travelled from the west coast by ox wagon, Baines's party fell ill with malaria and in 1863 abandoned the attempt, leaving the boat unassembled on the south bank of the river. During the 1870s, a number of hunters entered the middle reaches of the Zambezi, and Frederick Selous wrote about his hunting expeditions in a popular work *A Hunter's Wanderings in Africa*, which was published in 1881. It seems that in 1880 a man called Monks made a solo journey by canoe from below the Batoka gorge to the sea. No details of this somewhat mythical journey exist, though Monks does seem to have made a detailed map of his expedition.

Described in great detail was the attempt by Major Gibbons to take a steamer up the river from Cahora Bassa to Victoria Falls. He had two aluminium boats, cunningly designed so that they could be taken apart or lined up to make one boat. Somehow, he and seven companions got their boats through the Kariba and Mpata gorges and then struggled up the shallow, winding bed of the Gwembe valley as far as the Batoka gorge, where the boats were duly abandoned and the expedition dispersed. Gibbons's detailed account of his struggles to get his steamers up the river has something heroic about it and much that is simply futile and pointless.[1] He showed beyond any doubt, if doubt ever existed, that the Zambezi was not a viable waterway: the gorges were impossible at times of flood and the broad valley equally impossible during the dry season when water depths had to be measured in inches.

In 1903, Harold de Laessoe travelled from the Batoka gorge downstream to the sea, taking two boats with him. Somehow he managed to get his boats through the Cahora Bassa gorge, with the help of a little portering at certain points. The whole journey took only 2 months, but once again it was a statement of the inevitable: that the gorges of the Zambezi could not be navigated by anything much larger than a canoe.

However, while Europeans struggled with their advanced technology, the Africans who lived in the Gwembe valley and the reaches beyond Kariba did successfully navigate the river using traditional dugout canoes, employing their deep practical knowledge of the vagaries of the river. Wilfrid Robertson describes how skilled African canoemen took three dugouts through the Mpata gorge loaded with his hunting gear: "We were not the only travellers on the river for the Zambezi was the main highway of the country. Every mile or two we met other voyagers, pulling upstream against the current, natives passing from one riverine village to another or returning from their favourite fishing grounds."

The riverbed,

from one permanent bank to another, was quite three miles, an expanse at this season of the year made up of half a dozen channels, divided by sand banks and reed beds ... The pilots, however, knew their job; without hesitation they steered the flotilla down the primary channel.

As they approached the first rapid,

slowly my leading boat drifted towards the lip, the paddlers waiting the word of skipper. The bows of my boat reached the margin. "Washoo" shouted the steersman; the paddlers, galvanized into activity, sent the foam flying. Down we shot amid the troubled water, sweeping out a minute later onto a smooth surface once more ... Though the whole of the area was totally uninhabited by natives, the waterway was the only link between the up-river and the down-river villages and more than once we passed other travellers.

The sight of debris caught high in the rocks convinced Robertson that the passage through the gorge during the flood would be quite impossible. "A low roar in front came to my ears ... we had reached the main rapid that lies at the heart of the gorge." Here the canoes were unloaded and the empty dugouts taken through the rapids.

My head pilot here took charge, making his arrangements with the confidence of past experience ... His plan was to bring the empty vessels down singly, shooting down the rapid with the first boat, and returning on foot for the second and third ... In and out between fangs of rock projecting from the boiling rapid sped the first canoe, at times both dugout and occupants being hid from my sight by spouting water and whirling spray.[2]

All three boats were brought down safely, but darkness was falling and Robertson and his crew had to spend the night in the depth of the gorge on a small fall of stones on the edge of the water.

Donald Sutherland, who was also taken through the Mpata rapids by skilled local boatmen, described how

> the crack paddlers took command at the bows of each craft, thereby reversing the customary arrangement of the steersman occupying the stern position. The reason for this was that should a rock or suspicious ripple appear in the boat's path, all depended on a powerful stroke of a paddle by the front paddler to divert the dugout from the danger.[3]

Although he never quite admits the fact in so many words, Robertson makes it clear that the valley Tonga understood the river and how to navigate it, and what were its possibilities and impossibilities, making the heroics of European explorers with their aluminium, flatpack little steamboats somewhat absurd.

The Middle Zambezi under colonial rule

When the dust settled from the hectic days of the Scramble for Africa, the British South Africa Company found itself entrusted with the administration of two colonies separated by the Zambezi river, which thus formally became what it had always been to some extent: a frontier. The Company's plans were to exploit the mineral resources of its chartered territory and settle large parts of it with European colonists. White farmers were allocated extensive areas of both territories, but these were mostly the healthy plateau lands, and no one considered the valley of the Middle Zambezi to be an area where Europeans would want to settle.

In some ways, the Company—the new overlord of the region—can be compared with the African states it replaced. There was a new, ethnically distinct ruling elite which had arrived in the region from the south. The members of the new elite brought with them their own language which soon became the lingua franca of the region, as had happened with the Makololo and the Ndebele, and their Christianity, which became the dominant religion of the region. Tribute was taken in the form of native tax, and various pressures were applied to produce a servile class of labourers for the mines and white farms.

Such a comparison is, of course, superficial and takes no account of the totally alien culture, in particular as regards the literacy and technology, which characterised the new overlords. In one important respect, however, the comparison is valid. Except in areas allocated for white farmers, the 'small society' of the population remained relatively unchanged, as it had done under the rule of the Karanga, Marave, Ndebele and Lozi overlords in the past.

The 'small society' of the people who lived in the Zambezi valley—the Valley Tonga of the Gwembe valley, the Batoka of the region between the Falls and the Kafue and Shona-speaking Korekore of the stretch from Kariba down to the Portuguese frontier and beyond to Cahora Bassa—lived much as they had always done, though now without the fear of being raided. They were weak in political institutions, and the Tonga especially lived in communities that were effectively acephalous (without permanent established leaders). However, among the Korekore, prestigious spirit mediums with their 'provinces' largely took the place of political institutions.

David Lan has described eloquently the importance of ancestral spirits in the life of people who inhabit the valley:

> All women and men are expected to provide for and protect their families as best they can. Even when they die and leave their bodies in the grave they do not cease to care for their descendants ... Women and men with their limited powers, their ignorance and weaknesses have been transformed into ancestors or *midzimu*, who know the future before it happens and can cure every ill ... As with ordinary women and men so also with chiefs ... When a chief dies he is transformed into a *mhondoro* and becomes the source of the

fertility of the land itself. He provides rain for the fields and protects the crops as they grow. Rain will only be withheld if the *mhondoro's* laws are disobeyed.[4]

Spirit mediums, men or women, were selected according to various rituals to maintain contact with the spirit world, with ancestors or with the guardian spirits of nature and the land. There was a hierarchy of spirit mediums, some being largely of local significance while others had an overarching authority, attracting followers from a wide area of the country. These senior mediums spoke for the spirits of important past rulers—in particular the Monomotapas of the sixteenth and seventeenth centuries—and among these the mediums of Matope and Mutota, the founders of the Monomotapa dynasty, were particularly influential in the lives of the valley people. Spirit mediums are mentioned in the earliest Portuguese writings, but it was not until Albino Manuel Pacheco described the mediums he met on his journey from Tete to Zumbo in 1861 that a detailed account appeared of how they operated.

In the Zambezi valley, colonial rule made little impact on the influence of these powerful figures. And, although they had clearly been a very significant organising influence during the rebellions of 1896–7, it was not until the 1950s that their importance was seriously studied by anthropologists like Kingsley Garbett and Donald Abraham. It was found that not only did the mediums act as arbiters in all kinds of local land disputes and in the selection of chiefs and headmen, but they could also act as spokesmen for the ancestors when important decisions had to be made, like the location of villages, the suitability of marriages or, more importantly, how local people were to respond to the demands of the colonial governments. In the Zambezi valley, little challenged the prestige of the mediums, and returning migrant labourers who had worked on European farms or in the mines or urban occupations fitted back easily into this traditional world.

The power of the mediums was the power of the spirit world and the power of the ancestors, and it was part of their role to represent the spirit world to the people still living in the area where they operated. This accounts for the mediums' role as the 'historians' of the particular ancestors with whom they were in contact, making them a rich repository of oral tradition. The complexity of the beliefs in the active presence of the spirit world in everyday affairs can be seen in the widespread assumption that the spirits of the dead can inhabit the bodies of lions, and in the all-pervading belief in the activity of witches and in the malevolence of those who can control evil forces.

The Zambezi valley was supervised on both banks by District Officers with the backing of small contingents of African police, but this impinged little on the pervasive, age-old traditions represented by the spirit mediums. The colonial governments operated a sort of indirect rule by which the everyday life of the population was regulated by traditional authorities, appointed and approved by the Native Affairs Department. Among the Valley Tonga, the Northern Rhodesian authorities introduced 'chiefs' among people who had never had such a person directing their lives but otherwise interfered little in the way communities arranged their affairs.

The Middle Zambezi valley then was left very much undeveloped and its inhabitants relatively undisturbed in their ancient village way of life. Although, since Livingstone's day, a number of people had passed along the river valley between the Luangwa confluence and the Victoria Falls, this stretch of the river remained relatively unknown, and there was no crossing point except for the Victoria Falls bridge (which was completed in 1905), until in 1934 the Alfred Beit Trust paid for the construction of the road bridge at Chirundu, which carried the road which connected Salisbury to Lusaka. Donald Sutherland graphically describes the isolation of the valley at the beginning of his book on hunting big game, which was published in 1935:

It [the Zambezi Valley] is entirely innocent of roads, wheels have never turned within its confines, and the roars of a motor horn would be nothing short of sacrilege ... The Valley is approached via Salisbury, the capital town of Southern Rhodesia, and thence by a branch line to Sinoia railhead, a distance of eighty miles. From now on walking must be the means of progress ... the foot of the escarpment can be reached in about two days from Sipolilo; thence the journey over the range presents difficulties in the way of water supplies ... Six carriers should prove ample for the average hunter, and are readily obtainable from any Native Commissioner. The rate of pay varies from fifteen shillings to one pound per month ... It should be borne in mind that, as one penetrates further into the Valley, the kraals become fewer and sometimes are long distances apart; consequently food for carriers becomes a problem. On reaching the northern edge of this range, the Zambesi Valley can be seen far below, a vast purple carpet stretching sixty miles to the Livingstone Range; and on a very clear day the Zambesi River threads a silver ribbon at the foot of the mountains.[5]

The Tonga of the Gwembe valley

The Gwembe valley was the 230-mile stretch of the Zambezi which extended downriver from the Victoria Falls to the Kariba gorge, a stretch of the river that would be largely drowned by the formation of Lake Kariba. The Portuguese probably traded ivory beyond the Kariba gorge in the seventeenth century, but they left almost no records of this. By the nineteenth century, the valley had become a frontier zone between the Batoka plateau in the north, nominally subject to the rulers of Barotseland, and the southern plateau which formed part of the Rosvi and subsequently the Ndebele kingdoms. Later, this valley was to form the frontier between Northern and Southern Rhodesia and then between Zambia and Zimbabwe.

This floodplain of the Middle Zambezi was always relatively thickly populated, as the inundations of the river—beginning around December and occurring again in April when floodwater from higher up the river reached Gwembe—allowed the sowing of two crops, whereas the surrounding escarpment allowed only a single sowing after the start of the rains in October. The proximity of the river also assured water supplies that could be relied on even in years of drought.

Elizabeth Colson, the anthropologist who worked in the valley at the time of the building of the Kariba dam at the end of the 1950s, observed that the pattern of settlement in the floodplain differed in some important respects from the pattern lower down the river. Through the Gwembe valley, the Zambezi flows quite fast and is compressed at intervals by narrows that force the current onwards. During the floods, the swiftly flowing river was not suitable for navigation by the comparatively small canoes possessed by the inhabitants, who therefore did not use the river to navigate up- and downstream.

However, these canoes could be used to cross the river from one side to the other. This meant that village settlements were often isolated from those upstream and downstream on the same bank but had close connections with those on the opposite shore, where village inhabitants had kin and might even go to till fields. Further down the Zambezi, conversely, the width of the river makes contact with the opposite bank more difficult, while river boats are able to navigate along the river up- and downstream.

The people of the Gwembe valley shared a common Tonga language and in the anthropological literature were always known as Valley Tonga. They were matrilineal in their social organisation and were clearly related culturally to the people of the northern plateau, known as the Plateau Tonga. When periodically droughts affected the valley settlements, or when raiders appeared looking for slaves, people would escape to the escarpment and the plateau. However, although they shared a common language, the Tonga population of the valley was not entirely undifferentiated and, when Europeans came to describe the region, they discovered groups calling themselves by many different group names. In particular, groups known as We or BaWe ('people of the east'), Goba and Leya, Namainga, Mambi and Mwemba. The Goba even spoke a dialect related to Shona along with the universal Chitonga.[6]

The lineage-based villages of the Tonga depended on agriculture, as the climate and disease environment were not suitable for cattle rearing. Villages were grouped into neighbourhoods with which people identified and which could number up to 2,000 persons. However, there appears never to have been any move to establish a system of political overrule, and there were no invasions of ruling dynasties from outside, such as those which formed the Karanga and Marave states of the lower river. The difficult climate of the valley, where summer temperatures regularly reach 115 degrees, and the inhospitable nature of the escarpment, lacking in secure water supplies, always discouraged settlement by outsiders.

Elizabeth Colson described the situation when colonial rule first came to the Gwembe valley at the very end of the nineteenth century:

> When Europeans came to the Valley, they found themselves faced with a people who were both extremely parochial and largely egalitarian. Authority was diffused rather than concentrated in the hands of a single representative of the community. Common action and the settlement of disputes could be obtained only after negotiation and interminable discussions in which all elders had a right to have their say.[7]

However, the lack of any centralised political organisation had made the population of the region vulnerable to raiders. Warfare along all reaches of the river often centred on the capture of slaves, especially women and children, and the Gwembe populations suffered from these slave raids, especially in the nineteenth century, when records tell of attacks by the Ndebele, the Lozi from upstream and the *chicunda* coming from the Portuguese settlements downriver.

Periodic droughts had always meant that people had to be prepared to move in order to survive, while the insecurity resulting from raiding in the nineteenth century meant that many Tonga were prepared to take opportunities to migrate in search of work. As a result, in the early twentieth century, many of the Gwembe Valley Tonga joined the migrations to the copper mines and to the gold mines of South Africa. The end of raiding, which was one of the results of the establishment of colonial rule, also led to a rapid growth in the population, with the result that by the end of the colonial period the Tonga had become the second-largest ethnic group in Northern Rhodesia. In the 2010 census in Zambia, the Tonga formed 13.6 per cent of the population, exceeded only by the Bemba with 21 per cent.

Life below the escarpment

The Middle Zambezi valley was hemmed in on both its north and south sides by the mountains of the escarpment. In spite of the best efforts of adventurers who had braved the rapids and shallows, no viable river route had been discovered, and the river remained a very visible frontier between Northern and Southern Rhodesia but not a highway to provide a passage for the modern world. As mines, farms and modern cities gradually took shape on the plateaux, the valley remained ignored and largely inaccessible. Few roads were built through the escarpment, and the valley communities remained ignored and largely forgotten by all except the big-game hunters who set out to slaughter animals and bring back what they called 'trophies' from an area still very rich in Africa's magnificent wildlife. The hunting culture was immensely destructive, as in many areas near the river animals were killed in large numbers. The depredations of the hunters were matched by periodic campaigns against the tsetse fly organised by a colonial bureaucracy that believed that the mass slaughter of wild animals would lead to the fly disappearing; it didn't.

The river valleys, including those of the Kafue and Luangwa, became for the European settlers places where they could go 'on safari' to pursue their favourite hobby of killing. A large literature grew up around these adventures in which authors put on display their masculinity with tales of life in the bush and, to the modern sensibility, cruel and horrific tales of slaughter.

The figure of the 'white hunter' was brilliantly satirised by P.G. Wodehouse in his story 'A Mixed Threesome':

> Denton was one of those lean, hard-bitten men with smouldering eyes and a brick red complexion ... He had the wiry frame and strong jaw without which no explorer is complete ... "In the morning they took me down to the river. At this point it widens into a *kongo*, or pool, and it was here, they told me, that the crocodile mostly lived, subsisting on the native oxen—the short-horned *jongos*—which, swept away by the current while crossing the ford above, were carried down to the *longos*, or rapids. It was not, however, till the second evening that I managed to catch sight of his ugly snout above the surface ... He was certainly a monster—fully thirty—you have never been in Central Africa, have you Miss Weston? No? You ought to go there!—fully fifty feet from tip to tail ..."
>
> "And what did you do then, Mr Denton" asked Betty, breathlessly
>
> "Eh? Oh?," he said, carelessly, "I swam across and shot him".[8]

However, 40 years after the white settlers had conquered the kingdom of the Ndebele and established their control over the regions where the Ndebele had traditionally raided and demanded tribute, some change in attitude was beginning to take place, and the protection of wild animals was slowly gaining acceptability. Shooting game with the camera rather than the rifle was becoming more common.

In 1936, Wilfrid Robertson—who was born two years after Rhodes's Pioneer Column had entered the country and who had taken up a land concession, which he described as being a ranch of 27 square miles—published an account of hunting and travel in the valley, called *Zambezi Days*. The year before, he had written an autobiographical novel, *Rhodesian Rancher*, which covered many of the same themes. *Zambezi Days* is well written and not only lays bare the deep contradictions embedded in the minds of the white settlers but describes, perhaps for the last time, a traditional African world which, if not exactly unchanged, strongly resembles the world depicted in the Portuguese writings of 300 years earlier. Robertson starts his account of hunting in the valley with pitching his camp for breakfast:

> Around lay the rolling forests of the Zambezi valley, bathed in the rays of the African sun, and, except for a couple of eagles circling high above, showing no sign of life; for every wild creature had sought the refuge of its deepest shades from the daytime heat. Twenty miles to the north lay the great Zambezi river; the same distance to the south the bastions of the escarpment rose against the sky, that mighty wall of hill and cliff which upholds the southern plateau above the elephant-haunted floor.[9]

Immediately, he embarked on one of his favourite themes, the relations of white settlers with the African population. Here it is a relationship one to one with the local village headman: "I knew the value of being clean and smart when dealing with natives. Savages are quick at detecting small things, shrewdly they argue that a white chief who does not respect his own appearance is not entitled to a great deal of respect from them."[10]

There are contradictions already: the Africans are 'savages' but at the same time 'shrewd' observers of the human scene. This contrast dominates so much of the culture of colonialism. Africans are always 'savages', but they have unusual skills and virtues that are amply illustrated as the book progresses. The whites are, of course, the representatives of civilisation, but also the bringers of new vices and new relationships. In short, it is the civilisation of the white settlers that has destroyed the much-admired virtues of traditional African life. Why do missionaries insist on people being clothed? "Is His work bettered by being covered with the cast-off rags of civilisation?"[11]

> Idly I mused on the inborn conservatism of the native. For instance, the case of my own personal boy. For me he could cook exceedingly well—the meal I had just eaten had been excellent—while for himself he prepared much the same ingredients in a way that would turn the stomach of a civilised being. His own food was prepared in precisely the same way as that of the other carriers in the identical fashion indeed that his ancestors had done for untold generations. Stiff and soggy maize porridge, and bits of meat impaled on sticks and scorched in the ashes.[12]

The same deep-seated contradictions colour how he sees the wilderness of the Zambezi valley and its animals. Everywhere he admires the grace of the antelopes, the power of the buffaloes and elephants and the savage fighting strength of the leopards, but killing them 'for the pot' or as 'trophies' is somehow quite legitimate and indeed a manly exercise. Nor does Robertson resist the temptation to kill for sport whenever he has the opportunity. Having washed himself in the river and put his clothes back on, he sees two crocodiles further out in the stream. They have not attacked him or endangered him in any way.

> Quietly I picked up the rifle, aimed and fired. The bullet struck with a clap that rang across the pool; and the crocodile—shot in the head just below the projecting eye-socket leaped clean out of the water, turned over in mid-air, and struck the surface again with a huge splash ... Another shot; and it turned belly upwards and sank to the bottom.[13]

And it is quite clear that the 'unspoiled native' of the valley is also one of the natural fauna of the region. "To the passing glance, a native woman in Africa never appears to be nude, any more than an antelope or bullock seems to be so." The 'native' is to be admired and appreciated, but also utilised as unskilled labour—under compulsions that are hardly acknowledged—and disciplined with the whip.

Although the idea of an unchanging Africa is long-since defunct, there are always continuities which can be followed over the centuries. It is interesting to compare Robertson's compendium of wildlife lore with a similar account written by a Jesuit 300 years earlier. For instance, both of them speak of traditions surrounding baboons molesting women and kidnapping children, and of being able to speak. Here is Robertson:

> Natives are convinced that the great apes have a definite and recognizable language of their own; and there are men who contend not only that they can understand what is said, but can hold converse with them. Certainly they are feared, especially by the women; and though I have never encountered a case, there are many reports of native women, caught alone in the forest, being attacked by one of these creatures. Certainly there are authentic cases of child stealing.[14]

The Jesuit António Gomes wrote in 1648,

> Some monstrosities have been born, but the cafres kill them because, they say, if they did not do this, they would all become monkeys ... They think that they [the monkeys] are people who do not want to come to the village for fear that they will be made to work and that their king has told them not to talk because, if it is known that they can talk, war will be made on them to capture them and make them work. Elsewhere I have described how they pick up the children and take them up into the trees.[15]

Both writers also comment on the honeyguide bird. As Robertson says, "it has found a wild bees' hive; twittering and

dipping from tree to tree it flutters in front of the traveller, trying to enlist his co-operation in raiding the honey", and, according to Gomes three hundred years earlier,

> There is a kind of very small bird that feeds on honey and as the
> bees know them, they have a great war with them and defend them-
> selves. They [the birds] watch the paths for people and when they
> see someone, they chirp very enthusiastically and fly from branch to
> branch singing their song. They fly and stop until they guide the
> cafre to the honeycomb, fly twice round it and then stop and go on
> singing while the cafres take the honeycomb, and they do this
> because they are interested in the little pieces that are left.

Robertson records how, when travelling near a village in the
valley, the villagers called out to them, and "my people answered
back with jokes and laughter and scraps of information about the
journey". Gomes records, "in the places where they arrive or
where they see people working in the fields, they greet them and
start digging with them. While digging they tell where they have
come from, where they are going to and what has happened to
them etc.".[16]

Robertson records how two man-eating lions

> took up their quarters in the dense surrounding forest; and in three
> weeks or so they accounted for fourteen or fifteen natives ... In the
> end the natives abandoned the village and fled; returning to live
> there only when they were sure that the man-eaters had grown tired
> of prowling round the empty huts.

Compare this with Gomes:

> Travelling through a certain place, I found entire villages recently
> abandoned because of the lions. The houses contained food, chickens
> and tools belonging to people the lions had killed and to other people
> who had fled and left everything behind because they say the lions
> will follow the scent on the tools and come for them ... [People]
> there advised us to move to a different place because the previous

night the lions had taken two people. So, we crossed the river to the other side by boat and a lion came during the night and took a young cafre aged seventeen or eighteen years and stayed nearby, growling in a frightening way, as a cat will do with a mouse.[17]

Livingstone and the railway

The Victoria Falls with its bridge and railway crossing soon saw the development of the important European town of Livingstone. This was only the second major town, after Tete, to be built on the Zambezi, and in 1907 it became the capital of Northern Rhodesia. In 1923, the administration of the colony was transferred from the British South Africa Company to the Colonial Office when it was declared that the interests of the African population would be paramount, thereby virtually putting an end to any idea that it would develop, like Southern Rhodesia, into a white settler-dominated regime. The railway across the gorge remained Northern Rhodesia's main link to the outside world, connecting it to the southern African railway system. Livingstone became not only a major administrative centre but also saw the emergence of a number of industries which grew up beside the railway that provided access to the commercial centres of Southern Rhodesia and the Copper Belt in the north.

With copper prices low during the Great Depression, Northern Rhodesia had few resources to invest in anything except basic administration. The development of road transport remained hampered by the broad floods of the Zambezi and its major feeder rivers, the Kafue and the Luangwa. These rivers needed to be bridged before a road transport network could reach across the Zambezi valley. In 1934, the Beit Trust funded the building of the Chirundu bridge across the Zambezi to complete the highway from Salisbury to Lusaka, which after 1935 replaced Livingstone as the capital of the colony. The Zambezi now had two crossings in its 1,600-mile stretch, both of them linking the two Rhodesias. The Beit Trust, whose priorities at that time were the building of transport infrastructure, also constructed numerous smaller bridges so that the transport network of the two Rhodesias grew web-like through the plateau country north and south of the Zambezi.

Once the capital was moved, Livingstone suffered a decline, to be revived when it became one of the destinations for the growing number of tourists heading for the Falls. Another tourist town, simply called Victoria Falls, grew up on the Southern Rhodesian side of the gorge.

The Kariba dam

In 1953, the British government established the Central African Federation (CAF), hoping thereby to provide a more prosperous future for its three central African territories. The concept was not hopeless, as the four colonies that made up South Africa had been brought together in 1910 to form the Union of South Africa, and earlier there had been similar unions that had created Canada and Australia. Moreover, the economic case was a strong one, as the Federation would, in theory, be able to link the industrial expertise that existed in Southern Rhodesia (where the country was even able to build its own railway locomotives) with the copper mines of Northern Rhodesia. Development funding would now be available for Northern Rhodesia and Nyasaland, which had for so long been starved of investment.

However, the politics of the scheme were less secure, and from the start it was widely opposed not only by Africans—who saw in it a plot to establish white settler domination north of the Zambezi—but even by the white settler population in self-governing Southern Rhodesia, who were deeply suspicious of the multiracial Federal institutions which they saw as undermining white civilised standards. In retrospect, it is possible to see that the centuries-old frontier which the river had formed between lands and peoples to the north and south had already established fundamental cultural divisions that could not easily be overcome.

Nevertheless, in its 10 years of existence, the CAF went ahead with creating a raft of institutions aimed at building a common citizenship and a common future, among them the Federal University, located in Salisbury.

However, the greatest monument to the Federation—and one that, for better or worse, came to symbolise all that the CAF stood for—was the building of a giant dam on the Zambezi. Downstream from the Victoria Falls, the Zambezi flowed through a number of gorges which the river had cut through mountain barriers, and the idea of damming one of these gorges was suggested quite early in the twentieth century. The Northern Rhodesian authorities wanted to build a dam on the Kafue to supply electricity to the Copper Belt and irrigate the drylands of the plateau, but instead the decision was made to go ahead with a dam on the Zambezi, a decision which was made largely for political reasons. Located on the river that formed the border, the dam would serve both Northern and Southern Rhodesia and would be symbolic of the co-operation that the CAF was supposed to bring.

Work on the site began in 1955 and construction of the dam itself in 1956. It was designed by French engineer—Andre Coyne, who designed seventy other dams—and was built by the Italian Impresit Consortium. It was a 'double curvature concrete arch dam' with walls 128 metres high and 24 metres thick at the base. One million cubic metres of concrete were poured, and, when completed, it had an overall length of 161.3 metres and carried a roadway across the river. The water imprisoned by the dam created what, at the time, was the largest man-made lake in the world. It took 4 years, until 1963, for the lake to fill to an overall length of 280 kilometres. The lake covered 6,000 square kilometres and, as a reservoir, held 185 cubic kilometres of water. When fully in operation, 10 million litres of water passed through the dam every second. During the filling of the lake, twenty large earth tremors were recorded.

In 1959, the year the dam was completed, the Malpasset dam in France—also designed by Coyne—suddenly collapsed, swamping the town of Fréjus and killing more than 400 people. Coyne himself died a year later.

The Kariba dam initially cost 135 million dollars, but this was only the beginning. The capacity of the dam was expanded in the 1970s, and the north bank power station was built for an additional 480 million dollars. A further expansion planned for 2014–18, with Chinese help, was estimated to cost 533 million dollars. By that time, a vast operation was underway to stabilise the dam, whose foundations were being undermined. All in all, Kariba has turned out to be a very expensive way of providing central Africa with cheap electricity, and in 1967 Zambia went ahead with the Kafue dam that it had wanted to build in the first place.

In preparation for the flooding of the valley behind the Kariba dam, bulldozers stripped an estimated 954 square kilometres of surface vegetation, and 57,000 Tonga villagers were told they would have to move. Not surprisingly, there was widespread resistance which spilled over into some violence, with up to eight villagers being killed by police. The Tonga received no compensation, and resettlement beyond the lake shore did little to remedy the total destruction of a way of life that had depended on the seasonal rise and fall of the river. Initially, the Valley Tonga who had been evacuated were allowed sole fishing rights in the lake, but in 1963 this exclusive right was ended and commercial fishing began.

In 2001, a Tonga spokesman, Dominic Muntanga, summed up the feelings of many people a generation after the population had been resettled: "For the local Tonga, it buried their ancestors under the water, separated their families and failed to bring irrigation to their arid farmlands."[18] It is clear that, when costing the dam, little account had been taken of the human cost or the longer-term costs to the environment.

The Tonga protest had centred on the river spirit Nyaminyami, who was believed to be the protector of the river. As the dam was constructed, Nyaminyami's displeasure was manifested in the two immense floods of 1957 and 1958 which swamped the coffer dams. His power was further demonstrated when the bodies of three of the dam's workforce, who had been killed during the construction, miraculously reappeared at the river's edge for burial. In popular belief, Nyaminyami has withdrawn in displeasure at the building of the dam, but the image of a river snake, supposedly his, has been used to fill the shelves of tourist craft shops.

A rescue operation known as 'Operation Noah' was mounted to remove large game animals from the rising water. An estimated 6,000 animals were rescued, but this was a small percentage of those countless animals, large and small, killed by the rising waters. Most of the rescued animals were brought to the Southern Rhodesian side of the valley, while most of the Tonga expelled from their homes went to the Northern Rhodesian side.

There were other consequences for the environment as well. The infestation of so-called Kariba weed threatened for a long time to choke the lake. Eventually the problem stabilised itself, but the other environmental consequences were more long-lasting. The dam had the effect of moderating the flow of water downstream, evening out the floods and periods of low water. It also greatly reduced the amount of silt that was carried downstream. The effects of this were mostly felt on the Lower Zambezi and in the delta, where the flat, grassy plains no longer received the annual floods which had maintained the rich grassland and alluvial soils. The ecology of the delta began to change in unforeseen ways.

Then, in 2014, the dam began to experience severe structural problems, just as climate change began to affect the river's flow, a crisis that will be considered in more depth in Chapter 12.

11

BALOVALE AND THE UPPER ZAMBEZI

The Lunda empire[1]

From the location near Kalene hill where it rises, the Zambezi flows south for 600 miles through the floodplains of the upper river before turning eastwards. These upper reaches of the river have provided an open highway for the migration of people from the forested areas in the north, and from the sixteenth century onwards this migration route has been followed by people from the Luba and Lunda states beyond the great watershed of the Zambezi and Zaire. The traditions of the peoples of the Upper Zambezi, and those of their neighbours across the watershed in the drainage basin of the Zaire, describe the establishment of the Luba and Lunda states in the sixteenth and seventeenth centuries. This was an overrule imposed by an organised elite whose military power and lucrative participation in trade, principally the trade in textiles and slaves, enabled them progressively to subdue the populations of a considerable area of central Africa on both sides of the great Zaire–Zambezi divide.

The Lunda kingdom came into existence as an offshoot of the neighbouring Luba kingdom, its first recorded king, Chibinda

Ilunga, being a Luba-speaking aristocrat who married a Lunda woman. The kingdom he established east of the great Kasai tributary of the Zaire had its capital at Mussumba on the Nkalanyi, another river flowing north towards the Zaire beyond the Zambezi–Zaire watershed. Ilunga, or his successors, are supposed to have introduced Luba ideas of kingship where the belief in the divine nature of kings, perpetuated in the shrines to dead rulers, underpinned the royal authority.

The king bore the title of Mwant Yaav (Muata Yamvo, as the Portuguese rendered it). The king's power was modified by a council of elders who advised him and by the institution of the 'mother-queen', who had her own 'capital' and exerted extensive authority over the domestic affairs of the kingdom, including the question of the succession which always proved so dangerous and destructive to other African monarchies. Other characteristics of the Lunda monarchy were the naming of an heir apparent during the lifetime of the reigning king and the institution of *cilolos*, a class of nobles who held privileged status throughout the kingdom. These institutions are characteristic not only of the Luba/Lunda kingdoms but also their offshoot, the Lozi kingdom of Barotseland. However, parallels can also be seen in the kingdoms of the Karanga and Marave on the lower reaches of the Zambezi, which shared with the Lunda many of what became the key characteristics of central African monarchies.

Lunda wars of conquest may account for the sixteenth-century migrations and invasions—attributed by the Portuguese to Jaga and Imbangala—which devastated the Kongo kingdom, but it was in the mid-seventeenth century that the main Lunda expansion, recorded in their traditions, really began. Gradually, the Lunda subdued and incorporated into the monarchy the small and often acephalous communities of the river valleys to the west and the north. However, apart from the heartland around its capital, the Lunda kingdom was never very centralised.

Conquered peoples were allowed a large degree of autonomy as long as tribute was paid to the Lunda king, while Lunda-appointed officials, known as *kawatta*, were permanently resident in the outlying areas, reporting back to the centre about local affairs and such matters as the state of trade and the regular payment of tribute.

The expansion of the Lunda kingdom was in part driven by economics. To the north lay what John Thornton called the 'textile belt', where the weaving of cloth from the fibres of the raffia palms was a major industry, while to the west the Atlantic slave trade system, presided over by creole Portuguese, was becoming increasingly important. As the Lunda elites conquered and incorporated more and more people, the tribute they exacted increasingly took the form either of slaves—who were either retained or sent towards the Atlantic—or textiles, which formed part of the patrimonial wealth-sharing that maintained the prestige and hence the stability of the monarchy. The main focus of expansion was in the north, and by the middle of the eighteenth century the Lunda king ruled—in the sense that he took tribute from—a huge area west of the Kasai.

In the middle of the seventeenth century, sections of the Lunda elite began to turn their attention south and eastwards. A group, later to call themselves Luyana, had reached the headwaters of the Zambezi and from there had used the highway provided by the great river to establish their control 400 miles downstream over the Barotse floodplain. There they set up a typical Luba/Lunda style of kingdom with councils of elders, the figure of the mother-queen and the appointment of officials throughout the region to organise information flows and the payment of tribute. Over time, the Lunda connection was largely forgotten and was replaced by a new ethnic identity, that of the Lozi.

Another group established themselves on the central African plateau and over time acquired a separate ethnic identity, becoming known as Bemba. Equally impressive was the founding of the Kazembe kingdom by another group of Lunda who left the central state core sometime in the early eighteenth century and established a kingdom astride the Luapula, another tributary of the Zaire. With the consolidation of this Kazembe kingdom, trade relations grew up with the east African coast, and Arab and Portuguese creole traders made their way from there to buy Kazembe's ivory. Kazembe's kingdom was visited and described in detail by two Portuguese trade missions in 1798 and 1832, and it is largely through the records of these expeditions that knowledge of the structure and politics of these Lunda states is known.

The Lunda-related kingdoms shared key institutions and recognised an ancestral relationship with the founder of the Lunda kingdom and its ruling dynasty. They all shared a common way of relating to the people they conquered. These peoples were incorporated into the Lunda-related monarchies according to their geographical locations and the skills of their people. Some, who dwelt near the forests in the north, were recognised as expert hunters, others along the rivers were known as the makers of canoes, others yet again were iron workers or skilled in woodwork. Some were recognised as artists, and their carvings were appropriated and adapted to the rituals of Lunda kingship. Others yet again were servile people who not only paid their tribute in slaves, often children, but who could be summoned to labour for the ruling elites.

It seems that the power of the Lunda kings reached its fullest extent in the early nineteenth century, the kingdom stretching 1,000 kilometres from the Kwango river to Lake Mweru in the east. The ruling Mwant Yaav, named Yavu, took significant steps to develop the trade with the Portuguese of Angola, and from the beginning of the century increasing numbers of *pombeiros* from Angola, often accompanied by Portuguese traders, began to visit Lunda. In 1843, an Angolan coffee-plantation owner named

Joaquim Rodrigues Graça had organised an expedition to the capital of the Lunda king and had declared his intention of reaching the headwaters of the Zambezi. His expedition only reached the Lunda court in 1846 and got no further. Graça had no official position and was not able to negotiate any permanent treaty with the king.

The growing trade of the Lunda with Portuguese Angola seems to have hastened the disintegration of a monarchy which was anyway too large and unwieldy to remain stable. Regional *cilolos* were increasingly able to assert their independence from the centre and trade directly with the Portuguese. The new Mwant Yaav, Nawej, who had succeeded to the throne after the death of Yavu in 1820, engaged in constant warfare as he tried to maintain the tribute-paying status of outlying regions. In order to strengthen his position at the centre, Nawej is supposed to have involved Cokwe hunters, who became an increasingly powerful group in the kingdom.

The Cokwe were, in origin, another subgroup within the Lunda empire who specialised in hunting and trade. Trade with the Portuguese enabled them to buy guns with which they not only freed themselves from Lunda control but effectively broke up the extended Lunda empire. With the defeat of the Lunda, the vast, decentralised structure of overrule fell apart, and subject groups which had paid tribute to the Lunda paramount king asserted their independence. Nawej's hold on the kingdom gradually relaxed, and in 1852 he was 'sent to his ancestors', a traditional form of royal euthanasia practised by many of the central African monarchies and described as early as the seventeenth century by the Jesuit António Gomes.[2] With the death of Nawej, the Lunda empire ceased to exist, though the empty rituals around the holder of the royal title lingered on.

In 1884, Henrique de Carvalho was commissioned by the Portuguese to go on a mission to Lunda and make treaties with the Mwant Yaav. Carvalho's expedition, which continued until 1887, found that the old Lunda empire no longer existed and the Mwant Yaav title was an empty formality held by insignificant figures who wielded little or no real power. Although he visited the site of the old Lunda capital at Mussumba, where there were the remains of a once-large town, he found nothing but a disorganised population with no leadership, at the mercy of Cokwe raiders who actually visited Mussumba while he was there and went off with the slaves they captured.[3]

The disintegration of the Lunda empire has parallels in the gradual disintegration and disappearance of other Zambezi systems of overrule. The Marave kings who had once been considered powerful enough to be called 'emperors' by the Portuguese, and who ruled over the peoples on the north side of the Lower Zambezi, dwindled in power until they became little more than figureheads with prestigious titles. The same happened to the Monomotapa 'empire', which by the nineteenth century had shrunk so drastically that the Monomotapa was little more than a disputed title held by rulers of a small sector of the Zambezi valley. These apparently impressive central African monarchies had for the most part been little more than ritual titles, supported by a more or less effective system for exacting tribute from their subjects. As Nowell put it, summarising Carvalho's opinion,

> the famed Muatianvua [Mwant Yaav] power, even in its heyday, had been more of a fiction than a fact. The territory directly governed by this ruler had always been small but somehow his name and title had been blown up out of all proportion to the reality. Chiefs, supposedly subordinate but really their own agents, had collected tribute on his ostensible behalf, though little of it ever reached him.[4]

Livingstone visits the Lunda ruler, Shinte

Livingstone travelled through the southern regions of the Lunda empire in 1854 when the kingdom was visibly breaking up and

the Lunda rulers along the Zambezi were, to all intents and purposes, already independent. He recalled a memorable meeting
with a female ruler of one section of the Lunda close to the
junction of the Zambezi with the Kabompo river. This must have
been the most southerly point of Lunda expansion, as populations were close enough to the Makololo of the Baroste floodplain to be raided by them for slaves.

According to Livingstone, Shinte, who was the most important Lunda ruler in this region of the Upper Zambezi, had a
Zulu wife, who must have come via diplomatic relations with the
Makololo. Through trade with the Mambari (Ovimbundu from
Angola), the Lunda had imported European-made cloth, but
Shinte's niece, Manenko, who Livingstone described as "a tall,
strapping woman about twenty", met Livingstone clad only in
red ochre and grease, "with a profusion of ornaments and medicines hung round her person".[5] Livingstone was, perhaps for the
first time in his life, somewhat taken aback and referred to her
costume as one of "frightful nudity". She was clearly a formidable
woman who forced Livingstone to leave his canoes and his preferred mode of travel by river and to visit her uncle following a
route by land. In pouring rain, Livingstone and his party strag-
gled after Manenko.

> Her husband used various incantations and vociferations to drive
> away the rain, but down it poured incessantly, and on our Amazon
> went, in the very lightest marching order, and at a pace that few of
> the men could keep up with. [I] asked her why she did not clothe
> herself during the rain, and learned that it is not considered proper
> for a chief to appear effeminate. He or she must always wear the
> appearance of robust youth.

Livingstone and his party stayed for some days at Shinte's
capital. Livingstone's description of the town and the ceremony
at the Lunda ruler's court is a rare description of a Lunda state
in operation and can be compared only with the descriptions of

Kazembe's capital given by Lacerda and Gamitto, the Portuguese who travelled there earlier in the century. The town lay in a valley and Livingstone described it as "embowered in banana and other tropical trees". The streets were straight and the huts were square in shape (unlike those built by the Lozi or the Makololo), and the fences surrounding them were interwoven with grass. "In the courts were small plantations of tobacco and a little solanasceous plant which the Balonda use as a relish, also sugar cane and bananas." The next day there was a grand reception attended by Portuguese and Mambari traders who came with their guns to fire a salute to Shinte.

> The kotla or place of audience, was about a hundred yards square, and two graceful specimens of banian stood near one end; under one of these sat Shinte, on a sort of throne covered with a leopard's skin. He had on a checked jacket, and a kilt of scarlet baize edged with green; many strings of large beads hung from his neck, and his limbs were covered with iron and copper armlets and bracelets, on his head he wore a helmet made of beads woven neatly together and crowned with a great bunch of goose-feathers. Close to him sat three lads with large sheaves of arrows over their shoulders.

Behind Shinte sat his chief wife and about a hundred women who chanted during the orations which followed.

The ceremony began with headmen coming forward to greet the chief, followed by armed men who rushed threateningly at Livingstone's party before veering away. Dancers then appeared imitating the actions of warriors. Livingstone was then formally introduced, and drummers and marimba players performed. In all, Livingstone estimated there were about 1,000 people present, in addition to 300 soldiers.

Shinte had a woman who "occupies the office of drawer of water ... she rings a bell as she passes along to give warning to all to keep out of her way" so that no one could "exercise an evil influence by his presence on the drink of the chief". Shinte offered a 10-year-old girl to Livingstone "to bring me water, [saying] that a great man ought to have a child for the purpose, yet I had none". When Livingstone refused the gift, he was offered an older girl whom he also refused. It is difficult not to recall the Jesuit missionary, Gonçalo da Silveira, also being offered women by the Monomotapa in 1560, an offer which he, like Livingstone, refused. Was it just as water carriers that distinguished visitors were offered these gifts of young women?

Later holders of the Shinte title were to be recognised as 'chiefs' of the Lunda by the British colonial administration.

These were the last days of relative peace for the Lunda. Everywhere Livingstone saw and heard evidence of the slave trade, and he described the encampment of the Mambari who were at Shinte's town:

> There were many Mambari with them [the Portuguese] and the establishment was conducted with that military order which pervades all the arrangements of the Portuguese colonists. A drum was beaten, and trumpet sounded at certain hours, quite in military fashion. It was the first time my men had seen slaves in chains ... they had a gang of young female slaves in a chain, hoeing the ground in front of their encampment.[6]

The Lunda along the Upper Zambezi were living in a state of great insecurity. Their villages were heavily fortified:

> Each house of these hamlets has a palisade of thick stakes around it, and the door is made to resemble the rest of the stockade; the door is never seen open; when the owner wishes to enter, he removes a stake or two, squeezes his body in, then plants them again in their places, so that an enemy coming in the night would find it difficult to discover the entrance.[7]

Livingstone noted the very hospitable custom by which "the inhabitants lent us the roofs of their huts". Apparently, the roofs of huts could be easily lifted off and brought to where travellers were encamped and there re-erected to provide some shelter.

THE ZAMBEZI

Lovale

In 1854, Manenko had given as one of the reasons why Livingstone should not proceed by river, that the "Balobale" who inhabited the land west of the Zambezi would be hostile, and, even if they did not kill Livingstone himself, they would kill his Makololo followers. Already, it seems, hostility between the Lovale and Lunda was a looming danger for the peoples of the Upper Zambezi.

When Lunda armies began to penetrate south to the upper reaches of the Zambezi at the end of the eighteenth century, they were confronted with a state which appeared in Portuguese records as 'Lobal' or 'Lovar'. Nothing much is known of this state, which the Portuguese record as being large and ruled over by a king with the title of Chinyama, with eighteen *sobas* (local rulers) subject to it. The population of this state would later be known as Lovale or Lwena, although there was also a population group known as Mbwela who were recognised as original inhabitants of the valley.

Lunda armies occupied this region between 1794 and 1797 and established there a typical pattern of Lunda overrule.[8] The Lwena/Lovale had two important royal titles, Chinyama and Kakende, but in practice authority was dispersed, often down to the level of the village. Among the Lwena clans, there was one which was recognised as conferring ruler status. As the Lwena were matrilineal, this status was passed through the female line and was enjoyed by all the female offspring but not the male. C.M.N. White, who made a lifetime study of Lovale/Lwena customs in the mid-twentieth century, explained how this worked:

> Lovale chiefs may be male or female, and the daughters of a female chief are themselves members of the chiefly lineage by matrilineal descent and eligible to become female chiefs ... the chiefly lineage came late on the scene and established itself in a chiefless society ... The royal lineage depends upon the fertility of its female members

to perpetuate itself ... the Lovale princesses traditionally select themselves a man they want as a husband and the latter does not make
approaches for the hand of a royal girl.[9]

It is probable that most of the people who lived in the valley
of the Zambezi were at one time organised on the basis of individual lineage-based villages, with some acknowledgement of
wider clan loyalties. Most of them practised a matrilineal social
organisation which recognised the primacy of the mother's lineage. However, this Lovale/Lwena custom of recognising all
females of one clan as potential rulers produced a system that led
to a great degree of fragmentation of political authority, and in
practice each village tended to be largely self-governing.

The rise in importance of the Cokwe and the spread of the
slave trade in the second half of the nineteenth century brought
about a reversal of previous roles with Lunda-speakers, who, no
longer protected by the state structure of the Lunda empire,
were now frequently the victims of slave raiding. Among their
principal enemies were the Lovale/Lwena. The Lovale occupied
land on the right bank of the Zambezi and had been trading with
the Mambari from Angola since at least the 1830s. The Lovale
used the expansion of trade to purchase guns, unlike the Lunda
who were slow to adopt the new technology. By the middle of
the century, Lovale hunters had eliminated all elephants on the
right bank of the river, at which point they crossed to hunt on
the left bank where the majority of the population were Lunda
speakers. Hunting marched hand in hand with slave raiding, and
the Lovale became among the biggest suppliers of slaves to the
Angolan markets in the last years of the trade.[10] The Lovale were
also accomplished fishermen and, again unlike the Lunda, were
at home on the rivers of the Upper Zambezi valley.

The slave raiding and conflict which followed the death of the
Lunda paramount ruler Nawej in 1852, and the breakup of the
Lunda state, were known as the Wars of Ulamba. Slaving imposed

new patterns on political and social relations. The possession of guns and a continuing market for slaves allowed powerful figures to emerge who could offer protection, and who purchased slaves to build up their own followings. The situation of disorder enhanced ethnic differences, which had previously been ill-defined amid a rich diversity of dialects and clan rituals. Now, consciously defined ethnic identity became a source of communal protection. When, in 1885, the Plymouth Brother Frederick Arnot travelled through the country inhabited by the Lovale and Lunda on the Upper Zambezi, his diary entries recording his journey to the capital of Msiri in modern Katanga give a clear picture of the increasing dominance of the Lovale in what had originally been part of the Lunda empire.

> Dec 3rd The Balovale people ... are in many respects superior to the Bachiboke [Cokwe], in the sense that they make better inhabitants of a country, being less wandering. I am amused to see how fond they are of singing-birds ... their neatly made cages are to be seen hanging about all their villages. I notice here, close by my camp, that they have made a large fish-dam. I have never before seen natives untaught by whites, dam a river for any purpose. Kangombe is quite a powerful man, the leader of all the Balovale and many of the Bachibokwe in war.

> Dec 5th I met some of the Balovale before at the Barotse, and I retain the opinion first formed of them—that they are a race of exceptionally manly-looking people.

> Dec 16th This is now Lunda country, although the Balovale are everywhere to be met.

> Dec 20th Camped at Kapwita. Here no less than three chiefs turned up. One called himself the chief of the Lunda residents; another, the chief of the Lovale residents; and the third the 'man of the country' ... In spite of their troublesome ways there is much about these Balunda I like. Their villages are kept clean, and they have good gardens, and the men work in the fields as well as the women; this

is also common among the Balovale. They seem to be more 'religious' than their neighbours. One sees continually in the forests small clearings about the trunk of some immense tree, with a double rail round, and some 'fetish thing' in front, in the shape of a horn or image, and there the people come to offer to their forefathers.

Dec 28th Camped on the east bank of the Luvua ... Here there is a Lovale colony under a chief named Fela. They have established themselves in the Lunda country by sheer force.

Jan 12 1886 Reached Sacindinga ... Here I met with a few wandering Balunda, but the country is practically desolate. Remains of former town and large cultivated fields, now all weeds, exist on all sides. War parties from the Lovale ... have wrought these devastations.[11]

In 1892, Lewanika, the Lozi king, was invited to intervene in these conflicts by some factions among the Lunda. Although his forces met little success, this campaign laid the foundation for Lozi claims to overlordship of the whole Upper Zambezi region.

It is often maintained by historians that slavery in Africa was quite different from the sort of slavery that was prevalent in the New World or the islands of the Indian Ocean, and that it encompassed various forms of serfdom, debt peonage, adoption, the incorporation of captured women into lineages and so on. However, this did not mean that African rulers were any the less eager to sell slaves to traders from the west coast and into a wholly different kind of slavery. They even sold people from their own ethnic groups.

Robert Papstein explains how Lovale rulers engaged with Mambari slavers: "As a general rule Ovimbundu [Mambari] were not interested in taking slaves themselves, but preferred instead to buy them for guns, cloth and jewellery ... By the mid-nineteenth century ... virtually all of the major chiefs were also important slave traders." Slaving led to the emergence of

> big men able to take advantage of international trade ... the relative
> Luvale monopoly of firearms, and the aggressive expansionist policy

which Luvale chiefs were following meant that any defenceless group was subject to enslavement. Luvale traditions are quite explicit in stating that many Luvale—in addition to the Lunda—were enslaved, and sometimes by their own chiefs.[12]

The establishment of colonial rule

Tempting as it may be to make a clean conceptual break between the colonial and the pre-colonial period in African history, the realities were never that simple. The interaction of African societies with the traders, missionaries, hunters and concession seekers coming from beyond their borders evolved gradually over the best part of a century. The first traders from the Atlantic coast of Africa reached the Upper Zambezi at least as early as the seventeenth century, and the impact of this long-distance trade to the Atlantic coast built up gradually through the eighteenth and nineteenth centuries. From the 1840s onwards, a trade route was also opened towards the south. So African societies in the Upper Zambezi region had already had to adapt to the arrival of outsiders and their trade long before the European powers crudely divided up the African continent in a series of agreements from which Africans themselves were excluded. These treaties were often dangerously vague, and the details of this partition had to be worked out over the next 10 to 20 years, with further adjustments after the First World War. The map of the partition of Africa was not finalised until the 1920s.

The region of the Upper Zambezi had been divided in a series of agreements involving Germany, Britain, Portugal and King Leopold of the Congo Free State. The agreement between Portugal and Britain in 1891 purported to draw a frontier between their respective spheres of influence and the line was drawn down the centre of the Zambezi from its source to the boundaries of the Barotse kingdom. So far so good, but no one knew for certain what the boundaries of the Barotse kingdom were, especially as the Barotse king mounted a major campaign in 1892 to make the Lunda and Lovale of the upper river pay tribute. Significantly, this was *after* the agreement with Portugal had been signed. So the border between Portuguese and British spheres continued to be disputed, and caught up in the dispute was the control over the Zambezi river itself.

Eventually, in 1903, the question was referred to the arbitration of the king of Italy. His judgement, delivered the following year, makes interesting reading. He judged that, in determining the extent of an African ruler's sovereignty, a distinction had to be made between areas ruled by the king and regions from which he merely took tribute. The king of Italy decided that the boundaries of the kingdom ruled by Lewanika did not include most of the upper reaches of the river, and, as the Portuguese had been active in this part of the upper Zambezi, his boundary award gave to Angola the large square extension that became the province of Moxico, which included a 200-mile stretch of the river.[13]

The Portuguese had already tried to occupy the Moxico area, and in 1894 it had been decided to establish a penal colony there. At that time, the Portuguese thought this was the best way to found a European settlement, and an expedition was sent to build a fort which would form some kind of nucleus around which a colonial presence could be made. Ricardo Roque describes what happened:

> According to the captain and colonial governor, the expedition of occupation included banished people transformed into soldiers (around seventy two), many more carriers (around one thousand) and a further collection of mules, ox-carts, food supplies, textiles (as gifts to the natives), and some guns. But during the journey, his collective chronically fell apart. The soldiers either died or ran away; native carriers frequently disappeared into the jungle, sometimes

under the influence of indigenous leaders. All defectors pilfered the expedition supplies. Oxen died of disease.[14]

The penal colony attracted criminals, drifters, bush traders and every kind of lawless element. In 1902, the whole area flared up in a rebellion which spread across the central plateau of Angola and became known as the Bailundu War. Eventually the Portuguese regained some sort of control, and in 1904 the penal colony was discontinued. In that year, when the Italian arbitration finally awarded this stretch of the Zambezi to Portugal, "the state administration was practically absent, no roads, or bridges were constructed, [and] no credible maps of the region were available". According to Ricardo Roque, "Portuguese Moxico during the times of occupation was more an international convention than a concrete reality, for the border was only a passage to some lands that British indirect rule also left carelessly administered."[15]

The new frontier had not only chopped the upper reaches of the Zambezi river into three sections (because the source of the river near Kalene Hill was located in Northern Rhodesia), it had also split up the various ethnic groups, Lunda, Lovale/Lwena, Cokwe and Luchazi. As the frontier had no real existence, there was a great deal of movement of people backwards and forwards, and, when the Portuguese began to organise a forced-labour regime, refugees from Moxico entered Northern Rhodesia in considerable numbers.

From this time, the Lovale and the Lunda were divided between the Congo Free State, Northern Rhodesia and Angola. When the Portuguese and British colonial authorities established administrative districts covering the Upper Zambezi (in British Northern Rhodesia, these were the districts of Balovale and Mwinilunga) in the early twentieth century, another system of overrule—taking tribute in the form of tax and labour services—was established where once the Lunda empire had held sway. The new rulers brought with them their languages, which were gradually imposed as the lingua franca over a wide area, just as the conquering Makololo had done 70 years earlier in the Barotse floodplain.

F.S. Arnot had clearly been an admirer of the Lovale/Lwena people, and his positive opinion of them carried over into the colonial period when a skeleton administration was finally established by the Northern Rhodesian government. In 1935, R.S. Hudson, a colonial official, wrote an account of the Upper Zambezi region. The Lovale/Lwena still had no transport links with the outside world. No roads had been built, and its only connection to regions in the south was by navigation on the Zambezi. It took 3 weeks to travel the 400 miles downstream to Livingstone.

As it entered Zambia, after its passage through Angola, the Zambezi cut the district in two, the Lovale/Lwena people predominating on the right bank and the Lunda on the left. Hudson described how villages were sited near the rivers and thick forest often divided the river valleys from each other. Lovale settlements were large and could number 200–300 huts, but Hudson thought that the population was not growing and the Lovale had low birthrates. As a result, other people were moving into the region, notably Cokwe and Luchazi from Angola, as the comparative peace and relatively light hand of the Northern Rhodesian administration attracted migrants from the Portuguese colony where forced labour was increasingly being enforced.

Little in the way of modern technology had penetrated the region. Hudson commented that "the plough has not yet been seen in the district" and "nowhere in the district is water used for irrigation and there are no canals". Instead, villages depended on traditional hoe agriculture, and village sites were frequently moved, less because of problems with the fertility of the soil and more as a way of suppressing epidemic disease.[16]

In 1948, C.M.N. White—another colonial official who wrote about all aspects of the culture of the region and who was, among other things, an expert on ornithology—described the people of the region in terms of distinct 'tribal' identities. This, of course, suited the purposes of colonial administrators who, according to the precepts of indirect rule, liked to identify people as belonging to clear and distinct categories which could then be placed under the rule of an approved chief. White referred to the people who inhabited the upper reaches of the Zambezi as the Balovale 'tribes'—the Lovale/Lwena, Lunda, Cokwe and Luchazi—each of them placed in a neatly defined tribal pigeonhole:

> The conservative, rather unprogressive Lunda with his tradition of hunting: the enterprising irrepressible Lwena, who lived by fishing: the often primitive argumentatively stubborn and very industrious Luchazi: and the self-confident Chokwe with his mixed background of highway robbery and trading, and today often with his touch of Portuguese culture—and all with their own distinct languages.

The Lunda speakers specialised in making canoes and pre-ferred smaller villages where, they claimed, there was less likeli-hood of quarrels and social conflict. The Lwena/Lovale, on the other hand, had a reputation as skilled fishermen, as befitted those whose deep history had been lived along the great river, and dried fish was for them an important marketable product. They were adept at fishing with a bow, spearing the fish with their arrows from a distance with the needle-sharp points.

When White was writing, the rituals of Lunda kingship were already receding in people's memories, and objects which had at one time played an important part in upholding royal power were now preserved largely as family heirlooms.

> Reference has been made from time to time above to royal insignia: the bead coronet used by Lunda chiefs, the beheading knife, to which may be added the ngoma yamukupelo of the Lovale—a drum

carried slung round the neck with a skin at either end and beaten with both hands. No mention, however, would be complete without reference to the *lukano* or crowning bracelet of the Lunda-Lovale chiefs. This is composed of human genitalia. It is kept in a small house along with the other royal emblems and guarded by an old man. It is produced on the day of formally installing the new chief and slipped over his hand and wrist. In theory each new chief should add a new link to the *lukano* on his accession.[17]

Balovale in the colonial era

During the colonial era, Balovale was the name given to the principal town of the Balovale district. It was built on rising ground on the right bank of the Zambezi and was one of the remotest administrative stations in colonial Africa. It could only be reached by river from Mongu, the principal administrative centre in the Barotse floodplain which itself was 200 miles from the former colonial capital in Livingstone. Boats took 15 days travelling up the river and, according to Margaret Beet writing after the Second World War, mail arrived carried by a runner over the last 100 miles. There was an airstrip, built in 1935, but planes were a rarity and did not provide any regular transport service.

Remote as it was, Balovale was nevertheless the point from which the Pax Britannica spread throughout the upper river region. The area had seen the rivalries of Lunda and Lovale, which towards the end of the nineteenth century had become increasingly violent, while the Lozi king continued to assert his paramountcy in the face of obvious hostility from the population who claimed never to have been under Lozi rule. Historians often comment on how remarkable it was that, at the height of the British empire, India was ruled by only 2,000 British civil servants. Just as remarkable in its small way, the Balovale district—which until the mid-1890s was the scene of regular slave raids and endemic warfare—was now administered peacefully by a group of four European officials, including the doctor. It was at Balovale that, from the early 1930s, the District Commissioner had his offices—known inevitably as the Boma—and there also was a hospital and leper colony under the supervision of a European doctor.

In 1935, Dr A.J. Board, newly arrived from Britain, filled the post of medical officer. For 2 years he recorded the events in the town and the surrounding area in letters to his family, providing a vivid picture of life in the Upper Zambezi region during the heyday of colonial rule.[18] In April 1935, he travelled from Livingstone up the river to Balovale by boat, a mode of travel which had scarcely changed since the nineteenth century: "[Travel] is by canoe the whole way and takes about 5 weeks" (28 April 1935). Arriving at Sesheke, he wrote,

> I have just seen the first white man for four days—quite a thrill! Have been camping on the river bank, eating, sleeping and bathing out of doors ... Stayed with the Provincial Commissioner here last night—visited a wonderful mission hospital here run by a Swiss nurse ... The most difficult part of the trip is over—we have been struggling through rapids and swamps up to now, but shall soon be keeping to the river ... everywhere you call, you are inundated with patients directly they realize you are a doctor. There's room for thousands of medicos here!

At Mongu:

> This is the capital of Barotseland and quite a large town for this country—about 20 Europeans here—tennis courts and golf course (made by prisoners from the jail) ... The journey is becoming increasingly difficult owing to the floods dropping rapidly and cutting off our short cuts across flooded fields. We made our own bread on the river, cut our own hair, make our own butter, buy eggs from the villages where available, for salt. [2 June 1935]

This was Barotseland halfway through the colonial period, little changed since the nineteenth century. Ten days later at the Plymouth Brothers mission at Chitokoloki, Board wrote:

It's about 600 miles from Livingstone and from the nearest shop—
there are no shops at Mongu. Goods take over two months by river
from Livingstone—mail from 20 days upwards, according to the state
of the river ... the barge has a canopy of reed matting and propelled
by eighteen paddles, with a big chief (Induna) shouting encourage-
ment or abuse practically the whole time. It was tremendously hard
going against the flood, and periodically the crew had to get out and
tow us through the most difficult spots up to their waists in water,
but terrifically cheerful ... At other places owing to the rapids, we had
to unload completely and all the goods were carried over land (at one
point for 3 miles). Then the paddlers had to go back and tow the
barge through the rapids. After paddling through terrific heat at
about 30 strokes a minute for 8 hours, we would select a camp, and
they would carry the camp equipment ashore, fetch firewood and put
up a tent, finally they would settle down to cook their own food,
squatting round the fire, looking most picturesque, chattering, singing and dancing until about midnight. [13 June 1935]

The British South Africa Company had handed the colony
over to the Colonial Office in 1923, and the colonial presence in
Balovale was just beginning to take some sort of shape. The day
after Dr Board arrived,

the first aeroplane to land at our new aerodrome arrived with the
auditor ... I have got the lepers at work on the garden (paid for out
of the Balovale Occupation Scheme for lepers). I have a glorious
house on the side of a large wooded hill overlooking a bend in the
river, which is a quarter of a mile wide here ... In addition to the
cook I have two waiter boys, one of whom does the laundry excel-
lently, one garden boy, one water boy who draws the water from the
river and also waters the garden, also a piccaniny for taking messages
and as a ball boy for tennis. [21 June 1935]

The hospital was

just as beautifully situated as the house, but on the hill top. One
brick building with my office—dispensary—operating theatre—drug

store. The patients live in small huts to accommodate two—they won't even sleep on beds, as they are afraid of spirits coming in through the windows. The leper compound is about 400 yards away. The patients bring all their relations to hospital, and also any poultry they have—quite a holiday for them. I have five orderlies all very smart in khaki with a red cross on their chests and they wear fezzes, also a head orderly who ... typed my numerous returns, keeps the hospital records and gives anaesthetics ... The hospital is very popular with the natives here, and I get the most extraordinary cases, terrible burns, due to them smoking native tobacco round the fire, and then getting doped and falling in. I have at least twelve cases which would never have survived the shock at home—literally charred to the bone.

In spite of the arrival of the first aircraft, the mail continued to be brought by land. "Our postman wears a red fez with a red tassle and red uniform. He only comes once a week [and] carries the letters all the way from Mongu and it takes him five days, walking all day long."

The handful of Europeans were just beginning to make Balovale a town to their liking. "We are busy building two roads at the moment but are rather short of prisoners" (21 June 1935). When dirt roads were made, they became overgrown almost as soon as they were cleared. Dr Board somehow acquired a 5-year-old motorbike, but

there is no such thing as a road with a good surface—enormous potholes scattered everywhere where the trees have been removed to make it feaible to get through at all—then you have to leave the 'road' which is of such soft loose sand that you can't get out of bottom gear.

Much of the time Dr Board used an ordinary bicycle, accompanied by a "cycle boy [who] runs behind your bike, and when the sand gets [too] bad to ride or the road runs up hill, assists by pushing. If too bad to ride, he wheels the bike till matters improve" (5 May 1936).

BALOVALE AND THE UPPER ZAMBEZI

No British colonial society could exist without its sports, and in October 1936 Board wrote:

> I am trying to make a golf course, but the trouble is to clear the country sufficiently—it will mean pulling down dozens of enormous trees (60 footers) ... As far as the greens are concerned, we use sand greens, which are very accurate if kept well watered. [15 October 1935]

Dr Board also wrote about introducing football into the area:

> Just come back from the store, where we've been playing 'soccer'—bought a soccer ball recently and the game has caught on very rapidly amongst the black element here. The finer points are still however to be taught and at present the object of every nigger seems to be [to] try to kick the ball hard at one of the others and try to lay him out, thereby causing shrieks of laughter from the rest—the high spots of the game are sending fast shots into the crowd on the store verandah and seeing them disperse in all directions. [16 July 1936]

> Football is still very popular though with increasing enthusiasm there is usually a big queue of casualties to see me at the hospital the morning after. [23 July 1936]

The ever present river dominated the lives of Africans and Europeans. In 1935, Balovale was terrorised by crocodiles. On 4 December, Dr Board described a visit to Chavuma near the border with Angola:

> I didn't like the trip across the river by canoe as there have been several natives drowned there this year, and one of the missionaries. The currents are very bad at this spot, and it's jolly difficult to balance properly in the shallow native canoes. The other snag here is the crocs'—although it is practically an unheard of thing elsewhere, they attack canoes in this part of the river, sometimes snatching the occupants out of their canoe, and at other times capsizing the canoe first and grabbing their victim ... I had quite a job persuading my boys to come to Chavuma, as the reputation of the Chavuma crocs is a by word—dozens are taken every year.

Two months later he told his family, "the old Chavuma 'croc' is still busy, and has disposed of six natives during the past month. I'm afraid your howitzer idea won't work, as he never shows his nose above water and we shouldn't know where to fire."

What is clear from these letters is that, following the tenets of indirect rule, relatively little pressure was being exerted to change the traditional way of life of the local population. There were no motorcars, and very few motorboats operated on the river (in the end, Dr Board built his own). During the annual floods it was possible to travel all over the countryside by canoe. There were no white farmers in the region, and agriculture was carried on in traditional ways in traditional villages. Famine, in which some died of starvation, was common at the end of the season before new crops could be harvested. Then the hospital became in effect a relief point where food could be obtained for the patients and their families, while the lepers in their village not only were fed by the government but tilled their own gardens and were relatively comfortably off.

Balovale was the only government administrative centre, but there were two missions: Chavuma upstream and Chitokoloki downstream towards Mongu. Newspapers that eventually arrived were weeks old, and the outside world intruded little. However, one rumour caused a certain amount of local alarm. In 1935–6, there were persistent stories that the colony might be handed over to Germany after Hitler demanded that the former German colonies be returned. This seemed to prompt loud expressions of loyalty to Britain from the local population.

Soon after he arrived, Dr Board was made aware of the growing tension resulting from the fact that the region was nominally part of the Barotse kingdom, something which the local Lunda and Lovale/Lwena strongly resented. His letters add an interesting footnote to the history of the affair.

BALOVALE AND THE UPPER ZAMBEZI

Had the 'Prince of Wales' of Barotseland and his wife to see me this morning. He is the son of the Paramount Chief (Yeta III) of Mongu—speaks English well and is quite a rogue—hopelessly in debt and terribly unpopular, but just the type who would impress a visitor—can talk on any subject, is apparently an idealist—theoretically a Christian but actually I am afraid a waster. His father was glad to get rid of him and sent him up here out of the way. His wife is a very pleasant creature—came for treatment. There is a great deal of trouble locally between the Prince, and the chief Shinde ... The natives consider this territory is not under Yeta's regime and hence resent his son being planted here. Actually the government supported Yeta's caim and Yeta sent his son here to consolidate it. [17 July 1935]

In October, Dr Board returned to the issue:

Had chief Shinde in to-day for a little treatment, but I think the real motive was a chat. He is a nice old thing, but is being rather badly treated by the Barotse here since the advent of Kufuna [Yeta's heir], who incidentally has no right here, as we are not in Barotseland actually. The ground here north of the Kabompo and East of the Zambezi being Crown Land although a native reserve. Yeta has however been trying to squeeze in and the sending of his son here is just one more step in his attempt to squeeze out Shinde. Hazell [the District Commissioner] is however very keen on clearing up the situation, and I think eventually Shinde will get a square deal. It has all been happening so gradually that it is only recently the 'PC' [Provincial Commissioner] has become alive as to what the Barotse are up to. [21 October 1935]

In November, he mentions having breakfast with "Superior Chief Kafuna Daniel Yeta" (11 November 1935).

Dr Board saw a lot of Shinde, the senior Lunda authority, descended from the Shinte who had so impressed Livingstone. He reflected on Shinde's paternalist rule. His son, known incongruously by the name of Peter Dawson, had worked in Bulawayo and on his return built a dam to irrigate his garden.

Peter Dawson re-named himself after a trip to Bulawayo, where he was a hotel porter for some years. He returned here to help his father Shinde in his fight to retain his country against the peaceful penetration of the Barotse. The Paramount chief sent his son here to set up a court of appeal, and to 'help' the people, but it has been the thin edge of the wedge, as the Barotse have no right to this country and are very much disliked by the Baluena [Lovale] and Balunda. At long last the Government have made a big effort to clarify the position. Shinde has hitherto ruined his chances by always contriving to be drunk when called in to the Boma but his son (Peter Dawson) who is well educated for a Lunda has helped considerably. [26 March 1936]

Then in June the situation came unexpectedly to a head.

It appears the Nawinda khotla (Barotse) had sent for chief Shinde and his son (Peter Dawson). In the khotla the Barotse indunas assaulted Dawson and there was a free fight. Afterwards Shinde, who left separately from his son, was overtaken by Kufuna and assaulted. Kufuna attacked him with a pocket knife, saying he would kill him—he was pulled off by some of his friends and then said he wouldn't kill him as he was an old man but that if he could find his son (Dawson) he would kill him. Shinde fled into the bush to hide and a messenger was sent here to report the two incidents ... the messenger went to all the neighbouring villages and sent various messages to the local chiefs saying there would be a war against Barotze on Monday.

Shinde apparently calmed everyone down, "and the upshot of the whole matter is that Kufuna is being taken to Mongu this week to stand his trial by the Provincial Commissioner". Dr Board finishes by saying there is likely to be some bloodshed "unless the Paramount chief is properly kept in his place" (8 June 1936).

In the end, the British decided in 1941 to remove the whole area from Barotse jurisdiction: in Lozi eyes, the final excision of territory from their historic kingdom.

BALOVALE AND THE UPPER ZAMBEZI

In 1966, two years after Zambia became independent, Balovale was renamed 'Zambezi', as the name Balovale was thought to exacerbate tensions between the Lovale and the Lunda. A footbridge bridge was built across the Zambezi, and a largely Lunda township grew up on the left bank. And here history comes full circle. As mentioned in Chapter 2, the Dominican priest, João dos Santos, describing the Zambezi in his book published in 1609, wrote, "this river is called Zambesi because upon issuing from the lake it runs through a large cafre town so called, and from this the river takes the same name as the town".

12

WAR AND THE CAHORA BASSA DAM[1]

The Zambezi valley had frequently been a battleground where
warring kingdoms clashed and petty warlords established their
domains with the help of their slave armies. For a brief period
from 1900 to 1960, the very short period of colonial control, the
upper and middle reaches of the river had enjoyed a period of
peace, and the lower river the same from 1920. Then, from about
1970, the Zambezi valley once again became a theatre of warfare,
which continued until 2002.

The Cahora Bassa dam

In 1964, Frelimo, the party pressing for independence for
Mozambique, initiated an armed struggle. At first, the Zambezi
region was not affected, and Frelimo won little support among
the plantation workers of the lower river. All the fighting took
place in the north of the country. However, influenced by the
changing political situation brought about by the nationalist
campaign, plans were already being discussed for a radical transformation of the river valley in its middle reaches. In 1953, the

Portuguese had published a development plan which envisaged considerable investment in the country's infrastructure, with new railways planned that would link the Mozambique ports to Rhodesia and Nyasaland. Projects also included a Limpopo barrage to provide irrigation for a large *colonato* (agricultural settlement). Among the projects envisaged was a dam on the Zambezi. Building such a dam was a hugely ambitious idea presenting unprecedented engineering challenges as well as vast cost beyond the scope of Portugal's economy to finance. However, the scheme was given credibility by the decision of Mozambique's neighbour, the Central African Federation, to go ahead with the Kariba dam in 1956.

It is worth recalling that Portugal, as well as Spain, had a lot of expertise in dam and hydroelectric projects, as the Salazar and Franco regimes had built a number of such schemes in the mountains of the Iberian peninsula. As a result, Portugal had a whole cadre of professional engineers, used to working on hydroelectricity projects, on whom it could draw. Any dam that was built was going to be a Portuguese dam. In the 1950s, few people in the world seriously contested the importance of giant engineering projects as the keys to development. Moreover, the confidence that man's control of nature was somehow an inherently desirable thing had few critics.

Portugal now set up an organisation to investigate the possibility of building a dam at Cahora Bassa. Geological surveys were undertaken, and the purpose of the dam and its role in the future of Mozambique was elaborated upon. It was to be the centrepiece of ambitious plans to develop irrigated agriculture in the Tete district, to exploit the mineral resources of the area, to create a transport corridor along the middle river and to provide Mozambique more widely with cheap electricity. However, plans for the dam moved very slowly. The preliminary reports were only completed in 1961 and published in 1966. The Portuguese

Council of Ministers only backed the proposal in 1967 when Salazar was finally won over to support it.

For all the talk about the economic development that would follow its construction, from the start the dam was—in part at least—a political project. It was seen as a statement of Portugal's commitment to modern economic development which would give substance to Portugal's often-repeated claims that it had a civilising mission in Africa. By 1967, the dam had also assumed an importance in the context of the independence struggle that had broken out in Mozambique and Angola. The dam was a highly public statement of Portugal's determination to stay in Africa.

However, politics would not pay for the dam, and over the next 2 to 3 years finance was sought in a complex series of negotiations which involved giant multinational companies, notably the Anglo-American Corporation of South Africa. Private financing, however, had to be backed by state guarantees and eventually a package of loans and guarantees was put together. A consortium, Zamco, won the tendering and undertook the construction of the dam.

Why so many major companies, backed by their governments, agreed to build the dam in the middle of the independence war, when it was clear to most observers that sooner rather than later Mozambique would become independent, remains a mystery. As with so many great projects that ultimately result in major changes to the course of history, there was no one single moment when key decisions were made. The major participants were, to some extent, swept along by a tide of events to which no single one of them was able to call a halt. The fact that Zamco involved Germany, South Africa, France, Italy and Portugal as major participants also complicated decision-making, as political considerations and international relations meant that calculations of a purely commercial or financial nature could not come effectively into play.

The economic case for financing the dam, in the end, came to rest on the sale of its electricity to South Africa, and the dam was built entirely on this assumption, with the plans for economic development in Mozambique being quietly shelved.

The dam was designed by the Portuguese company Hydro-Technica Portuguesa. It was a novel design, showing how far dam design had moved on since Kariba. For instance, at a height of 171 metres the dam was much higher than Kariba (thus having far larger generating capacity), and the dam wall only half as thick. Its construction involved diverting the flow of the Zambezi through two tunnels carved through the mountains to enable the coffer dams to be constructed. The turbine chambers that were constructed on the south bank were so vast that it was estimated that St Paul's cathedral could fit twice over inside them. The dam had four spillways for the river, each able to take the equivalent of the flow of the Danube. The Kariba dam suffered from the hollowing out of the riverbed by the water release, so Cahora Bassa was designed for the water from the dam to be propelled 600 metres downstream.

The construction of the dam began in 1969 and was built to a tight schedule, as the financiers wanted the electricity to come on stream at the earliest possible date. This led to intense pressure being put on contractors and the workforce, and there is plenty of evidence of shortcuts being taken on safety and the living conditions of African workers. There were a number of accidents as heavy equipment slid off roads and rockfalls caused numerous casualties. Keith Middlemas, in his book on the dam which was published in 1975, claimed blandly that all workers were volunteers and that they were being paid and treated better than they would be in other industries. However, the notion of volunteering has to be understood in the context of a colonial system which was able to put all kinds of pressures on people to enter the labour market. Moreover, once he arrived at the dam, no worker was free to leave no matter what the conditions in which he found he had to work.

Meanwhile, the Portuguese also went ahead with a road bridge to replace the ferry crossing at Tete. However, the bridge was a suspension bridge and was not designed to take the sort of heavy traffic needed for the Cahora Bassa dam. It was only completed in 1973, shortly before the dam itself. This bridge provided for the first time a key link in the main road from Zimbabwe to Malawi.

To house the workforce constructing the dam, a large town was built at Songo, the local population being removed to make space for engineering operations. Songo also became the site of one of the converter stations. From at least 1970, the region where the dam was being constructed became a war zone. The dam site was protected by barbed wire and minefields, and the workers' freedom of movement was severely curtailed. However, the access roads to and from the dam were vulnerable. Frelimo mounted an international 'Dam Busters' campaign, ostensibly to prevent the dam from being built, but this had relatively little success except for one Swedish company that withdrew from the project. The dam was completed on time in December 1974.

In the case of the Kariba dam, some attempt had been made to study the ecological impact and prepare for the evacuation of people and animals from the flooding. In the case of Cahora Bassa, studies were only undertaken in 1973, and any implementation of well-thought-out policies was made virtually impossible by the warfare which had engulfed the Tete region.

When completed, the Cahora Bassa dam was the fifth largest, in terms of generating capacity, of any hydroelectric project in the world. The lake, when filled, was 250 kilometres long and covered 2,700 square kilometres of the valley, half the area of Lake Kariba. Although built as a great symbol of Portugal's colonial might, once it was eventually completed, it was handed over to newly independent Mozambique, which was run by the

Frelimo government that had fought so hard to prevent the dam from being built.

The two Zambezi dams were designed at approximately the same time—and both had room for the expansion of generating capacity in the future—though in the 1950s no one had yet heard of climate change! The dams had turned large sections of the valley into vast lakes, stilling the flow of the river and removing the seasonal rhythms of low water and flood along the whole middle and lower reaches of the Zambezi, rhythms which had marked its history for thousands of years. The longer-term effects of the dams on the ecology of the valley soon became apparent. There were no locks for the passage of boats, and the dams interfered with the natural fish stocks, as there were no fish ladders of any kind to allow the migration of fish.

The Rhodesians introduced new fish into Lake Kariba, notably the kapenta, and some of these apparently escaped through the slipways and turbines to create a population in the Cahora Bassa lake as well. As a result, a large fishery developed and in 2003 the catch was alleged to be as much as 10,000 tons. There were also strange anomalies. Eels apparently found ways of moving up the river past the dams in order to reach breeding grounds, and it appears that some bull sharks, which can live in fresh water, were trapped upriver by the Cahora Bassa dam and formed an inland, freshwater shark population.

Unlike Lake Kariba, which had filled relatively slowly over a period of four years, the lake behind the Cahora Bassa dam filled in only four months because the dam authorities virtually closed down the flow of the river through the spillways. Then, when the April floods poured down from upriver, the sluices were opened and a vast flood swept through the lower reaches of the valley. It appears there was no body with the authority or vision to regulate the way that Hidroeléctrica de Cahora Bassa (HCB) managed the dam and its impact on the lower reaches of the river.

WAR AND THE CAHORA BASSA DAM

The main effect of the dam was to replace the well-understood pattern of flood and low water with a highly unpredictable regime, in which flooding might occur at any time that the HCB decided to release water, making life almost impossible for the downriver agricultural communities. Meanwhile, the ending of the annual flooding of the delta meant that lakes and rivers of that vast wetland began to dry up, and the strong flows of fresh water that held back the invasion of the sea were interrupted. Over the decades since the building of the dams, the irregular floods have destroyed much of the ecosystem of the lower valley, including the fish and bird life, which had depended on the natural cycle of the annual rise and fall of the river.

What is so significant is that the builders of the dam—and, since independence, the Frelimo government—have shown little knowledge of, or concern for, the ecological consequences of building a high dam. This is not just the result of ignorance but of the peculiar conditions under which the Cahora Bassa dam operated. It was completed in December 1974, just as Portugal was handing over the country to Frelimo. However, although Portugal gave Mozambique its independence, it retained possession of the dam and HCB continued to manage it.

After independence, Portugal continued to own 82 per cent of the dam and Mozambique 18 per cent. According to the agreements reached with South Africa, the electricity generated by the dam had to be sold at a very low price, and the management of the huge debt incurred meant that electricity had to be sold to South Africa in as large a quantity as possible. It was not until 2007 that Portugal finally passed the dam back to Mozambique control (receiving 750 million Euros and retaining a 15 per cent stake) and South Africa agreed to increase the amount it paid for the dam's electricity. Even so, South Africa's demands continue to be the prime consideration in the management of the dam. The welfare of the ecology of the lower river and the people who live in the region were largely ignored. And virtually none of the electricity generated by the dam went to the downriver communities.

From about 2014, the Zambezi began to feel the effects of global warming. Rainfall declined, flows of the river and its feeder streams diminished and the levels of Lakes Kariba and Cahora Bassa fell. In 2015–16, the level of the lake dropped 5 metres, and it remained only 31 per cent full. This not only effected the amount of electricity that could be produced but drastically reduced the downstream flow of the river.

The Mozambique war of independence

The Portuguese were aware of the problems that had arisen with relocating the Tonga population from the valley in advance of the flooding of Lake Kariba. They had drawn up plans for a gradual relocation of the valley population to new villages and farms which would have been prepared in advance. However, the spread of guerrilla activity in the Tete region to the north and south of the river meant that relocation for the valley population was caught up with a wider movement of the whole rural population into fortified villages (*aldeamentos*) carried out by the military. This mass relocation took place rapidly and with little advance preparation, and, once settled into the *aldeamentos*, the population was in fact imprisoned in fortified settlements surrounded by barbed wire and mines. Wars always involve huge restrictions on the liberty of ordinary people and, as guerrillas always try to hide among the local population, it is impossible to insulate ordinary civilians from the full effects of fighting. Civilians are invariably caught up in the conflict, and loss of liberty is probably the least of the consequences they have to face.

As the war got closer to the river and the Frelimo fighters hid themselves among the civilian population, the latter were thrust into the frontline of the struggle. Unable to disentangle Frelimo fighters from innocent villagers, if indeed such a distinction was made at all, the Portuguese took their counterinsurgency to the villages and on 16 December 1972, an incident took place that came to symbolise the brutality of the war and, in retrospect, can be seen as one of the events that precipitated the final collapse of the Portuguese colonial regime.

Portugal had been 'Africanising' its forces, and in May of that year a commando unit was sent to 'clean up' the village settlements around Wiriyamu near the confluence of the Zambezi and the Luenha, not far from the site of Massangano where the Zambezi Wars had been fought in the previous century. The result was a massacre that led to the deaths of 385 men and women. This incident was not the only one of its kind but acquired a unique importance because the massacre was made known to the global public by a Catholic priest just as the prime minister of Portugal, Marcello Caetano, was visiting Britain. It was made worse by the fact that Portugal tried, without any success, to deny that it had ever happened. The full details of the incident had to wait until 2016, when Mustafah Dhada published his book *The Portuguese Massacre of Wiriyamu in Colonial Mozambique, 1964–2013*.

War in Rhodesia

Soon after Ian Smith declared Rhodesia's independence from Britain in November 1965, a desultory guerrilla war began. The Zambezi valley became an infiltration route for guerrillas entering Rhodesia from the north, but the valley and escarpment—which had been left largely untouched by colonial rule—was sparsely populated and at first proved difficult for guerrillas to penetrate. However, it became the policy of the guerrillas to seek support among the population of the valley and the escarpment, and they soon found allies among the spirit mediums. Colonial rule had turned local chiefs into the agents of the government, and they had increasingly lost influence to the spirit mediums that had kept themselves aloof from the government and from all aspects of the modern world that were threatening to undermine traditional values. By focussing on the restoration of land lost to white settlers, the guerrillas were able to ally themselves with the mediums and the traditional values that they represented. Once these influential traditional authorities were on their side, the guerrillas were able to move freely in the valley, and they received very good intelligence from the village communities. As David Lan wrote, "everywhere and in all circumstances peasants and guerrillas felt themselves in the presence and under the protection of their ancestors."[2]

The Rhodesian security forces patrolled the river and carried out search-and-destroy operations in the dense bush, eventually building a road through the valley. Rhodesian forces even began to help the Portuguese protect their Zambezi defence line. However, following the April 1974 revolution in Portugal, the war in Mozambique came to an end and Portuguese forces were withdrawn. This opened new opportunities for guerrillas to infiltrate Rhodesia using the now-extended frontier between newly independent Mozambique and Rhodesia's eastern highlands. In retaliation, the Rhodesian forces carried out missions deep inside Mozambique, in effect continuing the war which Frelimo had hoped would end when the Portuguese withdrew.

Higher up the Zambezi, the mouth of the Chobe river where the frontiers of four countries met became a crucial crossing point for Africans fleeing South Africa and for fighters heading in the other direction. There was a narrow passage which linked Botswana with its northern neighbour, Zambia, through which refugees could cross.

The white regime in Rhodesia finally came to an end with a negotiated settlement in 1980, and ZANU took power in the country. However, this did not bring peace, for the next stage of warfare had already begun.

Renamo and civil war in Mozambique

Frelimo had not hesitated to take its revenge on those who had opposed it during the war of liberation. After it had taken power in 1975, rival nationalist leaders were killed, opposition figures were sent to concentration camps and soldiers who had fought for the Portuguese—notably units of the elite *flechas*—took refuge in Rhodesia and started to launch attacks across the border in the name of a movement which went under the initials of MNR (Mozambique National Resistance). When Rhodesia became independent in 1980, these soldiers moved to South Africa and were organised as a guerrilla army by the South African military. By 1981, they were launching attacks on Mozambique government installations and the attacks spread rapidly in the country south of the Zambezi and along the river.

The South African strategic plan for Renamo (as MNR was now called) was to destabilise the country and discredit Frelimo in every way it could so that a weakened Mozambique would become totally dependent on South Africa and cease to be a base for nationalists seeking to overthrow the apartheid regime. Once firmly established, however, Renamo acquired a dynamic of its own and began to take possession of large tracts of the country.

The tactics pursued by Renamo involved repeated attacks on the easy targets of the Lower Zambezi. One of the earliest was to sabotage the Lower Zambezi Bridge by rigging explosives to bring down one of the sections. Then it was the turn of the fixed installations of the sugar and tea plantations. Attacked and plundered, the managers decamped and the working population fled. The plantation sector was effectively ruined. The population of the valley was particularly affected. Frelimo forces, which had operated successfully against the Portuguese, were quite unable in their turn to control the Renamo guerrillas who operated at will throughout the valley. In particular, the guerrillas were targeting the population concentrations in the *aldeamentos* and the transport corridor between Zimbabwe and Malawi, which used the newly completed bridge at Tete.

The war continued throughout the 1980s. Troops from Zimbabwe were invited to defend the railway to Beira and the Tete corridor and the installations of the Cahora Bassa dam were also protected, though many of the electricity pylons were damaged (as many as 1895 being totally destroyed) cutting off the flow of electricity to South Africa, which was not fully restored until 1997.

After 1986, the war intensified as Renamo took over and effectively controlled large sections of the country and other armed bands that were only loosely connected with Renamo, took advantage of the disorder to plunder what was left, kidnap women and recruit boys as child soldiers. The Zambezi region reverted to the state it had been in when the slave-trading warlords had dominated most of the middle river from their stockades in the nineteenth century. In many respects, Renamo acted in the same way as the old Zambezi warlords, in particular in their habit of capturing civilians, who were forced to work for them or act as sexual slaves, and in their demanding food supplies as a form of tribute.

In 1989, the war in Zambezia province took an unexpected turn. A young man named Manuel António, who was a traditional healer, began to attract followers to his spiritual army. Manuel António declared that he had risen from the dead (having died earlier in his life from measles). His followers received medicine, in the form of ashes that were rubbed into incisions made with a razor, which made them immune to bullets. This medicine was called Naparama, which was also the name assumed by those who had received the medicine. Armed only with traditional weapons—spears, machetes and so on—the Naparama army successfully expelled Renamo forces from large areas of the province during the year 1990.

In 1991, the journalist Jeremy Harding travelled to Zambezia province to meet Manuel António and recorded what António was told about his origin. The period after he had risen from the grave

> had been followed by a long sojourn with wild beasts and spirits on a mountain in Nampula province, at the end of which Manuel António had received divine instruction to go down to the plain and perform Christ's work in Mozambique. The task in hand was a holy war against Renamo and the crucial battle ground would be Zambezia.

Frelimo was uncertain how to react to Naparama: "Had Manuel António emerged from his seclusion a decade earlier, they would have driven him straight back into the bush, for he was a paragon of *obscurantismo*. Now they hailed this resurrected prophet as a 'person of influence'."

Eventually Harding ran Manuel António to earth. "Manuel António's house was long and narrow, ten disciples sat around the porch using their traditional weapons to crack open hairy grey coconuts." A lorry approached loaded with sacks of grain:

> stacked on these ... stood a hundred cases of South African lager. At the top of the heap sat the prophet and a group of followers ... [he was] a small inconspicuous man in battle fatigues and a military beret with a wooden cross fastened to its front. His hands were clasped firmly around a box of Pink Harmony china teaware.

Harding followed him into the house and was able to record some of what followed. "'Listen', said Manuel António, 'the government of Mozambique will not help us. Why not? Ever since I came to the province nothing is left of the bandits [i.e., Renamo].'"

This was the commander of an army speaking; the words of the prophet followed:

> "I was reborn. I stayed six months in the mountain. I am the son of Jesus Christ ... Renamo has many sins in this world. I don't kill anybody, I don't act like a soldier. I capture Renamo and hand them to Frelimo, this is a simple thing ... Besides all this, I treat the sick."

Harding wanted to know if Naparama was still an effective force, to which António replied, "'You journalists, you mustn't play with *naparama*, you must stop asking foolish questions. I can turn into any animal and deal with you if I have to. Your work is to tell Renamo that wherever they go, they are sure to suffer.'"[3]

The story of Manuel António is not just an episode in the long, drawn-out civil war, but a story that belongs to the whole history of the peoples of the Zambezi. Faced with the displays of modern weaponry from white Rhodesians and black Frelimo military forces, the ordinary people of the Zambezi valley had turned to the spirit world of their ancestors for the protection the modern state was unable to provide. The spirit mediums of the Dande region of Southern Rhodesia/Zimbabwe offered this protection, as did Manuel António to the people of the Zambezia province displaced by the war. The spirit mediums had demanded that their followers reject the consumer goods of the modern world, just as Manuel António had told his followers to use only traditional weapons. And these movements find echoes in other quasi-messianic movements in Africa. Manuel António's medicine, which made his followers immune to bullets, recalls similar promises, for example those made to fighters who took on the Germans in the so-called Maji Maji rising in German East Africa in 1905–7. Likewise, Manuel António's narrative of resurrection and his claim that he was the son of Jesus show how Christianity merged with the traditional beliefs, held by so many Africans in the Zambezi valley, that after death their chiefs returned to inhabit the bodies of lions and rule the spirit realm which provided protection to the living.

These movements linked to spirit mediums and purveyors of traditional medicine may have been allies of the African nationalist guerrillas of ZANU and the military of Frelimo, but they were uneasy allies. As Stephen Emerson put it,

> Yes, the movement had provided a huge boost in rolling back the Renamo presence in key areas, but it had done so at the expense of the government's credibility. And many civilians developed faith in Naprama they had lost in FAM troops, as the populace increasingly came to view Naprama, not government troops, as their savior. Moreover the movement had empowered local communities and their sense of independence, thus laying the groundwork for an alternative system of political power outside of Frelimo control.[4]

Manuel António was killed in action in December 1991, and the Naparama army evaporated but the civil war in Mozambique finally came to an end with the Peace Accord signed in 1992.

"History may not repeat itself but it often rhymes," as Mark Twain probably did not say, but those who like to find strange coincidences in history that may or may not have meaning, might recall that in 1638, when social revolt broke out in southern Portugal against Castilian taxation and Castilian rule, "there were rumours of a mysterious young man, known as *manuelinho*, appearing as leader of the revolt—another manifestation of the messianism that was always liable to appear when the wider population was stirred to political action".[5]

The Angolan civil war

In spite of the 1992 Peace Accord, which brought an end to warfare on the Lower Zambezi, war on the Upper Zambezi continued. Ever since gaining its independence from Portugal in 1975, Angola had been torn by civil war. The Moxico region where the Zambezi flowed for 200 miles through Angolan territory was a part of the country where, during the war against Portugal, Jonas Savimbi's nationalist movement, UNITA, had been able to operate from bases in Zambia. When civil war followed the departure of the Portuguese in 1975, UNITA remained strong in the eastern parts of the country as well as on the central plateau. Although fighting paused briefly in the early 1990s when the UN negotiated elections to try to resolve the conflict, the civil war reignited in 1994 and raged for another 8 years, fuelled by illegal diamond sales and the interventions of white and black mercenaries. Moxico remained an area that UNITA continued to dominate, but it was there in 2002 that Jonas Savimbi was at last cornered and killed. Along with 21 of his bodyguard, Savimbi died, gun in hand, near the Luvuei river about 80 kilometres from the Zambian border.

Savimbi's death ended 40 years of continuous warfare on the Zambezi. On 4 April 2002, the so-called Luena Memorandum was signed following the Angolan government's unilateral decision to implement a ceasefire. The UNITA generals quickly followed suit. Savimbi was buried in the public cemetery of Luena, the capital of Moxico province, and, after his grave was vandalised, he was reburied in 2019 in a public ceremony.

EPILOGUE

How have the Zambezi river and the people who live along its banks fared in the 20 years since the culmination of the wars that accompanied the end of the colonial era?

While the wars were being fought, a narrative was created and widely disseminated that saw the colonial period as one of exploitation and oppression, with the ordinary African the principal victim of cheap compulsory labour, forced relocations, military violence and the lack of basic facilities in health or schooling. It was assumed that all this would fade into the past when popular, nationalist governments took control. Naturally, these new regimes would remedy the neglect and exploitation of the colonial era, and their prime concern would be the interests of the ordinary African.

Looking at what happened in the seven countries that border the Zambezi river, it is difficult to see that the ordinary villager making a living along the valley has experienced any change for the better (except, of course, for the psychological liberation of not being oppressed by people of a different skin colour and culture). This should be no surprise to a historian, as history has time and again shown that continuity in political culture—and in social and economic practice—has survived even the most radical-seeming revolutions. The Zambezia kingdoms of the past were based on the dominance of a ruling elite who took tribute from the population, monopolised the use of violence and attempted to control external trade. As has already been argued, colonial rule to some extent replicated this pattern, and it is not surprising that the post-colonial regimes should continue this tradition. This is only too clear in the case of Mozambique.

Vail and White in their book *Colonialism and Capitalism in Mozambique* reflect on how the seigneurial relationship of the *prazos* passed into the era of company rule and then into the era when local authority was wielded by Frelimo party cadres. The use of local *régulos* (chiefs) to control the population during Mozambique's colonial period was reintroduced by Frelimo after the 1992 Peace Accord; the old colonial *cartaz* (pass) system was copied with the issue of *guias de marcha* to control population movement; the Portuguese policy of distinguishing between educated urban populations and the so-called *indígenas* (natives) of the rural areas found an echo in the decision to limit full citizenship rights (for example, the election of town councils) to urban areas, leaving rural areas under the control of government-appointed *régulos*. The old Portuguese *aldeamentos*, so oppressive in the anti-colonial narrative, were continued in the policy of moving people into communal villages, in many cases with the same level of violence and lack of consultation. The *assimilado* of the Portuguese era was replicated in the ideal of the scientifically educated, modern Mozambican extolled by Samora Machel.

And the continuities go on. The populations, forcibly relocated when the Cahora Bassa dam was built, have not been compensated. Nor have the tens of thousands of those who live below the dam and whose way of life has been drastically altered by the way the dam's waters are regulated, while the South African segregated township of Songo has continued to be a township dominated by the foreign specialists who maintain the dam. As more and more capital-intensive projects are undertaken (another hangover from colonial times), the works are carried out by highly paid foreigners, with Mozambicans employed only in menial and unskilled work, where they are employed at all. A similar situation exists with the Kariba dam, where the Tonga population displaced by the Kariba lake during the era of the Central African Federation have not received any compensation from the ZANU government or even much benefit from the dam 50 years after its completion.

Moreover, the Frelimo regime in Mozambique acts in many respects like the old colonial regime. Contracts are awarded to associates of the ruling elite; ordinary people are not consulted about so-called development projects, nor are they adequately compensated when they are relocated to enable vast mining operations to go ahead. It was one of the scandals of the colonial regime that so little was done for African education or to provide rural communities with basic services. Today, Mozambique still ranks among the poorest countries in the world, with one of the highest rates of illiteracy and lowest percentages of connectivity to electricity. This is not, of course, to argue, that anyone would want the colonial regime to be restored. If you are going to be exploited by a corrupt government dominated by a small elite, it is without doubt better that this government be made up of people of the same skin colour, who may even speak your language and share some of your cultural assumptions.

However, if the Frelimo regime in so many ways replicates the colonial regime it replaced, the world outside has moved on. Nowhere can the interplay of continuity and change be seen more clearly than in the tortuous process of building the third Zambezi dam.

Mphanda Nkuwa[1]

When the Cahora Bassa dam was being designed, plans were already being laid for a second dam, 60 kilometres downstream, which would make further use of the water released by Cahora Bassa; the electricity produced would also be sold to South Africa. Once the Peace Accord was signed in 1992 and the elections held, these plans were dusted off, and in 2000 firm proposals for a third Zambezi dam were presented to the government. The dam was to be smaller than Cahora Bassa, with a very much smaller reservoir lake. It was to operate in conjunction with water released from the dam upstream. Once again, international finance was sought and the sale of the electricity to South Africa was indicated as the way the loans would be serviced.

But the process was not straightforward. The World Bank was not convinced, and a major campaign was launched both within and outside of Mozambique highlighting the damage which a new dam would cause to the downstream communities and to the ecology of the lower river. These were lessons that had been learned from 25 years of the Cahora Bassa dam being in operation. In response to these objections, it was suggested that the damage wrought by the new dam might be alleviated if the release of water from the dams could replicate the natural cycle of flooding that the Kariba and Cahora Bassa major dams had interrupted.

Supporters of the dam now had to make a case on environmental grounds rather than a crude cost-benefit analysis of the old kind, where no cost was ascribed to environmental damage and very little to compensating displaced people.

Moreover, there was a growing realisation throughout the world that there were major problems with big dams, not least from a series of studies of the effects of the Hoover dam in the United States. Development economists were beginning to look with some scepticism at large dam projects, not least in a comparison of costs between big projects and a raft of smaller schemes that might be rolled out to benefit local communities. At the source of the Zambezi itself, at Kalene Hill, a mission had been established in 1905 with its own hospital. This became the centre of a community, as people moved to the protection the mission offered, but its isolation proved to be a problem. In 2001, a small-scale hydroelectric station was built, funded by missionary societies outside Zambia and built by the North West Zambia Development Trust. This is an example of a different and far less damaging kind of development project.

Nevertheless, the decision was eventually taken to build the Mphanda Nkua dam, with work due to commence in 2024, more than two decades after it was first seriously proposed.

This decision is not surprising, as Frelimo has supported a series of massive projects to exploit coal and natural gas reserves. These, together with the new dam, follow a pattern by which multinational companies extract Mozambique's resources, providing external finance and engineering expertise, with most of the profits being used to service the financing and a percentage only being paid in royalties to the Frelimo government. Compensation for people who lose their homes and livelihoods is seldom adequate and very often not paid at all, and benefits in the form of training, education, local employment and even extra purchasing power in the local economy are negligible.

One of the lessons of Cahora Bassa was that, even had South Africa allowed significant amounts of the power to be distributed to Mozambique, there was no infrastructure of powerlines in place to serve the rest of the country. No provisions have been made to remedy that in the case of Mphanda Nkuwa, and most of the power generated will once again be sold to South Africa. The downstream communities, meanwhile, will bear all the environmental and social costs in their daily lives.

In Zimbabwe, the Tonga—who were moved out of the Gwembe valley when it was flooded by the Kariba dam and who have waited not only for compensation but also for any of the modern developments to improve their lives—have begun to organise. The Binga region south of the Kariba lake has seen Tonga frustrations harnessed by various community organisations—notably the Basilwizi Trust, which was established in 2002—to try to gain some development funding from the Zimbabwe government.

Batoka gorge hydro-electric scheme and other projects

As early as the 1990s, a dam was proposed for the Batoka gorge downstream of the Victoria Falls. This has been strongly opposed, particularly by local people who earn a living from tourism. However, the Zambezi River Authority now proposes to go ahead with the scheme, which would entail the construction of a dam 47 kilometres downstream from the Victoria Falls and flood the gorge up to 650 metres from the Falls. It is expected to take 9 years to complete. Once again, the main consumer of the electricity generated will be South Africa. The Zambezi River Authority now has at least six more so-called run-of-the river schemes proposed, as well as a dam in the Mpata gorge. In addition to these, there are five schemes to divert the waters of the Zambezi to Namibia and South Africa, as well as a large number of schemes to use the waters for irrigated agriculture. One estimate suggests that irrigated agriculture alone would use as much Zambezi water as evaporates from the Kariba and Cahora Bassa lakes.

One reads the optimistic reports of the Zambezi River Authority with a sense of despair. The uncertainties surrounding future rainfall patterns and climate change do not seem to have altered the default assumptions that the waters of the Zambezi can be exploited as an unlimited resource. Although the word 'ecology' frequently appears, no economist has found a way of satisfactorily including ecological and environmental impact into the economic modelling that so blithely recommends water transfer, run-of-the-river hydro projects and irrigated agriculture.

EPILOGUE

Kariba dam rehabilitation

Although the vast reservoir of Lake Kariba had been designed to cope with the fluctuations of the river's floods and dry seasons, these have proved difficult to manage. During the building of the dam, the coffer dams were twice swamped by the annual floods, and in subsequent years heavy flooding—for example, in 2000 and 2008—meant that the dam had to release more water than had been intended in the original designs, and large numbers of people downstream had to be removed to safety.

In 2014, the Zambezi River Authority, which operated the dam, was warned that there were problems with the dam's structure. The most serious of these was the fact that the release of water from the dam had scoured a huge hole in the bed of the river, called a plunge pool, which was estimated to be 300 feet deep. It was feared that any further growth of this cavernous pit would endanger the foundation of the dam and might even lead to its collapse. The repair of the dam was costed at a further 200 million dollars. The plan was to isolate the pool with a coffer dam, pump out the plunge pool and then excavate an extension of it downstream. At the same time, rehabilitation work would be carried out on the spillways and other structures of a dam that was showing its age and even becoming dangerous.

Tourism

The building of the dams has consigned the Zambezi valley's wild remoteness to historical memory. To build the dams, major road systems had to be laid out and airfields constructed. It is difficult to imagine a greater transformation of the river, or a greater reimagining of it as a factor in the history of the region. The flooding of the Gwembe valley ended the isolation of the Zambezi valley. The region now had road access, and townships were built on both sides of the lake. As the lakes grew, they provided opportunities for the lake shores to be developed for tourism. Where once intrepid hunters trekked into the valley followed by porters loaded with their tents, camping gear and hipbaths, modern tourist lodges and houseboats attract the wealthy, who fly in to witness wildlife or fish for the famous Zambezi tiger fish.

There are many objections to large-scale tourism, especially when it is the cause of major building projects or diversion of local resources to serve wealthy internationals. However, in the case of the reservoir lakes, the major construction that now attracts so many tourists was caused not by tourism but by the hydroelectric schemes. Tourism has grown on the back of the dam development. It provides some local employment, mostly of an unskilled or semi-skilled kind, but perhaps its greatest impact has been to persuade uninterested governments to make some gesture towards conserving the regions' wildlife. Without Africa's wild animals, there would be very few tourists. So a range of nature reserves have been laid out, the most famous being the Mana Pools National Park 100 kilometres downstream of Kariba, and the Matusadona National Park near Kariba Town in Zimbabwe.

A prospectus from the travel firm Wild Zambezi gives an idea of how the twenty-first century views a part of Africa that was, until recently, wild and remote. The town of Kariba, originally built for the construction of the dam, is now a tourist resort.

> There are a number of small hotels, lodges, holiday cottages, self-catering facilities and campsites dotted among the hills, bays and shorelines of Kariba town from where views of the lake are stunning. Many people visit Kariba briefly as a stopping off point prior to setting out from one of its four main harbours on boats across the lake either to stay in the safari and fishing camps on the southern shore mainland, in the Matusadona National Park or on the islands, or to

spend a few tranquil days fishing, game-viewing, birding, sunbathing or simply relaxing on board a houseboat. Kariba has lots of these 'floating hotels' of various sizes, shapes and degrees of comfort. They can be hired either on a full-board or self-catering basis and are usually equipped with an efficient and hard-working crew who will do everything to provide you with a holiday of a lifetime. The most popular destination for houseboat holidays out of Kariba is the Matusadona National Park, about 30kms across the lake, where there are islands, tranquil bays and creeks teeming with wildlife against the magnificent backdrop of the Zambezi escarpment mountains. If you are lucky, you can see a variety of large African mammal species, including elephant, buffalo, lion and cheetah and a staggering variety of waterbirds.[2]

From being a forbidding, remote and dangerous frontier river, the Zambezi had been tamed into being a playground for tourists, a transformation without parallel in the millennia of its existence.

Bridge building

Nor is there now any difficulty crossing the Zambezi. Gone are the days when to cross the lower river with a land rover it was necessary to drive to Dona Anna on the northern bank and hire a steam locomotive and a truck to take you across. Three road crossings of the Middle Zambezi were built in colonial times: the Victoria Falls Bridge, opened in 1905; the Chirundu bridge in 1934; and the Kariba dam roadway in 1959. There was no road bridge on the lower river until the 1973 Tete bridge was constructed in the last year of colonial rule and the Cahora Bassa dam was finished in 1974.

After the Peace Accord of 1992 and the end of warfare throughout the valley in 2002, bridges have been built up and down the river, ending to some extent the role the Zambezi played as a frontier between the lands and peoples to the north and the south. The Lower Zambezi bridge was restored with funds provided by USAID and was briefly converted into a road bridge across the Zambezi. Then, in 2006, further work on the bridge returned it to rail operation with a parallel footway for pedestrians. This was followed by the Kazungula bridge, the Guebuza bridge downriver from Dona Anna and the Cazombo bridge in Angola, vital for traffic on the route between Angola and Zambia.

In 2008, 35 years after its completion, the bridge at Tete (renamed the Samora Machel bridge) had to undergo extensive repairs as some of the cables had broken. Then, in 2014, another bridge, called the Kassuende bridge, was built across the Zambezi, 6 kilometres further downstream, so that traffic would not have to pass through Tete town. There is even a pedestrian-only bridge that has been built at Zambezi, as the old town of Balovale has been renamed. Both the big dams act as road crossings. Bridges have contributed as much as the dams to the transformation and the taming of the river. Perhaps only the Upper Zambezi and in particular the Barotse floodplain retain something of the ancient character of the river that shaped the lives and cultures of people along its banks.

Global warming

When the two major dams were being designed, no one had heard of global warming and the dislocation of climate that accompanies it. Calculations were made on the basis of historical data and the fluctuations in rainfall and flow in the river that were known at the time. The pattern appeared stable enough, with major floods in 2000 and 2008 serving to keep the lake reservoirs full. However, it was the effects of these floods on coastal and valley communities that helped awaken people throughout the world to the realities of climate change and its potential effects.

Supported by the sympathies of the world and with aid coming from forty different countries, Mozambique put in place policies aimed at making those most at risk of climate change 'more resilient'. This included the population of the Lower Zambezi and, through an organisation called the Instituto Nacional de Gestão de Calamidades, a policy of relocating the population was put in place. Over the next 6 years, over 100,000 people were relocated. As with the relocations connected with the Cahora Bassa dam, the idea was that people would be voluntarily relocated, but soon old colonial habits resurfaced and 'persuasion', bribery and compulsion were being used. As the process was carried out in full view of the NGOs and other observers, it soon became clear that the government was pursuing other agendas in trying to lure people into the communal villages, where they would be easier to control.

Meanwhile, other voices were raised, suggesting that the valley peoples knew how to manage the river floods and that what was needed was a different regime of control over the Cahora Bassa waters. As Alex Arnall, one of those who carried out research in the region, wrote:

> most international donors present in the country accept the inevitability of extreme weather impacts and view resettlement as an unfortunate and, in some cases necessary, step to increase peoples' 'resilience', thus rationalising the top-down imposition of unpopular social policies and a depoliticised interpretation of climate change can deflect attention away from underlying drivers of vulnerability and poverty, as well as obscure the interests of governments that are intent on reordering poor and vulnerable populations.[3]

A report dated 2011 concluded,

> current water abundance in most parts of the ZRB [Zambezi River Basin] is unlikely to last ... climatic changes are likely to have only

relatively small effects on water availability, population and economic growth as well as expansion of irrigated agriculture and water transfers are likely to have very important transboundary impacts. Such impacts involve drastically reduced run off in the dry season.[4]

Then, starting around 2013, the Zambezi valley began to experience a dry phase with rainfall and river flows falling off. By 2016, the lakes were emptying and the generation of electricity from the dams was being cut. Aerial photographs showed clearly the 'ring' that was growing around the shore of the Cahora Bassa lake. Between 2016 and 2019, lake levels fell dramatically to a point where it was barely possible to operate the turbines. In December 2019, official statistics indicated that the lake was less than 9 per cent full, a figure which had recovered to 19 per cent by the following year. In 2019, there appeared dramatic, and terrifying, pictures that showed the Victoria Falls as a bare rock face with only the smallest trickle of water reaching the lip of the falls. There have been similar periods of drought in the past, not least in the 1820s, and it is possible that 'normal' rainfall patterns will return, but it is equally likely that the Zambezi valley and the whole central African plateau will enter a prolonged dry period.

Given the enormous demand for its waters, it seems possible that the Zambezi will become the first of the world's great rivers to run dry.

NOTES

1. RHYTHMS OF HISTORY

1. F.S. Arnot, *Garenganze: Seven Years Pioneer Mission Work in Central Africa*, Hawkins (London, 1889), 158, 159–60.
2. Matthew Hannaford, 'The consequences of past climate change for state formation and security in southern Africa', PhD thesis (University of Sheffield, 2015).
3. António Gomes, *Journey which Father António Gomes of the Company of Jesus made to the Empire of Manomotapa; and his presence for some years in the said lands*, Malyn Newitt ed., British Academy and OUP (Oxford, 2021), 161.
4. Francisco de Lacerda e Almeida, *Travessia de África*, Manuel Múrias, ed., Agência Geral das Colonias (Lisbon, 1936), 86.
5. Richard Hasler, *Agriculture, Foraging and Wildlife Resource Use in Africa*, Kegan Paul International (London, 1996), 47–8.
6. Lawrence S. Flint, 'State-building in central southern Africa: citizenship and subjectivity in Barotsekand and Caprivi', *International Journal of African Historical Studies*, vol. 36 (2003), 394.

2. THE LOWER ZAMBEZI BEFORE THE 19th CENTURY

1. D.N. Beach, *The Shona and Zimbabwe, 900–1850*, Heinemann (London, 1980), ch. 2.
2. 'Summary of letters from António Carneiro to the king', *Documents on the Portuguese in Mozambique and Central Africa*, A. da Silva Rego,

T.W. Baxter and E.E. Burke, eds, 9 vols, Centro de Estudos Históricos Ultramarinos (Lisbon, 1962–75). Henceforward *DPMCA*, vol. iii, 15.

3. Diogo Couto, *Da Asia* [On Asia], in Theal, G.M., *Records of South Eastern Africa*, 9 vols, Government of Cape Colony (Cape Town 1898–1903), 2nd edition, Struik (Cape Town, 1964). Henceforward *RSEA*, vol. 6, 370.

4. João de Barros, *Da Asia* [On Asia], Theal, *RSEA*, vol. 6, 265.

5. Frei João dos, Santos, *Etiópia Oriental, e Varia História de Cousas Notáveis do Oriente* [Oriental Africa and various histories of notable things in the East], (Évora, 1609). Extracts published in Theal, *RSEA*, vol. 7, 1–370. Quotations from 253.

6. Manuel Barretto, 'Informação do estado e conquista dos Rios de Cuama [Information on the state and conquest of the Rivers of Cuama]', in Theal, *RSEA*, vol. 3, 504.

7. Manuel Barretto, 'Informação do estado e conquista dos Rios de Cuama [Information on the state and conquest of the Rivers of Cuama]', in Theal, *RSEA*, vol. 3, 466.

8. António da Conceição, *Treatise on the Rivers of Cuama*, Malyn Newitt, ed., British Academy and OUP (Oxford, 2009), 7.

9. Francisco Monclaro, *Relação da viagem q fizerão os padres da Companhia de Jesus com Francisco Barreto* [An account of the journey which the Fathers of the Company of Jesus made with Francisco Barreto], in Theal, *RSEA*, vol. 3, 220.

10. Monclaro, *Relação da viagem* [An account of the journey], Theal, *RSEA*, vol. 3, 222.

11. Monclaro, *Relação da viagem* [An account of the journey], Theal, *RSEA*, vol. 3, 226.

12. Santos, *Etiópia Oriental* [Oriental Africa], Theal, *RSEA*, vol. 7, 255.

13. António Bocarro, *Decada 13 da História da India* [Thirteenth decade of the history of India], in Theal, *RSEA*, vol. 3, 353.

14. Santos, *Etiópia Oriental* [Oriental Africa], Theal, *RSEA*, vol. 7, 254.

15. Bocarro, *Decada*, Theal, *RSEA*, vol. 3, 401.

16. Barretto, 'Informação do estado e conquista dos Rios de Cuama [Information on the state and conquest of the Rivers of Cuama]', Theal, *RSEA*, vol. 3, 476.

17. Santos, *Etiópia Oriental* [Oriental Africa], Theal, *RSEA*, vol. 7, 263, 359.

18. Santos, *Etiópia Oriental* [Oriental Africa], Theal, *RSEA*, vol. 7, 255.

19. Santos, *Etiópia Oriental* [Oriental Africa], Theal, *RSEA*, vol. 7, 255.

20. Monclaro, *Relação da viagem* [An account of the journey], Theal, *RSEA*, vol. 3, 220.

21. Gomes, *Journey*, 137.

22. Leroy Vail and Landeg White, *Capitalism and Colonialism in Mozambique*, Heinemann (London, 1980), 72.

23. Gomes, *Journey*, 141.

24. Gomes, *Journey*, 146.

25. Gomes, *Journey*, 135.

26. Santos, *Etiópia Oriental* [Oriental Africa], Theal, *RSEA*, vol. 7, 261.

27. Eric Allina, 'The Zimba, the Portuguese, and other cannibals in late sixteenth-century south-east Africa', *Journal of Southern African Studies*, vol. 37, no. 2 (2011), 211–27. See discussion in Gomes, *Journey*, xxxvii–xxxix.

28. Gomes, *Journey*, 130–1.

29. Pedro Barretto de Rezende, *Livro do Estado da India* [The book of the Estado da India], Theal, *RSEA*, vol. 2, 408.

30. Malyn Newitt, *A History of Mozambique*, Hurst (London, 1995), 61–78, 207–11.

31. See discussion in Conceição, *Treatise on the Rivers of Cuama*, xxv–xxxi.

32. Santos, *Etiópia Oriental* [Oriental Africa], Theal, *RSEA*, vol. 7, 214.

33. D. Andres de Vides y Albarado to the king, *Livros das Monções* [Monsoon books], 41, fols 13–14; 'Declaration of Domingos Henriques', Sena 31/7/1632 in 'Legal testimonies taken about the matter of the mines by D. Andres de Vides y Albarado', *Livros das Monções* [Monsoon books], 41, fols 15–16v.

34. Bocarro, António, 'Livro das plantas de todas as fortalezas, cidades e povoações do Estado da India Oriental [The book of the plans of all the fortresses, cities and settlements of the state of Estado da India', in A.B. Bragança Pereira, *Arquivo Português Oriental*, vol. II, pt 1 (Bastora, 1937), 30.

35. Gomes, *Journey*, 110.

36. AHU Moç Cx 2, Monomotapa to the king, Zimbabwe, 28/6/1679.

37. Souza, Francisco de, *O Oriente Conquistado a Jesu Christo* [The Orient conquered for Christ], 2nd ed. (1710), Examiner Typographia (Bombay, 1881), 39.

38. Gomes, *Journey*, 112.

3. THE CREOLE STATE ON THE LOWER ZAMBEZI

1. Monclaro, *Relação da viagem* [An account of the journey], Theal, *RSEA*, vol. 3, 235.

2. Luiz Froes, 'Da Viagem do Padre D. Gonçalo da Silveira ao Reino de Manamotapa e do seu felice transito [Of the journey of Father D. Gonçalo da Silveira to the kingdom of Manamotapa and his happy arrival], Theal, *RSEA*, vol. 2, 104–28; quotation from 118.

3. Monclaro, *Relação da Viagem* [An account of the journey], Theal, *RSEA*, vol. 3, 235.

4. Santos, *Etiópia Oriental* [Oriental Africa], Theal, *RSEA*, vol. 7, 291.

5. Santos, *Etiópia Oriental* [Oriental Africa], Theal, *RSEA*, vol. 7, 292–3.

6. Santos, *Etiópia Oriental* [Oriental Africa], Theal, *RSEA*, vol. 7, p. 292.

7. Rezende, 'Livro do Estado da Índia [The book of the Estado da India]', Theal, *RSEA*, vol. 2, 392.

8. Rezende, Theal, 'Livro do Estado da Índia [The book of the Estado da India]', Theal, *RSEA*, vol. 2, 390.

9. Rezende, 'Livro do Estado da Índia [The book of the Estado da India]', Theal, *RSEA*, vol. 2, 424.

10. Barretto, 'Informação do estado e conquista dos Rios de Cuama [Information on the state and conquest of the Rios de Cuama]', Theal, *RSEA*, vol. 3, 466.

11. Rezende, 'Livro do Estado da Índia [The book of the Estado da India]', Theal, *RSEA*, vol. 2, 408.

12. Gomes, *Journey*, 96.

13. Gomes, *Journey*, 107.

14. Conceição, *Treatise on the Rivers of Cuama*, 15.

15. Rodrigues, Eugénia, 'Mercadores, Conquistadores e Foreiros: A Construção dos Prazos nos Rios de Cuama na Primeira Metade do Século XVII [Merchants, conquistadores and landowners: the creation

of the prazos in the Rivers of Cuama in the first half of the seventeenth century]', *Vasco da Gama Homens, Viagens e Culturas*, 2 vols, Comissão Nacional para as Comemorações dos Descobrimentos Portugueses (Lisbon, 2001), 445–79.

16. António Pinto de Miranda, 'Memoria sobre a Costa de Africa [Memoir on the Coast of Africa]', in A.A. de Andrade, *Relações de Moçambique Setecentista* [Accounts of eighteenth-century Mozambique], Agência Geral do Ultramar (Lisbon, 1955), 231–312.

17. Gomes, *Journey*, 104.

18. Gomes, *Journey*, 180–1.

19. António de Vilas Boas Truão, *Estatística da Capitania dos Rios de Senna do anno de 1806* [Statistics on the captaincy of the Rios de Senna for the year 1806] (Lisbon, 1889), 8.

20. Vitorino Magalhães Godinho, *Os Descobrimentos e a Economia Mundial* [The discoveries and the world economy], 2 vols, Arcádia (Lisbon, 1963), vol. 1, 231.

21. Gomes, *Journey*, 97.

22. Gomes, *Journey*, 104.

23. Gomes, *Journey*, 101.

24. Gomes, *Journey*, 101.

25. Gomes, *Journey*, 182.

26. Gomes, *Journey*, 161–2.

27. Rezende, 'Livro do Estado da Índia [The book of the Estado da India]', Theal, *RSEA*, vol. 2, 418.

28. Gomes, *Journey*, 121.

29. A.C.P. Gamitto, *King Kazembe*, Ian Cunnison, ed., 2 vols, Junta de Investigações do Ultramar (Lisbon, 1960), 145.

30. Santos, *Etiópia Oriental* [Oriental Africa], Theal, *RSEA*, vol. 7, 291.

4. THE MIDDLE ZAMBEZI: CAHORA BASSA TO VICTORIA FALLS

1. Conceição, *Treatise on the Rivers of Cuama*, 29.

2. Barretto, 'Informação do estado e conquista dos Rios de Cuama [Information on the state and conquest of the Rios de Cuama]', 481.

3. Conceição, *Treatise on the Rivers of Cuama*, 29.

4. Albino Manuel Pacheco, *A Journey from Tete to Zumbo*, British Academy and OUP (Oxford, 2013), 117.

5. Figures from S.I. Mudenge, 'The Rozvi empire and the Feira of Zumbo', PhD thesis (London University, 1972). A *bare* of cloth amounted to 400 *panos*, each *pano* consisting of approximately 6 feet of cloth.

6. Augusto da Fonseca de Mesquita e Solla, 'Apontamentos sobre o Zumbo [Notes on Zumbo]', *Boletim da Sociedade de Geografia de Lisboa*, vol. 25 (1907), 252.

7. Mudenge, 'The Rosvi empire and the Feira of Zumbo', 263.

8. Nogueira de Andrade, Jeronimo José, 'Descripção do Estado em que ficavão os Negocios da Capitania de Mossambique nos fins de Novembro de 1789 com algumas Observaçoens, e reflecçoens sobre a causa da decadencia do Commercio dos Estabelecimentos Portugueses na Costa Oriental da Affrica: escrita no anno de 1790 [Description of the state of the commerce of the Captaincy of Mozambique at the end of November 1789 with some observations and reflections on the causes of the decadence of the commerce of the Portuguese settlements on the east coast of Africa, written in the year 1790]', *Arquivo das Colonias*, vol. 1, no. 2 (1917), 75–96, 116–34, 168–84, 213–35; vol. 2, no. 2 (1918), 32–48.

9. Pacheco, *Journey from Tete to Zumbo*, 122–5.

10. Pacheco, *Journey from Tete to Zumbo*, 49–57.

11. Pacheco, *Journey from Tete to Zumbo*, 17.

12. Pacheco, *Journey from Tete to Zumbo*, 19.

13. Pacheco, *Journey from Tete to Zumbo*, 89, 107.

14. Pacheco, *Journey from Tete to Zumbo*, 43–5.

15. Pacheco, *Journey from Tete to Zumbo*, 67.

16. Pacheco, *Journey from Tete to Zumbo*, 111.

17. Pacheco, *Journey from Tete to Zumbo*, 113.

18. Quoted in W.V. Brelsford, *The Tribes of Northern Rhodesia*, Government Printer (Lusaka, 1956), 52–3.

19. David Livingstone, *Travels and Researches in South Africa*, Amalgamated Press (London, 1905), 492.

20. I. Schapera, ed., *Livingstone's Private Journals 1851–1853*, Chatto & Windus (London, 1960), 234–5.

21. Livingstone, *Travels and Researches*, 472.

22. Livingstone, *Travels and Researches*, 489.

23. Livingstone, *Travels and Researches*, 496, 499.

24. Livingstone, *Travels and Researches*, 518.

25. Livingstone, *Travels and Researches*, 533.

26. David and Charles Livingstone, *Narrative of an Expedition to the Zambesi and Tributaries*, Duckworth (London, 2001).

27. Emil Holub, *Travels North of the Zambezi 1885–6*, Manchester University Press (1972), 13.

28. Livingstone, *Narrative of an Expedition*, 156.

29. Selous, F.C., *A Hunter's Wanderings in Africa*, Alexander Books (Alexander, NC, 2001). Originally published 1881. All quotations from Chapter 15.

30. Richard Hasler, *Agriculture, Foraging and Wildlife Resource Use in Africa*, Kegan Paul International (London, 1996), 52–63.

31. Quoted in Jeannie Boggie, *First Steps in Civilizing Rhodesia*, 4th edition, Kingston's Limited (Salisbury, Rhodesia, 1939), 268.

5. THE UPPER ZAMBEZI AND THE BAROTSE VALLEY

1. A.A. da Rocha de Serpa Pinto, *How I Crossed Africa*, vol. 2, Lippincott (Philadelphia, 1881), 86.

2. Arnot, *Garenganze*, 80–1.

3. Arnot, *Garenganze*, 50.

4. Livingstone, *Travels and Researches*, 164.

5. Holub, *Travels North of the Zambezi*, 12.

6. Holub, *Travels North of the Zambezi*, 7.

7. Schapera, *Livingstone's Private Journals*, 214.

8. A. St H. Gibbons, *Explorations and Hunting in Central Africa, 1895–96*, Methuen (London, 1898), 3–4, 60.

9. Livingstone, *Travels and Researches*, 190.

10. Livingstone, *Travels and Researches*, 196.

11. Gibbons, *Explorations*, 38.

12. Quoted in Ernest Baker, *Arnot: A Knight of Africa*, Seeley Service & Co. (London, 1923), 184.

13. Gibbons, *Explorations*, 100–1.

14. Mutumba Mainga, *Bulozi Under the Luyana Kings: Political Evolution*

and State Formation in Pre-Colonial Zambia, Longman (London, 1973), 55.

15. Mainga, *Bulozi Under the Luyana Kings*, 56.
16. Livingstone, *Travels and Researches*, 75.
17. Livingstone, *Travels and Researches*, 76.
18. Mainga, *Bulozi Under the Luyana Kings*, 61–2.
19. Schapera, *Livingstone's Private Journals*, 223.
20. Livingstone, *Travels and Researches*, 183–4.
21. Schapera, *Livingstone's Private Journals*, 181–3.
22. Livingstone, *Travels and Researches*, 190.
23. Schapera, *Livingstone's Private Journals*, 205.
24. Schapera, *Livingstone's Private Journals*, 226.
25. Schapera, *Livingstone's Private Journals*, 73.
26. Holub, *Travels North of the Zambezi*, 13.
27. Gibbons, *Explorations*, 138.
28. Giacomo Macola, 'Reassessing the significance of firearms in Central Africa: The case of north-western Zambia to the 1920s', *Journal of African History*, vol. 51 (2010), 310.
29. Serpa Pinto, *How I Crossed Africa*, 26.
30. Serpa Pinto, *How I Crossed Africa*, 27.
31. C.W. Mackintosh, *Coillard of the Zambesi*, Fisher Unwin (London, 1907), 316.
32. E.C. Tabler, ed., *Trade and Travel in Early Barotseland*, Chatto and Windus (London, 1963), 44–7.
33. Arnot, *Garenganze*, 257, 258.

6. THE ZAMBEZI WARS

1. Quoted in M. Newitt, 'Drought in Mozambique, 1823–1831', *Journal of Southern African Studies*, 15 (1988), 32–3.
2. Newitt, 'Drought in Mozambique', 20–1.
3. R. Foskett, ed., *The Zambesi Journal and Letters of Dr John Kirk*, 2 vols, Oliver and Boyd (London, 1963), 64.
4. Foskett, *The Zambesi Journal*, 66, 70.
5. F.L. Barnard, *A Three Years Cruize in the Mozambique Channel*, Richard Bentley (London, 1848), 137–8.

6. Foskett, *The Zambesi Journal*, 68.

7. Foskett, *The Zambesi Journal*, 72–4.

8. Foskett, *The Zambesi Journal*, 63, 66, 68, 70.

9. E.C. Tabler, ed., *The Zambezi Papers of Richard Thornton*, 2 vols, Chatto & Windus (London, 1963), 47–8.

10. Foskett, *The Zambesi Journal*, 75.

11. Foskett, *The Zambesi Journal*, 102–3.

12. Foskett, *The Zambesi Journal*, 103–4.

13. Foskett, *The Zambesi Journal*, 103–4.

14. A.C.P. Gamitto, *King Kazembe*, Ian Cunnison, ed., 2 vols, Junta de Investigações do Ultramar (Lisbon, 1960), 54, 113.

15. Foskett, *The Zambesi Journal*, 276.

16. José Capela, *Donas, Senhores e Escravos*, Afrontamento (Lisbon, 1995), 92, 93.

7. THE 'SCRAMBLE FOR AFRICA' AND THE ZAMBEZI

1. For the Rose-Coloured Map, see Charles Nowell, *The Rose Colored Map*, Junta de Investigações Científicas do Ultramar (Lisbon, 1982).

2. Lawrence S. Flint, 'State-building in central southern Africa: Citizenship and subjectivity in Barotsekand and Caprivi', *International Journal of African Historical Studies*, 36 (2003), 413.

8. BAROTSELAND IN THE 20th CENTURY

1. Gibbons, *Explorations*, 263.

2. Mackintosh, *Coillard*, 328.

3. Quoted in Mackintosh, *Coillard*, 330.

4. Gibbons, *Explorations*, 149.

5. Mackintosh, *Coillard*, 341.

6. Quoted in Mackintosh, *Coillard*, 341–2.

7. Quoted in Baker, *Arnot: A Knight of Africa*, 178–9.

8. Gibbons, *Explorations*, 150, 157, 165.

9. Gibbons, *Explorations*, 148.

10. Eric Stokes, 'Barotseland: The survival of an African State', in E. Stokes and R. Brown, eds, *The Zambesian Past*, Manchester University Press (Manchester, 1965), 261–301. Quotation from 271.

11. Stokes, 'Barotseland', 292.

12. Mainga, *Bulozi Under the Luyana Kings*, 138.

13. Max Gluckman, 'The Lozi of Barotseland in North-Western Rhodesia', in Elizabeth Colson and Max Gluckman, *Seven Tribes of British Central Africa*, OUP (Oxford, 1951), 1–162. Quotation from, 14.

14. Mainga, *Bulozi Under the Luyana Kings*, 52.

15. Gibbons, *Explorations*, 98–9.

16. Gibbons, *Explorations*, 10–12.

17. D.W. Stirke, *Barotseland. Eight Years Among the Barotse*, Bale and Danielsson (London, 1922), 43.

18. Stirke, *Barotseland*, 49.

19. Gibbons, *Explorations*, 127.

20. Mainga, *Bulozi Under the Luyana Kings*, 64.

21. Mackintosh, *Coillard*, 362.

22. Quoted in Mainga, *Bulozi Under the Luyana Kings*, 147.

23. Gluckman, 'The Lozi of Barotseland', 11.

24. Stirke, *Barotseland*, 12.

25. Flint, 'State-building in central southern Africa: Citizenship and subjectivity in Barotseland and Caprivi', 412.

9. THE LOWER ZAMBEZI IN THE 20th CENTURY

1. Quoted in M. Newitt, *Portuguese Settlement on the Zambesi*, Longman (London, 1973), 348.

2. For the Moçambique Company see Bárbara Direito, *Terra e Colonialismo em Moçambique: a região de Manica e Sofala sob a Companhia de Moçambique, 1892–1942* [Land and colonialism in Mozambique: The region of Manica and Sofala under the Mozambique Company], ICS (Lisbon, 2020).

3. R.C.F. Maugham, *Zambezia*, John Murray (London, 1910), 54, 55.

4. Michael Main, *Zambezi Journey of a River*, Southern (Cape Town, 1990), 267.

5. Owen Letcher, *The Bonds of Africa*, John Long (London, 1913), 142–4.

6. Maugham, *Zambezia*, 61, 63, 66.

7. Gomes, *Journey*, 175.

8. Maugham, *Zambezia*, 273.

9. Leroy Vail and Landeg White, *Capitalism and Colonialism in Mozambique*, Heinemann (London, 1980), 153.

10. Eric Allina, *Slavery by Any Other Name*, University of Virginia Press (Charlottesville, 2012).

11. Paul Lapperre, *Bitter Sweetness*, Paul Lapperre (2020), 79.

12. Wilfrid Robertson, *Zambezi Days*, Blackie (London, 1936), 121–3.

13. Vice-consul Rule, *Report on a Journey Made From Chinde to Tete*, Diplomatic and Consular Reports: Portugal HMSO (London, 1914), 6–7.

14. W.A. Handman, 'The Lower Zambezi Bridge', *Journal of the Institution of Civil Engineers*, (1936–7), 4.

15. Handman, 'The Lower Zambezi Bridge', 48.

16. Handman, 'The Lower Zambezi Bridge', 49.

17. Handman, 'The Lower Zambezi Bridge', 89.

18. C.F. Spence, 'The diary of a trip through Portuguese East Africa October and November 1943'. A typed copy of Spence's travel diary, which has not been published, is in the possession of the author. The original belongs to the Spence family.

19. Spence, 'The Diary of a Trip'.

10. THE MIDDLE ZAMBEZI: THE COLONIAL EXPERIENCE

1. A. St H. Gibbons, *Africa From South to North Through Marotseland*, 2 vols, John Lane (London, 1904).

2. Robertson, *Zambezi Days*, 105–15.

3. Donald Sutherland, *Zambesi Campfires*, Witherby (London, 1935), 112.

4. David Lan, *Guns & Rain*, James Currey (London, 1985), 31–2.

5. Sutherland, *Zambesi Camp Fires*, 9–15.

6. W.V. Brelsford, *The Tribes of Northern Rhodesia*, Government of Northern Rhodesia (Lusaka, 1956), 59.

7. Elizabeth Colson, *Social Organization of the Gwembe Tonga*, Manchester University Press (Manchester, 1960), 188.

8. P.G. Wodehouse, 'A Mixed Threesome', in P.G.Wodehouse, *The Golf Omnibus*, Hutchinson (London, 1981), 53–4.

9. Robertson, *Zambezi Days*, 1.

10. Robertson, *Zambezi Days*, 3.

11. Robertson, *Zambezi Days*, 36

12. Robertson, *Zambezi Days*, 32–3.

13. Robertson, *Zambezi Days*, 5.

14. Robertson, *Zambezi Days*, 72–3.

15. Gomes, *Journey*, 154.

16. Robertson, *Zambezi Days*, 36; Gomes, *Journey*, 115.

17. Robertson, *Zambezi Days*, 137; Gomes, *Journey*, 152.

18. Dominic Muntanga, mulonga.net http://www.mulonga.net/project/14-mission/14-on-the-domainname-mulonga.

11. BALOVALE AND THE UPPER ZAMBEZI

1. For much of what follows about the Lunda, see John K. Thornton, *History of West Central Africa to 1850*, Cambridge University Press (Cambridge, 2020).

2. Thornton, *A History of West Central Africa*, 350; Gomes, *Journey*, 135.

3. Nowell, *The Rose Colored Map*, 91–107.

4. Nowell, *The Rose Colored Map*, 107.

5. Livingstone, *Travels and Researches*, 257.

6. Livingstone, *Travels and Researches*, 270–4.

7. Livingstone, *Travels and Researches*, 264.

8. Thornton, *A History of West Central Africa*, 308–10.

9. C.M.N. White, *Tradition and Change in Luvale Marriage*, The Rhodes-Livingstone Papers No. 34 (Manchester University Press, 1962), 14–15.

10. Macola, 'Reassessing the significance of firearms in Central Africa: The case of north-western Zambia to the 1920s', 301–21.

11. Arnot, *Garenganze*, 155, 156, 158, 159, 161, 165.

12. Robert Papstein, 'From ethnic identity to tribalism: The Upper Zambezi region of Zambia 1830–1981', Leroy Vail, ed., *The Creation of Tribalism in Southern Africa*, James Currey (London, 1989) 372–94.

13. 'The Barotseland boundary case (Great Britain and Portugal), 30 May 1904'. *Report of International Arbitral Awards*, vol. xi, 59–69, United Nations (New York, 2006).

14. Ricardo Roque, 'The razor's edge: Portuguese imperial vulnerability in colonial Moxico, Angola', *International Journal of African Historical Studies*, 36 (2003), 105–24. Quotation from 120–1.

15. Roque, 'The razor's edge', 105, 107.

16. R.S. Hudson, 'The human geography of Balovale district, Northern Rhodesia', *Journal of the Royal Anthropological Institute of Great Britain and Ireland*, 65 (1935), 235–66. Quotations from 252, 259.

17. C.N.M. White, 'The material culture of the Lunda–Lovale peoples', *The Occasional Papers of the Rhodes-Livingstone Museum*, Manchester University Press (Manchester, 1974), 54–70. White's paper is dated 1948. Quotations from 55, 57, 66.

18. Dr Board's letters to his family are in the possession of the author.

12. WAR AND THE CAHORA BASSA DAM

1. Reference is made in this section to Keith Middlemas, *Cabora Bassa. Engineering and Politics in Southern Africa*, Weidenfeld and Nicolson (London, 1975); Allen and Barbara Isaacman, *Dams, Displacement, and the Delusion of Development*, Ohio University Press (Athens, 2013).

2. Lan, *Guns & Rain*, 134.

3. Jeremy Harding, *Small Wars, Small Mercies*, Viking (London, 1993), 298–304.

4. Stephen Emerson, *The Battle for Mozambique*, 30° South Publishers (Pinetown, South Africa, 2013), 192–3.

5. Malyn Newitt, *Portugal in European and World History*, Reaktion (London, 2009), 104.

EPILOGUE

1. For the controversies surrounding this dam, see Isaacman, *Dams, Displacement and the Delusion of Development*.

2. Kariba town, http://www.wildzambezi.com/locations/1/kariba-town

3. Alex Arnall 'A climate of control: Flooding displacement and planned resettlement in the Lower Zambezi Valley, Mozambique', *Geographical Journal*, vol. 180 (2014), 141–50. Quotation from 141.

4. Lucas Beck and Thomas Bernauer, 'How will combined changes in water demand and climate affect water availability in the Zambezi river basin?', *Global Environmental Change*, vol. 21, no. 3 (2011), 1061–72. Quotation from 1061.

BIBLIOGRAPHY

This bibliography consists only of works cited in the text.

Unpublished

Board, Dr A.J., 'The Letters of A.J. Board to his family, 1935–7'. Copies of these letters are in the possession of the author.

Hannaford, Matthew, 'The consequences of past climate change for state formation and security in southern Africa', PhD thesis (University of Sheffield, 2015).

Mudenge, S.I., 'The Rozvi empire and the Feira of Zumbo', PhD thesis (London University, 1972).

Spence, C.F., 'The diary of a trip through Portuguese East Africa, October and November 1943.' A typed copy of Spence's travel diary is in the possession of the author. The original belongs to the Spence family.

Published

Allina, Eric, 'The Zimba, the Portuguese, and other cannibals in late sixteenth-century south-east Africa', *Journal of Southern African Studies*, vol. 37 (2011), 211–27.

————, *Slavery by Any Other Name*, University of Virginia Press (Charlottesville, 2012).

Arnall, Alex, 'A climate of control: Flooding displacement and planned resettlement in the Lower Zambezi Valley, Mozambique', *Geographical Journal*, vol. 180 (2014), 141–50.

BIBLIOGRAPHY

Arnot, F.S., *Garenganze: Seven Years Pioneer Mission Work in Central Africa*, Hawkins (London, 1889).

Baker, Ernest, *Arnot: A Knight of Africa*, Seeley Service & Co. (London, 1923).

Barnard, F.L., *A Three Years Cruize in the Mozambique Channel*, Richard Bentley (London, 1848).

Barretto, Manuel, 'Informação do estado e conquista dos Rios de Cuama [Information on the state and conquest of the Rios de Cuama]', in Theal, G.M., *Records of South Eastern Africa*, vol. 3.

Barros, João de, *Da Asia* [On Asia], in Theal, G.M., *Records of South Eastern Africa*, vol. 6.

Beach, D.N., 'Ndebele raiders and Shona power', *Journal of African History*, vol. 15, no. 4 (1974), 633–51.

———, *The Shona and Zimbabwe, 900–1850*, Heinemann (London, 1980).

Beck, Lucas and Thomas Bernauer, 'How will combined changes in water demand and climate affect water availability in the Zambezi river basin?', *Global Environmental Change*, vol. 21 (2011), 1061–72.

Bocarro, António, 'Livro das Plantas de todas as fortalezas, cidades e povoações do Estado da India Oriental [The book of the plans of all the fortresses, cities and settlements of the Estado da India]', in A.B. Bragança Pereira, *Arquivo Português Oriental*, (Bastora, 1937), vol. II, pt 1.

———, *Decada 13 da História da India* [Thirteenth Decade of the History of India], in Theal, G.M., *Records of South Eastern Africa*, vol. 3.

Boggie, Jeannie, *First Steps in Civilizing Rhodesia*, 4th edition, Kingston's Limited (Salisbury, Rhodesia, 1939).

Brelsford, W.V., *The Tribes of Northern Rhodesia*, Government Printer (Lusaka, 1956).

Brown, Richard, 'The Ndebele Succession Crisis 1868–77', *Historians in Tropical Africa*, University College of Rhodesia and Nyasaland (Salisbury, Southern Rhodesia, 1962), 159–76.

Capela, José, *Donas, Senhores e Escravos* [Ladies, lords and slaves], Afrontamento (Lisbon, 1995).

Clarence Smith, W.G., 'The impact of the Spanish Civil War and the

BIBLIOGRAPHY

Second World War on Portuguese and Spanish Africa', *Journal of African History*, vol. 26 (1985), 309–26.

Colson, Elizabeth, *Social Organization of the Gwembe Tonga*, Manchester University Press (Manchester, 1960).

Conceição, António da, *Treatise on the Rivers of Cuama*, Malyn Newitt ed., British Academy and OUP (Oxford, 2009).

Couto, Diogo do, *Da Asia* [On Asia], in Theal, G.M., *Records of South Eastern Africa*, vol. 6.

Da Silva, A., T.W. Baxter and E.E. Burke, eds, *Documents on the Portuguese in Mozambique and Central Africa*, 9 vols, Centro de Estudos Históricos Ultramarinos (Lisbon, 1962–75).

Dhada, Mustafah, *The Portuguese Massacre of Wiriyamu in Colonial Mozambique, 1964–2013*, Bloomsbury (London, 2016).

Direito Bárbara, *Terra e Colonialismo em Moçambique: A região de Manica e Sofala sob a Companhia de Moçambique, 1892–1942* [Land and colonialism in Mozambique: the region of Manica and Sofala under the Mozambique Company], ICS (Lisbon, 2020).

Emerson, Stephen, *The Battle for Mozambique*, 30° South Publishers (Pine Town, South Africa, 2013).

Flint, Eric, 'Trade and politics in Barotseland during the Kololo period', *Journal of African History*, vol. 11 (1970), 71–86.

Flint, Lawrence S., 'State-building in central southern Africa: Citizenship and subjectivity in Barotsekand and Caprivi', *International Journal of African Historical Studies*, vol. 36 (2003), 393–428.

Foskett, R. ed., *The Zambesi Journal and Letters of Dr John Kirk*, 2 vols, Oliver and Boyd (London, 1963).

Gamitto, A.C.P., *King Kazembe*, Ian Cunnison ed., 2 vols, Junta de Investigações do Ultramar (Lisbon, 1960).

Gibbons, A. St H., *Explorations and Hunting in Central Africa, 1895–96*, Methuen (London, 1898).

———, *Africa From South to North Through Marotseland*, 2 vols, John Lane (London, 1904).

Gluckman, Max, 'The Lozi of Barotseland in North-Western Rhodesia', in Elizabeth Colson and Max Gluckman, *Seven Tribes of British Central Africa*, OUP (Oxford, 1951), 1–162.

Godinho, Vitorino Magalhães, *Os Descobrimentos e a Economia Mundial* [The discoveries and the world economy], 2 vols, Arcádia (Lisbon, 1963).

Gomes, António, *Journey which Father António Gomes of the Company of Jesus Made to the Empire of Manomotapa; and his presence for some years in the said lands*, Malyn Newitt ed., British Academy and OUP (Oxford, 2021).

Handman, F.W.A., 'The Lower Zambezi bridge', *Journal of the Institution of Civil Engineers*, (1936–7).

Harding, Jeremy, *Small Wars, Small Mercies*, Viking (London, 1993).

Hasler, Richard, *Agriculture, Foraging and Wildlife Resource Use in Africa*, Kegan Paul International (London, 1996).

Holub, Emil, *Travels North of the Zambezi 1885–6*, Manchester University Press (Manchester, 1972).

Hudson, R.S., 'The human geography of Balovale district, Northern Rhodesia', *Journal of the Royal Anthropological Institute of Great Britain and Ireland*, 65 (1935), 235–66.

Isaacman, Allen and Barbara, *Dams, Displacement, and the Delusion of Development*, Ohio University Press (Athens, 2013).

Kariba Town. http://www.wildzambezi.com/locations/1/kariba-town

Lacerda e Almeida, Francisco de, *Travessia de África* [The crossing of Africa], Manuel Múrias ed., Agência Geral das Colonias (Lisbon, 1936).

Lan, David, *Guns & Rain*, James Currey (London, 1985).

Lapperre, Paul, *Bitter Sweetness*, Paul Lapperre (2020).

Letcher, Owen, *The Bonds of Africa*, John Long (London, 1913).

Livingstone, David, *Travels and Researches in South Africa*, Amalgamated Press (London, 1905). Originally published as *Missionary Travels and Researches in South Africa*, Murray (London, 1857).

Livingstone, David and Charles, *Narrative of an Expedition to the Zambesi and Tributaries*, Duckworth (London, 2001). First published 1865.

Mackintosh, C.W., *Coillard of the Zambesi*, Fisher Unwin (London, 1907).

Macola, Giacomo, 'Reassessing the significance of firearms in Central Africa: The case of north-western Zambia to the 1920s', *Journal of African History*, vol. 51 (2010), 301–21.

Main, Michael, *Zambezi Journey of a River*, Southern (Cape Town, 1990).

Mainga, Mutumba, *Bulozi Under the Luyana Kings: Political Evolution and State Formation in Pre-Colonial Zambia*, Longman (London, 1973).

Mashingaidze, Terence, 'Beyond the Kariba dam induced displacements: The Zimbabwean Tonga's struggles for restitution 1990s–2000s', *International Journal on Minority Group Rights*, vol. 20 (2013), 381–404.

Maugham, R.C.F., *Zambezia*, John Murray (London, 1910).

Mesquita e Solla, Augusto da Fonseca de, 'Apontamentos sobre o Zumbo [Notes on Zumbo]', *Boletim da Sociedade de Geografia de Lisboa*, 25 (1907), 247–57, 274–87, 319–27, 340–56, 382–91, 436–56.

Middlemas, Keith, *Cabora Bassa. Engineering and Politics in Southern Africa*, Weidenfeld and Nicolson (London, 1975).

Monclaro, Francisco, *Relação da viagem que fizerão os padres da Companhia de Jesus com Francisco Barreto* ... [An account of the journey which the Fathers of the Company of Jesus made with Francisco Barreto], in Theal, G.M., *Records of South Eastern Africa*, vol 3.

Muntanga, Dominic, mulonga.net http://www.mulonga.net/project/14-mission/14-on-the-domainname-mulonga.

Mutonga, Sitwala, 'Agricultural dynamics in pre-colonial western Zambia in the nineteenth century', *Transafrican Journal of History*, vol. 24 (1995), 97–105.

Newitt, Malyn, *Portuguese Settlement on the Zambesi*, Longman (London, 1973).

————, 'Drought in Mozambique, 1823–1831', *Journal of Southern African Studies*, 15 (1988), 15–35.

————, *A History of Mozambique*, Hurst (London, 1995).

————, *Portugal in European and World History*, Reaktion (London, 2009), 104.

Nogueira de Andrade, Jerónimo José, 'Descripção do Estado em que ficavão os Negocios da Capitania de Mossambique nos fins de Novembro de 1789 com algumas Observaçoens, e reflecçoens sobre a causa da decadencia do Commercio dos Estabelecimentos Portugueses na Costa Oriental da Affrica: escrita no anno de 1790 [Description of the state of the commerce of the Captaincy of Mozambique at the end of November 1789 with some observations and reflections on the causes of the decadence of the commerce of the Portuguese settlements on the East coast of Africa, written in the year 1790]', *Arquivo das Colonias* 1917, vol. 1, no. 2, 75–96, 116–134, 168–184, 213–235; 1918, vol. 2, no. 2, 32–48.

Nowell, Charles, *The Rose Colored Map*, Junta de Investigações Científicas do Ultramar (Lisbon, 1982).

Pacheco, Albino Manuel, *A Journey from Tete to Zumbo*, Malyn Newitt ed., British Academy and OUP (Oxford, 2013).

Papstein, Robert, 'From ethnic identity to tribalism: The Upper Zambezi region of Zambia 1830–1981', Leroy Vail ed., *The Creation of Tribalism in Southern Africa*, James Currey (London, 1989), 372–94.

Pinto de Miranda, António, 'Memoria sobre a Costa de Africa [Memoir on the Coast of Africa]', in A.A. de Andrade, *Relações de Moçambique Setecentista* [Accounts of eighteenth-century Mozambique], Agência Geral do Ultramar (Lisbon, 1955), 231–312.

Robertson, Wilfrid, *Zambezi Days*, Blackie and Son (London, 1936).

Rodrigues, Eugénia, 'Mercadores, conquistadores e foreiros: A construção dos prazos nos rios de Cuama na primeira metade do século XVII [Merchants, conquistadores and landowners: The creation of the prazos in the Rivers of Cuama in the first half of the seventeenth century]', *Vasco da Gama Homens, Viagens e Culturas*, 2 vols, Comissão Nacional para as Comemorações dos Descobrimentos Portugueses (Lisbon, 2001), 445–79.

Roque, Ricardo, 'The razor's edge: Portuguese imperial vulnerability in colonial Moxico, Angola', *International Journal of African Historical Studies*, vol. 36 (2003), 105–24.

Rule, Vice-consul, *Report on a Journey Made From Chinde to Tete*, Diplomatic and Consular Reports: Portugal HMSO (London, 1914).

Santos, Frei João dos, *Etiópia Oriental, e Varia História de Cousas Notáveis do Oriente* [Eastern Africa, and various histories of noteworthy things in the East] (Evora, 1609). Extracts published in Theal, G.M., *Records of South Eastern Africa*, vol. 7, 1–370.

Schapera, I. ed., *Livingstone's Private Journals 1851–1853*, Chatto & Windus (London, 1960).

Selous, F.C., *A Hunter's Wanderings in Africa*, Alexander Books (Alexander, NC, 2001). Originally published 1881.

Serpa Pinto, A.A. da Rocha de, *How I Crossed Africa*, 2 vols, Lippincott (Philadelphia, 1881).

BIBLIOGRAPHY

Souza, Francisco de, *O Oriente Conquistado a Jesu Christo* [The Orient conquered for Christ] (1710), 2nd edition, Examiner Typographia (Bombay, 1881).

Stirke, D.W., *Barotseland. Eight Years Among the Barotse*, Bale and Danielsson (London, 1922).

Stokes, Eric, 'Barotseland: The survival of an African State', in E. Stokes and R. Brown eds, *The Zambesian Past*, Manchester University Press (Manchester, 1965), 261–301.

Sutherland, Donald, *Zambesi Campfires*, Witherby (London, 1935).

Tabler, E.C. ed., *Trade and Travel in Early Barotseland*, Chatto and Windus (London, 1963).

———, *The Zambezi Papers of Richard Thornton*, 2 vols, Chatto & Windus (London, 1963).

Theal, G.M., *Records of South Eastern Africa*, 9 vols, Government of Cape Colony (Cape Town, 1898–1903), 2nd edition, Struik (Cape Town, 1964).

Thornton, John K., *History of West Central Africa to 1850*, Cambridge University Press (Cambridge, 2020).

United Nations, 'The Barotseland boundary case (Great Britain and Portugal), 30 May 1904'. Report of International Arbitral Awards, vol. xi, 59–69 (United Nations, 2006).

Vail, Leroy, and Landeg White, *Capitalism and Colonialism in Mozambique*, Heinemann (London, 1980).

Vilas Boas Truão, António de, *Estatística da Capitania dos Rios de Senna do anno de 1806* [Statistics on the captaincy of the Rios de Senna for the year 1806], (Lisbon, 1889).

White, C.M.N., 'The material culture of the Lunda-Lovale peoples', *The Occasional Papers of the Rhodes-Livingstone Museum*, Manchester University Press (Manchester, 1974), 54–70. White's paper is dated 1948.

———, *Tradition and Change in Luvale Marriage*, The Rhodes-Livingstone Papers, No. 34 (Manchester University Press, 1962).

INDEX

INDEX

Arnot, Frederick 8, 109, 110–11, 113, 119, 127, 129, 182, 264, 269

Asena 74

assimilados 298

Ataide, Estevão de 47

Atlantic Islands 59, 63, 72

Augustinians 29, 56, 78

Aztecs 38

Bailundu war 268

Baines, Thomas 231

Baldwin, William 230

ballão 12

Balovale district 27, 266–79

Balovale town 271–9; bridge in 306; medical services in 272–8

Bambowe 113

Banyans 212–3; *see also* Indians

Barnard, Frederick 137

Barotse flood plain 8, 10, 104, 158, 172, 185, 191–3, 255, 259, 269, 271, 306

Barotseland 16, 93, 98, 104, 122, 136, 138, 144, 156, 161, 168, 170, 175–97; after independence 195–7; and colonial rule 183–97; described by European travellers 107–14; independence movement 196; kingdom of 15, 16–17, 18, 20, 108–30, 179, 266–7; Makololo invasion of 118–23; protectorate 174, 176, 177, 178, 179; 1884 rebellion in 127–9, 175, 187; relations

with Lunda 276–8; second kingdom 116–17, 187; slavery in 117–18

Barotseland Agreement 195

Barotseland Freedom Movement 196

Barotseland National Freedom Alliance 196

Barotseland National School 194

Barreto, Francisco 28–9, 35–6, 45, 51, 55, 61, 73, 74

Barretto, Manuel 27, 32, 47, 79

Barros, João de 26–7

Barue 38, 134, 150, 151, 164, 209, 213, 215; rebellion 217–19, 226

Basilwizi Trust 302

Batoka gorge 7, 10, 12, 231; dam 4, 302; plateau 92–8, 125, 130, 136, 176, 178, 182, 238

Beach, David 38

beads 79, 81

Beet, Margaret 271

Beira 208, 219, 220–1, 222, 224, 292

Belgian Congo 227; *see also* Congo Free State, Leopold

Bemba 241, 256

Beresford, Lord 139

Berlin Congress 129, 160, 162

Bertrand, A. 186

Bié 121, 127; *see also* Mambari, Mbunda

Binga region 302

Bisa 96–7

Bismarck, Otto von 160, 169, 170

INDEX

INDEX

INDEX

INDEX

INDEX

INDEX

INDEX

INDEX

INDEX